ENTERPRISE DIRECTORY AND SECURITY IMPLEMENTATION GUIDE

A Volume in The Korper and Ellis E-Commerce Books Series

ENTERPRISE DIRECTORY AND SECURITY IMPLEMENTATION GUIDE

DESIGNING AND IMPLEMENTING DIRECTORIES IN YOUR ORGANIZATION

Charles Carrington
Timothy Speed
Juanita Ellis
Steffano Korper

ACADEMIC PRESS
An imprint of Elsevier Science

Amsterdam Boston London New York Oxford Paris
San Diego San Francisco Singapore Sydney Tokyo

This book is printed on acid-free paper. ♾

Academic Press
An imprint of Elsevier Science
525 B Street, Suite 1900, San Diego, California 92101-4495, USA
http://www.academicpress.com

Academic Press
84 Theobolds Road, London WC1X 8RR, UK
http://www.academicpress.com

Library of Congress Catalog Card Number: 2002100202

International Standard Book Number: 0-12-160452-7

PRINTED IN THE UNITED STATES OF AMERICA
02 03 04 05 06 07 MB 9 8 7 6 5 4 3 2 1

To Rolinda Carrington-Rhone, Callie Rose Carrington and Miles Ellis Carrington

Charles Carrington

To Linda Speed, really *still my favorite wife*

Timothy Speed

Contents

Foreword **xi**

Acknowledgments **xv**

Company Copyright Notices and Statements **xix**

Chapter 1—Introduction **1**

1.1 Directories *1*
1.2 X.500 and LDAP *10*

Chapter 2—Directories, Security, and Tigers—Oh, My! **15**

2.1 Directory Types *15*
2.2 Directory Uses *17*
2.3 Directory Security *19*

Chapter 3—Directory Architecture **23**

3.1 Architecture Defined *24*
3.2 Critical Elements *26*
3.3 Implementations—Products and Vendors *27*
3.4 DAP and LDAP *28*
References *33*

Chapter 4—More on LDAP 35

4.1 Referrals *35*
4.2 Authentication and Authorization *36*
4.3 X.500 *39*
4.4 X.509 *40*
4.5 LDIF *40*

Chapter 5—Directories Within the Enterprise 41

5.1 Historical Perspective *41*
5.2 Directories and Privacy *44*
5.3 Directories and NOS/OS *45*
5.4 Directories and Messaging *46*

Chapter 6—Implementation Considerations for the Enterprise Directory 51

6.1 Directory Content, Design, DIT, and Attributes *51*
6.2 Authoritative Sources of the Directory Information *57*
6.3 Uniqueness Criteria *60*
6.4 Directory Aggregation *61*

Chapter 7—Enterprise Security 63

7.1 Bolt-on Security *64*
7.2 Process Security *64*
7.3 Competitive Asset *68*
7.4 Physical Security Policy *74*
7.5 Network Security Policy *77*
7.6 Acceptable Use Policy *81*

Chapter 8—The Security Strategy 87

8.1 The Security Committee *88*
8.2 The Corporate Security Policy Document *91*

Chapter 9—PKCS, PKIX, and LDAP 109

9.1 The Public-Private Key *109*
9.2 The CRL *125*
9.3 The LDAP *127*
9.4 Public-Key Cryptography Standards *130*
9.5 Cylink *136*
9.6 Certification Practice Statement *142*

Chapter 10—Enterprise Security Scenarios 159

10.1 Filtered Directory *160*
10.2 The 100 Percent LDAP Solution *161*

Chapter 11—Enterprise Security and Security Deployment Planning 173

11.1 Security Planning *173*
11.2 Security Hardware and Software Reference Guide *182*

Glossary 225

Index 235

Foreword

A customer stumbling upon this book in a bookstore might ask, "Why is a book on directories and security is so important?"

The Internet is connecting enterprises into a global economy, and the interaction of directories is critical to the success of the New Economy. Consider, for example, Internet commerce in the United States. According to a January, 2002 report from the Pew Internet & American Life Project (http://www.pewinternet.org), overall, 29 million American shoppers bought gifts online during the 2001 holiday season, spending an average of $392, up from $330 last year. A quarter of all U.S. Internet users did some of their buying online this year, versus a fifth of them last year. If Web-based retailers could not offer secure Web Services, then consumers would not feel safe on the Internet. As with any venture, security is as important as the venture itself. In order to communicate with the outside world, a company may need to securely publish part of their directory. This has certain risks and benefits: If a company's directory structure were compromised, the entire enterprise could be at risk.

Today, we live in a world of Internet technologies: messaging services, e-business enterprises, business-to-business value chain integrations, and now Web Services. The state-of-the-art value chain is now executed through both intranets and extranets. More and more of most companies' internal employee support systems (employee-initiated activities, such as registering for the company medical package, making a change to a personnel record, requesting help, etc.) are based on Internet technologies.

Consider, for a moment, all of the companies and workers on these intranets. The Internet is not just one network, but thousands of individual networks. These networks are most commonly connected by the TCP/IP network protocol, which provides the base communications for the information highway. Now a person may ask, "How does someone navigate through these networks?" The answer is, through *directories*.

Directories provide the road maps to the Internet. In most cases, each network has one or more directories. One of the best examples of these directories is the Internet Domain Name System (DNS). Directories, including

DNS, take the Internet from a series of numbers and protocols to actual names and locations. Consider, for example, the simple process of ordering a product from your favorite Web vendor and the directories that could be used in the transaction:

- A customer opens a URL to order a product (DNS directory used).
- A product is selected and submitted to a processing system (Internal routing directories used, such as server names, database names, and mail-in-services).
- The customer receives confirmation of the order (e-mail directories used, from both the vendor and consumer).
- The product is shipped to the customer (messages sent to a service vendor for delivery).

Many different directories could be used and accessed in any given transaction. If a hacker was able to gain access and make changes to these directories, e-mail addresses could be changed, messages could be routed to other sites, product deliveries could be rerouted, and servers could be impersonated. Businesses would not bring their wares to the Internet and customers would not want to do transactions there. The viability of the Internet itself would be called into question. Directory security is essential to business on the Internet.

The next iteration in today's Internet technologies is Web Services. This technology provides a mechanism that allows for the growth of network-based applications. Some of these Web Services include:

- UDDI—Universal Description Discovery and Integration
- SOAP—Simple Object Access Protocol
- WSDL—Web Services Description Language

These new technologies will provide the framework for application-to-application communications. Some of the parts directories will play in these new technologies include:

- Customer information
- Vendor information
- E-mail addresses
- Application registration

This book is aimed at providing the reader with the information needed to support and protect an *enterprise directory.* The authors understand that the primary objective of any business is to run a business and not just to install a security system. They emphasize the practical and pragmatic approaches to securing any Internet enabled business. This includes the directories services, authentication, and authorization.

Take the time to read this book, which gives the IT professional the information and tools needed to secure one of the most valuable network resources in the enterprise: The organization's directory.

Al Zollar
General Manager
Lotus Software, IBM Software Group, IBM Corporation

Al Zollar is responsible for the executive leadership of Lotus software. This includes overall strategy and day-to-day management of Lotus as a brand and a business within IBM. Lotus software is an established industry leader, empowering our customers to leverage their human capital through communications, advanced collaboration, and e-learning offerings to "enable the minds of e-business." Al oversees a worldwide organization that markets its products in over 80 countries.

Prior to joining the Lotus team, Al served as general manager of IBM's Network Computing Software Division, responsible for key internet infrastructure technologies, including networking, directory, security and Java technologies.

Since joining IBM in 1977 as a systems engineer trainee in San Francisco, Al has held several high-level positions within the company including senior management positions in every IBM Software Group division. He has served as general manager of IBM eNetwork software, senior vice president of development for IBM Tivoli software, and has held numerous key-management positions in IBM software development laboratories, including lab director for IBM Software Group in Raleigh, North Carolina, and DB2 Product Manager, Santa Teresa, California.

Most recently, Al was appointed to the Executive Committee of the Greater Boston Chamber of Commerce and is a board member of the Chubb Corporation. Additionally, Al is an advocate and supporter of business and community-based organizations aimed at expanding opportunities for minorities. He is a board member of the Executive Leadership Council, a co-chair of the IBM Black Family Technology Awareness project, and past member of the Durham, North Carolina Black Achievers Program Advisory Board. Al's also a member of the Leadership Council of the Center for Business and Government at the John F. Kennedy School for Government of Harvard University.

Al holds a master's degree in Applied Mathematics from the University of California at San Diego. He spends his free time with his family, reading, playing golf and listening to jazz.

Acknowledgments

Individual efforts aside, writing a book, like many worthwhile endeavors, relies on support. I've received tremendous support from my spouse and children during the course of work on this book, and I want to thank them for that, as well as their love. They were unstinting in allowing me to share time between them and the laptop.

I also want to thank my parents: My mother Raye, for allowing me to find my own way, and Walter for supporting me in my adventures. They truly helped to create the foundation that has allowed me to explore so widely and enjoy so much. My grandmother, Celia Sheppard (a teacher for 30 years and my first teacher), provided a fine example of the importance of teaching in order to learn; I thank her for all she has taught me by example over the years.

Special thanks to Aldo Grossi, Mike Bilger, and IBM for allowing me to coauthor this book, and to Juanita Ellis and Tim Speed, who made it possible and have offered so much guidance and support.

There's also a group of people whom I learned from over the years. They were managers, peers, and team members. While they did not contribute directly to this book, they made great contributions both to my professional life and to my understanding of directories and security. Their common quality was the remarkable way in which they freely shared their knowledge and their time. I appreciate them all deeply. They include: Bill Kilduff, Ciaran DellaFera, Chuck Reinehr, Erik Wilson, Chris Loesche, Frank Schimpf, Tom Macner, Phil Fritz, Tom Ballard, Jose Rodriguez, Diane Pierce, Jeff DeMent, Chris Mull, Roger Nash, Jim Sink, Dawn Branam, Dawn Rose, Linda Baschky, Greg Millet, Judi Flagg, Mike Guest, Rick Walters, Sridhar Muppidi, Keith Sams, Tim Hahn, Allison Dancy, John Mahony, Lisa Hirsch, Kimberley Merrell, Mark Griesi, Joe Shaulis, Rick Walters, Bill Bonneau, and Greg Pittman.

I also want to acknowledge some special customers, who taught me many lessons in the course of our relationship: Kenny Klepper, Grace Messina, Sam DeKay, Pam Ritz, and Dave Hanley.

Charles Carrington

Knowledge is based on many different facets—what you know, knowing where information can be found, and who you know. The information in this book is a combination of all these facets. Data sources have been referenced in this book, including references to people, URLs, and other books. But much of the knowledge that is in this book comes from very smart people. Although not all the people listed here actually participated in writing this book, they have all influenced and guided my life and this work. First and foremost I need to thank my wife for helping me with this book and providing some of the editing. Next I want to thank Johnny Speed, a great son who not only provided his support, but also edited various chapters in this book. I thank my daughter Katherine for tolerating me during the months that I worked on this. Next I want to thank my mother, Lillian Speed, for teaching me to "think big." It is great to have a mother's support. My brothers and sister have all been an inspiration to me and helped me to strive for a better life. Special thanks to Mike Speed for the inspiration to keep writing books. I am very grateful to Juanita Ellis for asking me to participate in writing this book. Special thanks to Julio G. Esperas, for project managing this and the previous book. Thanks to Joel Claypool for publishing this book. Special thanks to Lotus Development, Steve Mohr (previously with Lotus), Randy Parrett, Andy Nietupski, and Jamie Chisholm for allowing me to coauthor this book.

Now to talk about the really smart people. Due to legal issues, the people listed below could not directly contribute to this book, but I have learned a lot from these people through work and their friendship:

Dennis Archibald, Chip Coy, Catherine Yang, Lynn Pless, Dr. Rick Russo, Katherine Spanbauer, Alise Cashman, Deirdre O'Connor, Dee Fleming, Louis DePadova, Dorothy Kwapich, Michael Confoy, Ken Bugg, Steve and Tammy Stienbaugh, Bill King, Kevin Lynch, John McNamara, Brian Key, Randy Parrett, Rick Sizemore, Robert Nellis, Burk Buechler, Jesse Rodgers, Ted Lewis, Valerie Kunert, Mario Figueroa, Norma and Leonard Gomez, Clark and Stephanie Oberle, Jim and Diane Walker, Steve and Darla, and Ron Carmichael. Special thanks goes to Boris Vishnevsky for the inspiration to write this book! Boris is truly Mr. Directory.

Thanks to the following for helping get the approvals for Al Zolar to write the forward for the book:

Steve Robinson
Chris Ciotti
Brian Baker
Stacey Malin
Mark Harris

Thanks to Steve Robinson and Dennis Archibald for your help and support and to Brian Baker for helping with the foreword.

Special thanks to Al Zollar for writing the foreword.

And to friends lost and now found—Norman Zimmerman, Marvin Zimmerman, and Rita Zimmerman.

Finally, sorry if I missed you on this book, I will get you in the next.

Timothy Speed

Company Copyright Notices and Statements

Although the authors and editors have attempted to provide accurate information in this book, we assume no responsibility for the accuracy of the information. The following listing is not exhaustive. The names of actual companies and products mentioned herein may be the trademarks of their respective owners.

For the purposes of this book, the companies used as examples (e.g., The Company), as well as all organizations, products, people, and events depicted herein are fictitious. No association with any real company, organization, product, person, or event is intended or should be inferred.

Microsoft

Verisign

Armadillo Multimedia Enterprise LTD

http://www.armadillo.com.hk/legal.html

INTEL

http://www.intel.com/sites/corporate/tradmarx.htm?iid=intelhome+legal&

XEROX

http://www.xerox.com/go/xrx/template/004.jsp?view=Legal&Xcntry=USA &Xlang=en_US&Xseg=corp

DEC/Compaq

http://www.compaq.com/copyright.html

3COM

http://www.3com.com/legal/index.html

Spam (this is trademarked)

http://www.spam.com/ci/ci_in.htm

spam (this is not trademarked)

http://www.spam.com/ci/ci_in.htm

GE

http://www.ge.com/

Zone Labs

http://www.zonealarm.com/aboutus/legal.html

LinkSys

http://www.linksys.com/contact/coinfo.asp

Network ICE

APPLE

http://www.apple.com/legal/default.html

MICROWAREHOUSE

http://www2.warehouse.com/

IBM

The list for IBM is too extensive to present here. See this URL: http://www.ibm.com/legal/copytrade.phtml

RSA

For the purpose of promoting interoperability among products implementing S/MIME, the 'S/MIME-Enabled' logo is trademarked, http://www.rsasecurity.com/ and vendors must demonstrate S/MIME compliance before using the logo on product packaging, promotional materials, advertising, signage, and/or Web sites. See www.rsa.com for more information. The S/MIME logo can be found at http://www.rsasecurity.com/standards/smime/logos.html

Baltimore Technologies

Baltimore Technologies, Global E|Security, Global E-Security, E-Security, E|Security, TrustedWorld, PKI World, Zergo, ZSA, and Baltimore product names including UniCERT, MailSecure, PKI-Plus, W/Secure, X/Secure, and J/CRYPTO are all trademarks of Baltimore Technologies plc and its subsidiaries. http://www.baltimore.ie/legalnotices.html

Netscape

Netscape, Netscape Certificater Server, Netscape FastTrack Server, Netscape Navigator, Netscape ONE, SuiteSpot, and the Netscape N and Ship's Wheel logos are registered trademarks of Netscape Communications Corporation in the United States and other countries.

Netscape Trademarks

An ® following a name indicates that the trademark has been registered in the USA. This list is not exhaustive. Netscape may own other trademarks that are not included here.

AutoConfig, AutoUpdate, BeanConnect, Client Registry, Client Version Registry, Collabra®, Collabra Share®, Contact, CoolTalk, Expert Alliance, ExpertDesk, Expert-to-Expert, In-Box Direct, ISP Select®, Live 3D, LiveCall, LiveConnect, Live Objects, LiveType, LiveWire, LiveWire Pro, MailCaster, Mozilla, Netcaster, Netcenter, NetHelp, Netscape®, Netscape® Administration Kit, Netscape AffiliatePlus, Netscape® AgentXpert, Netscape Alliance, Netscape® AppFoundry, Netscape® Application Builder, Netscape® Application Server, Netscape® AutoAdmin, Netscape Business Community, Netscape Business Journal, Netscape® BuyerXpert, Netscape® Calendar, Netscape® Calendar Express, Netscape® Calendar Link, Netscape® Calendar Server, Netscape CaseTracker, Netscape® Cash Register, Netscape Catalog Server®, Netscape Certificate Server®, Netscape® Channel Finder, Netscape Charters Program, Netscape® Chat, Netscape® Client Customization Kit, Netscape® Collabra®, Netscape® Collabra® Server, Netscape® Commerce Server, Netscape® CommerceXpert, Netscape® Commercial Applications, Netscape® Communications Server, Netscape® Communicator, Netscape® Communicator Deluxe Edition, Netscape® Communicator Internet Access Edition, Netscape® Communicator News, Netscape Community, Netscape® Community System, Netscape® Compass Server, Netscape® Component Builder, Netscape® Composer, Netscape® Conference, Netscape® Console, Netscape® Content Management Server, Netscape DevEdge®, Netscape DevEdge® Application Builder, Netscape DevEdge® Online, Netscape DevEdge® Open Studio, Netscape® DeveloperXpert, Netscape Direct, Netscape® Directory Server, Netscape® ECXpert, Netscape® Enterprise News, Netscape® Enterprise Server, Netscape® Enterprise Server with FORTEZZA, Netscape® Extension Builder, Netscape FastTrack Server®, Netscape Guide, Netscape Industry Watch, Netscape Insight, Netscape® Install Builder, Netscape® Internet Applications, Netscape® Internet Foundation Classes, Netscape Internet Learning Academy, Netscape® Internet Service Broker, Netscape® Istore, Netscape® JAR Installation Manager, Netscape® JAR Packager, Netscape® LiveMedia, Netscape® LivePayment, Netscape® Mail, Netscape® Mail Server, Netscape® Mailing List Manager, Netscape® Media Converter, Netscape® Media Player, Netscape® Media Server, Netscape® Merchant System, Netscape® MerchantXpert, Netscape® Messaging Server, Netscape® Messenger, Netscape® Messenger Express, Netscape® Migration Toolkit, Netscape® Mission Control, Netscape® Mission Control Desktop, Netscape Navigator®, Netscape Navigator® with FORTEZZA, Netscape Navigator® Gold, Netscape Navigator® News, Netscape Navigator® Personal Edition, Netscape Netcenter, Netscape Netcenter Small Business Source, Netscape® News Server, Netscape ONE®, Netscape® Payment Kit, Netscape® Power Pack, Netscape® Process Manager, Netscape Professional Community, Netscape® Proxy Server, Netscape® Proxy Server with FORTEZZA, Netscape® Publishing Suite, Netscape® Publishing System, Netscape® PublishingXpert, Netscape® SellerXpert, Netscape Services Network, Netscape® Site Manager, Netscape Site Sampler, Netscape® SmartUpdate, Netscape Software Depot, Netscape Solution Expert, Netscape Subscribers Advantage, Netscape® SuiteTools, Netscape SupportEdge, Netscape® Update, Netscape Virtual Office, Netscape® WebTop, Netshare, ONE Stop Software, PowerStart®, ResponseDesk, ResponseLine, Secure Courier, ShopTalk Direct, SmartMarks, Suite Solutions, SuiteSpot®, SuiteSpot® Hosting Edition, and TechVision.

Netscape Trade Names

Following are Netscape trade names: Netscape; Netscape Communications; and Netscape Communications Corporation.

Cisco

See http://www.cisco.com/public/copyright/trademark.html for a list.

Sun

JavaScript is a trademark of Sun Microsystems, Inc., used under license for technology invented and implemented by Netscape.

CERT

CERT® is a registered trademark and service mark of Carnegie Mellon University.

Computer Security Institute

Copyright © 2000, Computer Security Institute, 600 Harrison Street, San Francisco, CA 94107. See http://www.gocsi.com/

SLAPD

Copyright © 1992–1996 Regents of the University of Michigan. All Rights Reserved. Redistribution and use in source and binary forms are permitted provided that this notice is preserved and that due credit is given to the University of Michigan at Ann Arbor. The name of the University may not be used to endorse or promote products derived from this software or documentation without specific prior written permission. This software is provided "as is" without any express or implied warranty. See http://www.umich.edu/~dirsvcs/ldap/

Open LDAP

Copyright © 1998–2000, The OpenLDAP Foundation, *All Rights Reserved.* See http://www.openldap.org/

Computer Associates International

Refer to http://www.cai.com/catrdmrk.htm for U.S. trademarks and registered trademarks owned by Computer Associates International, Inc. This list is provided for informational purposes only and may not contain all Computer Associates trademarks. Any questions concerning this list, the use of these trademarks or whether a name that does not appear on this list is in fact a trademark of CA should be referred to CA at 1-631-342-5224.

Excerpted from RFC2026:

ftp://ftp.isi.edu/in-notes/rfc2026.txt

(C) The following copyright notice and disclaimer shall be included in all ISOC standards-related documentation:

"Copyright (C) The Internet Society (date). All Rights Reserved.

This document and translations of it may be copied and furnished to others, and derivative works that comment on or otherwise explain it or assist in its implmentation may be prepared, copied, published and distributed, in whole or in part, without restriction of any kind, provided that the above copyright notice and this paragraph are included on all such copies and derivative works. However, this document itself may not be modified in any way, such as by removing the copyright notice or references to the Internet Society or other Internet organizations, except as needed for the purpose of developing Internet standards in which case the procedures for copyrights defined in the Internet Standards process must be followed, or as required to translate it into languages other than English.

The limited permissions granted above are perpetual and will not be revoked by the Internet Society or its successors or assigns.

Excerpted from RFC2223:

ftp://ftp.isi.edu/in-notes/rfc2223.txt

11. Copyright Section

Per BCP 9, RFC 2026 [2], "The following copyright notice and disclaimer shall be included in all ISOC standards-related documentation." The following statement should be placed on the last page of the RFC, as the "Full Copyright Statement."

"Copyright (C) The Internet Society (date). All Rights Reserved.

Warning and Disclaimer

Every effort has been made to make this book as complete and accurate as possible, but no warranty or fitness is implied. The security of any site is the responsibility of the owners. The authors and publishers are not liable for the security of any person, company or site. The authors and the publisher shall have neither liability nor responsibility to any person or entity with respect to loss or damages arising from the information contained in this book. Purchase and read this book at your own risk. Every effort has been attempted to obtain permissions for extracts and quotes whenever possible. See listed URLs for quote sources. The products referenced or mentioned in this book are listed for informational purposes only. The publisher and authors may have received demonstration copies to review. The publishers and authors have not received any compensation from the software or hardware vendors mentioned in the book. Many different vendors are mentioned in this book and many vendor products are used for reference. The publisher and authors do not recommend any product, software, or hardware. You, the owner of your hardware, software, and data are responsible for determining what is best for you. The authors DO advise that you take careful consideration in determining your security needs and review more than just one vendor. Remember, you own your security, we do not!

CHAPTER 1

Introduction

1.1 Directories

We all use some type of a directory. We look up a friend's or store's phone number in the phone book, or we send an e-mail to someone and then look up that name in the corporate directory. However, a directory is more than just a list of names; it can also provide information and perform a service. Directories supply standard information: names, addresses, phone numbers, and so on. Directory services can include automatic lookup and referrals, and they can even act as a binding agent for authentication. They help the end-user send e-mail. Imagine if you had to send a message to a number instead of a name. In the world of TCP/IP, you would need to remember both a list of numbers and a name—for example JoeB23465242@exampleemailserver.com. Although one address like this might not be hard to remember, what if you had to remember hundreds of addresses? With your address book, all you need to know is "Joe Bubba," and the address book would insert the actual address into the "Send To" field.

Let's consider this scenario. Your company has 3,000 employees who work in five different countries. Everyone must share his or her personal address book, and each employee has entries with customer information and e-mail addresses. Each employee could send or copy the addresses and send them to all the other employees as new contacts are made, but with 3,000 employees, this would be a mess! E-mail would be sent all over the place, or, in e-terms, this would be an "e-goofy." In this situation, an enterprise directory would help. The enterprise directory acts as a central repository that holds information about other employees in the company, customers, and even other resources—like conference rooms and projectors.

So now directories have grown from just a list of names and passwords into a ubiquitous systemic infrastructure. Today these directories contain not only user information but also security and access policies. Directories are an integral part of the new business-to-business structures that are being developed.

This book is a logical extension of the *Internet Security Guide Book, From Planning to Deployment.* It provides details about the directory, security requirements, and the functions a directory can offer security services. This book is also about messaging, since e-mail cannot work efficiently without a directory. It is geared toward all levels: from system administrator to CEO. It will help you design your directory and security architecture and then implement it.

The Internet is connecting enterprises into a global economy. The interaction of directories is critical to the success of this "new" economy. As with any venture, security is as important as the venture itself. Companies are exposing their directories. If the directory structure is compromised, the whole enterprise could be at risk. Directories play a large role in e-commerce security. The directory can be the central point that manages external and internal accounts. It can also enable the authorization and authentication processes.

Although some companies have only one directory, large enterprises have many different directories. Some companies refer to their sole "authoritative directory," which is the central source for all directory activities within the company. A company's payroll is an example of an authoritative directory. It is important that this directory be current and up to date so employees get their checks and those who have been terminated do not get a check. However, large organizations have several authoritative directories. Now this sounds like a paradox, since you would hope to have only one directory.

Today's business environment is complex and crosses many boundaries. There are mergers, joint ventures, and management buyouts. As a result, a company can have many authoritative directories. So how can a company use and manage these multiple directories? The answer is metadirectories. A metadirectory can connect many different directories both with one another and with various enterprise environments. These metasystems provide another layer of directory functionality that synchronizes and distributes as needed within a global enterprise. There are many different solutions offered for metadirectories. One example is a product from Critical Path (www.cp.net). The CP™ Meta-Directory Server automatically integrates directory data from various directories, database, and applications making the shared data consistent and current across systems.

In today's e-enterprise, you must be able to contact another member within your team or virtual team quickly. Directories enable "unified messaging." In the global enterprise, people will have several tools they can use for messaging (see Figure 1.1).

FIGURE 1.1 *Messaging Tools*

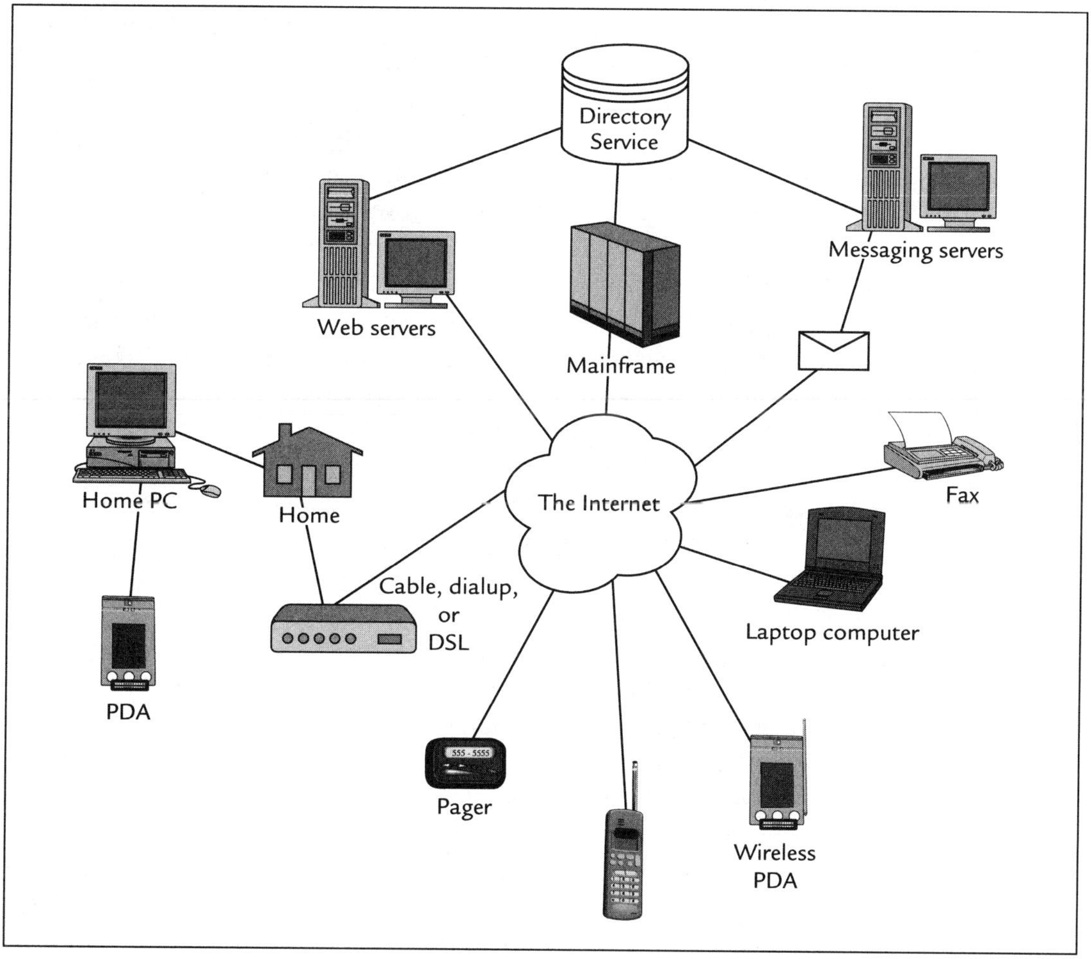

- Phone—In the office at their workplace or their home office, most employees have a phone. The enterprise directory will contain information about the user, the location of their workplace, and their phone number.
- Voice mail—This is typically tied to the phone number. Many companies offer a "find me" service, which provides a single phone number that the employee can give out to others and even put on a business card. This single number will route phone calls, voice messages, and pages to the targeted user.
- Paging service—With the advent of two-way paging, the directory is now very important. I have been in meetings where I sent a message to a partner in the meeting saying, "This speaker is really boring. I wish he would shut up." Now, as with mobile e-mail, it is necessary to carry your directory (or at least a part of your directory) with you.
- Home or office e-mail—Directories have been a part of e-mail since it was developed. With most e-mail systems there is a router service that actually moves the e-mail. The client sends the e-mail to the router service, which then delivers the e-mail. How does the router service know where the user really is? This is accomplished via a directory and a naming convention.
- Mobile e-mail—This is e-mail on the run. For example, when using a Wireless PDA, a message can be sent anytime and anywhere. The e-mail is an address either from the user's memory or a directory that is built into the device. When returning to the office (or home office), one can synchronize with a laptop and send the messages.
- Wireless mobile e-mail—The only difference between wireless and mobile e-mail is that messages can be sent immediately via a phone call. (There are other technologies that can provide immediate connections: WAP, GSM, and others.)
- Instant messaging—My company has rolled out instant messaging. I am totally addicted to this technology (I enter a treatment center next week.) I can contact team members quickly, host and attend meetings where we can share applications, or just chat to see how someone's weekend was. Guess what! I use a directory to find and establish communication with these users.
- Fax—Yes, even the lonely fax service can use a directory. This directory can be via DID to find users and deliver the fax directly to the desktop, or it can be just a simple directory embedded into the fax machine itself.

Directories are starting to be integrated into policy management. These directories can contain bandwidth and load-balancing allotment policies and can be the central point for distributing policy changes across the enterprise network. These directories are being integrated into network management as well, combining technologies with policy servers to enable a more granular division of network services.

Before we delve too deeply into directories, let's stop for a few minutes and discuss security. Here is the problem: A directory is no good to an enterprise if it cannot be trusted. One of the many features of a directory service is that it can provide authentication to an application environment. By using this same service, authorization can be controlled. So if the directory cannot be trusted, can you trust the security being given by the directory to your application? The answer is NO! Consequently, we will be looking at directories from two areas.

1. Using the directory as a service to provide security access and control.
2. Making the directory a trusted resource, or as we like to say, "Keep it safe from the bad dudes."

One of the most promising developments in the directory arena is the emergence of the Lightweight Directory Access Protocol (LDAP) standard. LDAP is quickly becoming a system that can provide a single universal interface for information retrieval across enterprise directories. Many products, including Microsoft Active Directory and Novel's NDS, support LDAP. The problem, however, is that hackers are already starting to look at the nuts and bolts of these new directories.

A directory is typically built from a set of **objects**. The directory object is normally a preset data structure that represents some type of entry in the directory. These entries can be users, groups, servers, resources (like a conference room, printer, or projector), and so on. Each object will have some type of definition assigned to it. These object definitions include a specification of properties (also known as attributes). In most cases, a directory object will have some type of identifier that makes it unique within the directory structure. This value can be a number, a name, or a combination of properties. Other object properties could include name, phone number, e-mail address, and so on. Typically each property will have a data type associated with each value: for example, phone number may be a data type of "number;" and name may be a data type of "string" or "text."

A directory will also have a **schema**, also known as the "definition" of the directory. This schema defines the basic structure of all directory objects and provides the rules used to enforce the relationships and definitions of an object. Furthermore, the schema defines what properties can be assigned to the objects and the syntax of the values that can be assigned. Ultimately, the schema defines how the directory is structured.

Once you have combined the object and the schema, you want to offer some services. Here are some of the basic qualities of a directory service.

- **Namespace**—A namespace is a collection of objects that reside within a common environment. In some cases, you can create an object that contains other objects. This is called a **container**. A container will have a set of rules, and if sets of objects follow those rules, then they "exist within that namespace." There are two general types of namespaces: flat and hierarchical.
  - *Flat names* are those in which the objects are held below a single authoritative object, which for the most part is a common container. For example, John Smith could be displayed in the directory as John or Smith or John Smith. In a small company, this would not be a problem unless you had John Smith's in Austin, Dallas, and Houston. In Figure 1.2 the three names in a single container display a representation of a flat directory structure, with each name different.
  - *Hierarchical names* are logically organized in a directory in a way that facilitates management of the directory. This tree structured organization can also assist with security and uniqueness management of the directory. For example, if you have John Smith/Dallas/The Company, John Smith in Houston, Dallas, and Austin would be unique in the directory. Figure 1.3 shows a hierarchical structure.
- **Distributed information system**—In many cases the directory service provides a system to distribute the directory across many different computers. Some directories partition themselves into different sections. In this way you can assign different parts of the directory to various administrators. For example, the administrators in China could update the directory for Hong Kong, but they could not edit or update the objects (records) for the directory in Dallas. At the same time, however, all users could read both the Hong Kong entries and the Dallas entries.
- **Search feature**—This is where you would hope that a directory service has some type of search feature or—even better—a robust search feature. This is not always the case, but in a perfect world you would be able to search on various attributes: last name, first name, unique key, or even location.

FIGURE 1.2 *Flat Directory*

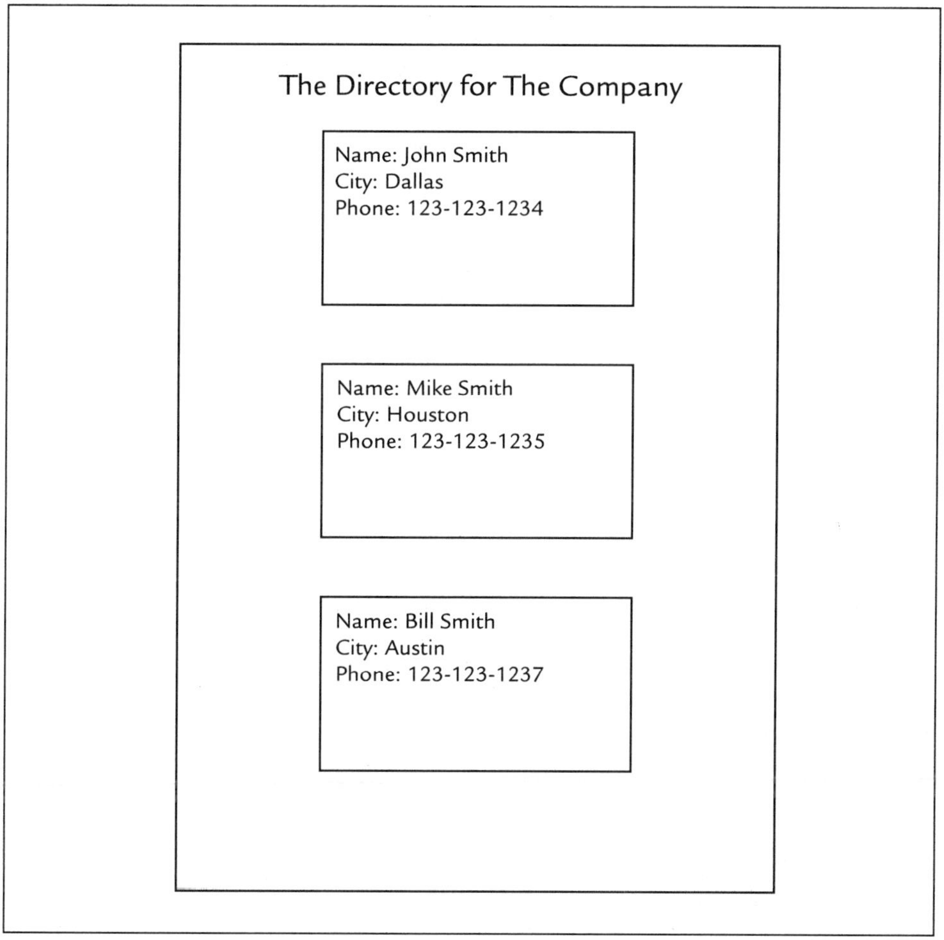

- **Replication**—This is where Lotus Notes (see Domino at www.lotus.com) has it down. These people know how to make replication work. One customer I worked with had 300,000 entries in his directory. Thanks to replication and a good infrastructure, this company could have any incremental update pushed out to 300 servers in 200 countries in under two hours. So you should hope that any directory service would have some type of data replication.
- **Extensible schema**—Most directory services have some type of "extension" to the directory schema. An extensible schema would give administrators and developers the ability to extend the native directory objects and implement new objects as needed.

FIGURE 1.3 *Hierarchical Directory*

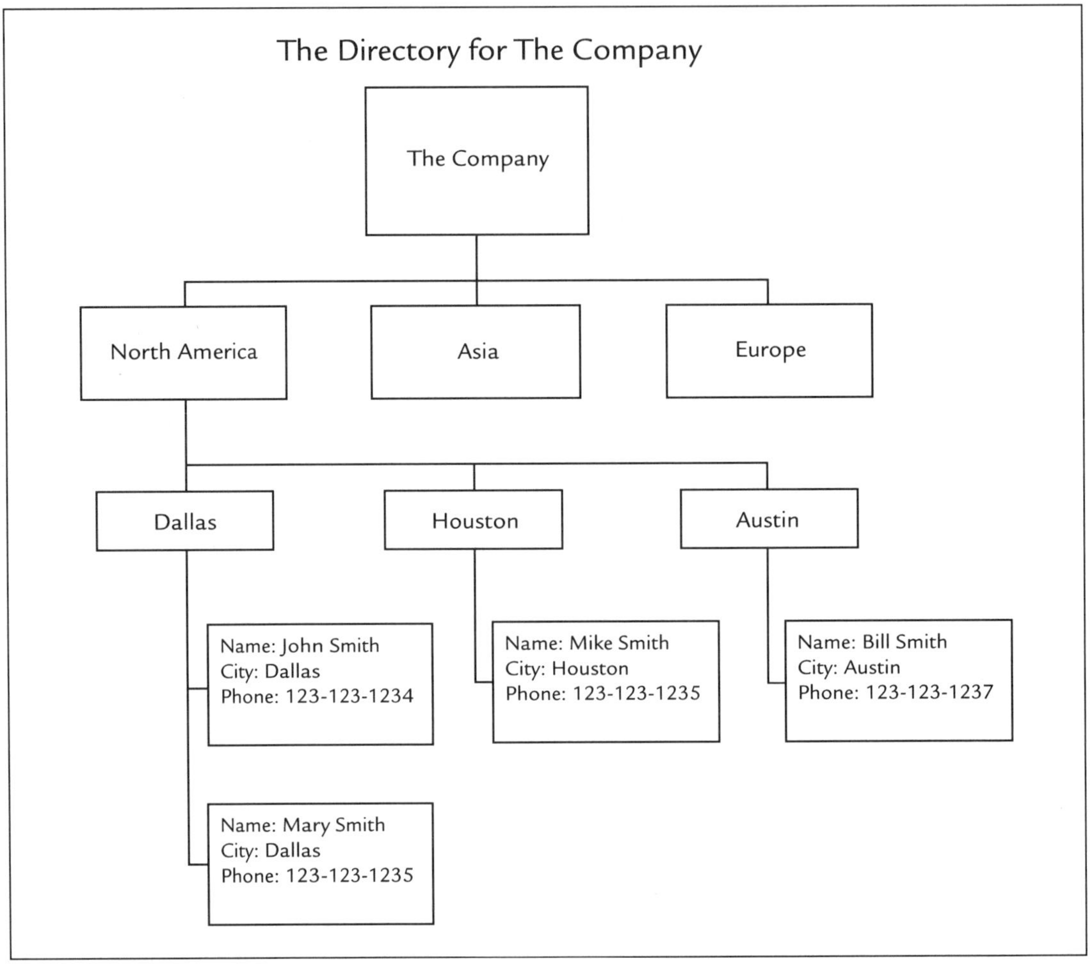

- **Ability to scale**—This be one of the most important features of the directory service. I have seen situations where a service works great for 30,000 users, but when you add another 30,000 due to a merger, the service breaks down. Make sure your service works just as well in a large environment as it does in a small environment.

  Now we'll examine where directories are used. Figure 1.4 shows each type.

- **OS/Network**—This is the directory that could be built into the OS. Microsoft NT, MS-NT has a directory that provides information about the user, his or her account, and the access level.

FIGURE 1.4 *Types of Directories*

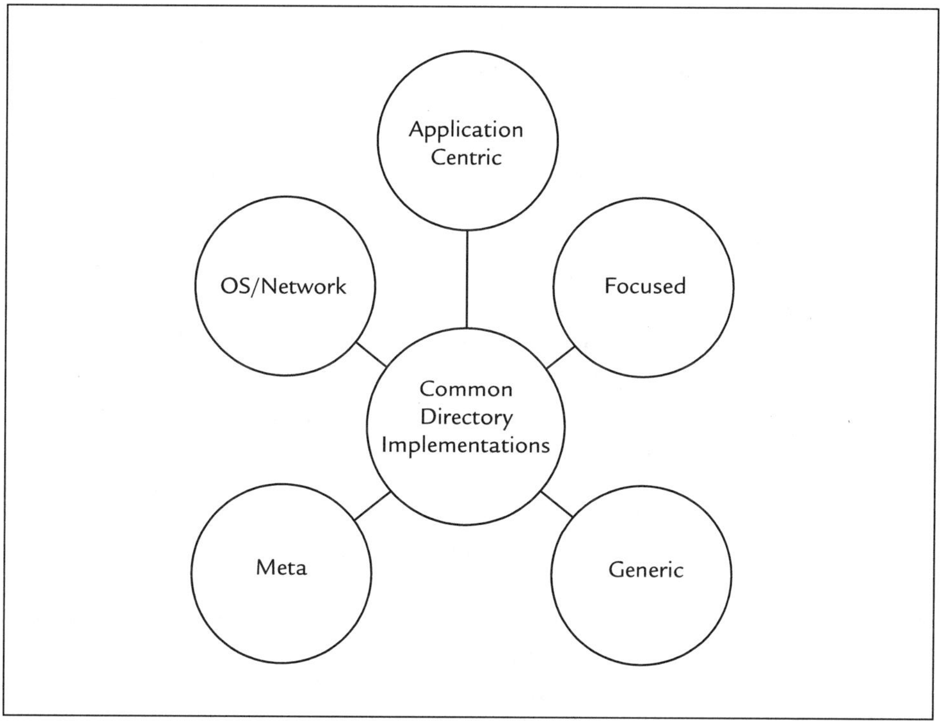

- **Application**—Some applications will keep user information embedded within the application. One example of this is Lotus Notes (Lotus Domino). This product keeps the information about the users in a separate database that is not directly tied to the operating system.
- **Focused**—These directories are designed to provide a service in a limited or focused environment. One example of this is the DNS system. The DNS system provides a directory of names in relation to IP addresses. The Internet would not work without it. Examples of focused directories include BigFoot (www.bigfoot.com), People Finder (http://www.peoplesite.com/), and Yahoo (http://people.yahoo.com/).
- **Generic**—These directories provide a wide range of services and information. An example of this type is LDAP, which we will discuss at length later on.
- **Metadirectories**—We have already discussed metadirectories, which will become more and more popular with larger enterprise companies via mergers and acquisitions.

1.2 X.500 and LDAP

X.500 is the name given to the standards produced by the International Telecommunications Union (ITU) (http://www.itu.int/).[1] ISO/ITU-T defined the protocols for a global directory service that is independent of computing application and network platforms. The X.500 standard was first released in 1988. This standard defines a specification for a distributed directory based on hierarchically named information objects (remember, we talked about directory objects) that users can search and browse. The X.500 directory service can provide access to data that is secure. This data can also be distributed or centralized. One part of the X.500 protocol is DAP. The Directory Access Protocol (DAP) provides a comprehensive protocol for accessing directory servers (which we'll see later). A significant part of the X.500 specification addresses the data and information model and the protocols needed to provide a fully distributed service based on a model of cooperating directory servers. Each server in this model would be responsible for a section of the overall Directory Information Base (DIB). These sections of the directory would be linked together, providing a single logical directory.

How do we get from X.500 to LDAP? LDAP emerged several years ago as a subset of the X.500 DAP specification. The idea was to use a lightweight client to access a X.500 "like" directory. Overall, X.500 did not take off in the Internet community. LDAP[2] has been readily accepted as a way to simplify access to a directory service and was modeled according to the X.500 standards. LDAP is increasingly being adopted as the Internet directory standard. The LDAP protocol provides a system for passing text-based queries from a client to an LDAP server over a TCP/IP network. The goal is to provide users an easy way to create and query directories to obtain user names, phone numbers, e-mail addresses, and other information.

LDAP was first developed in the 1990s when a complete OSI[3] solution like DAP would not fit on the desktop technology available at the time. LDAP v2 is defined in RFC1777. LDAPv3, RFC2251 is an update developed in the IETF[4] that addresses the limitations found during deployment of the

1. The ITU, headquartered in Geneva, Switzerland, is an international organization within it that governments the private sector coordinate global telecom networks and services.
2. Lightweight Directory Access Protocol—LDAP
3. Open Systems Interconnection (OSI) For more information see http://whatis.techtarget.com/WhatIs_Definition_Page/0,4152,212725,00.html.
4. Internet Engineering Task Force (IETF)

previous version of LDAP. This new version of LDAP also adds new features, improves compatibility with X.500 (1993), and specifies how LDAP can be used with non-X.500 and standalone directories. The major new features of LDAPv3 are in the areas of referrals, security, support for unicode characters, and extensibility.

The LDAPv3 core specifications contain the following.

- Protocol specification
- Attribute syntax definitions
- String representation of distinguished names
- String representation of search filters
- LDAP URL format
- X.500 schema definitions

LDAP v3 also defines a number of improvements to enable the client/server access model to be more efficiently implemented and more suitable for the new Internet model. Two examples of this are support for extended character sets and support for referrals to facilitate the hand-off from one server to another.

One big difference between LDAP v2 and v3 is in the security area. LDAP v2 only offers a simple clear text password authentication mechanism.[5] LDAP v3 describes a security model based on the Secure Sockets Layer (SSL).

As you can see, LDAP is a simplification of the X.500 directory access protocol that we had discussed in the first part of this chapter. As a result, LDAP can access X.500 directories and LDAP, and the X.500 servers can interoperate within the same environment. LDAP runs directly over TCP, eliminating the need for the complicated OSI stack.

The LDAP directory service model is based on specific and unique entries. An entry is a single collection of attributes with a single key (*key* means a parameter that can be used to look up something, not a key for encryption). In each entry there will be a name. As you recall, we have discussed DNs or distinguished names. The DN is used as a unique value that represents each collection or entry. Much like the X.500, each of the entry's attributes has a type and one or more values. Again, like the X.500 example that we have shown before, the LDAP directory entries are arranged in a

5. See Chapter 13 in *LDAP: Programming Directory-Enabled Applications with Lightweight Directory Access Protocol* (MacMillan Technology Series) This book has a great explanation of the authentication process and LDAP.

hierarchical treelike structure. This structure can reflect political, geographic, or organizational boundaries.

The LDAP directory service is based on a client-server model. A LDAP Server will offer the directory data via TCP/IP port 389, and SSL encrypted port 636 clients will access the LDAP server via a set of queries. The results of the queries can be used in messaging, applications, and authentication. One feature that is built into the protocol is that of a referral. If an answer is not available on the local server in the process of a query when it is configured, the LDAP server will attempt to connect to another server. If that server can service the request, then the result of the query will be returned to the client. One example of this could be name resolution. You may have a person's name but not his or her RFC821 Internet address (such as Bubba@exampleemailserver.com). See Figure 1.5. The client sends a request for "Bubba Duck." The first server performs a lookup and does not find the entry in its local DB. The server then sends a referral to the X.500 server, and the entry is found. A lookup is performed for "Bubba Duck," the

FIGURE 1.5 *LDAP Server*

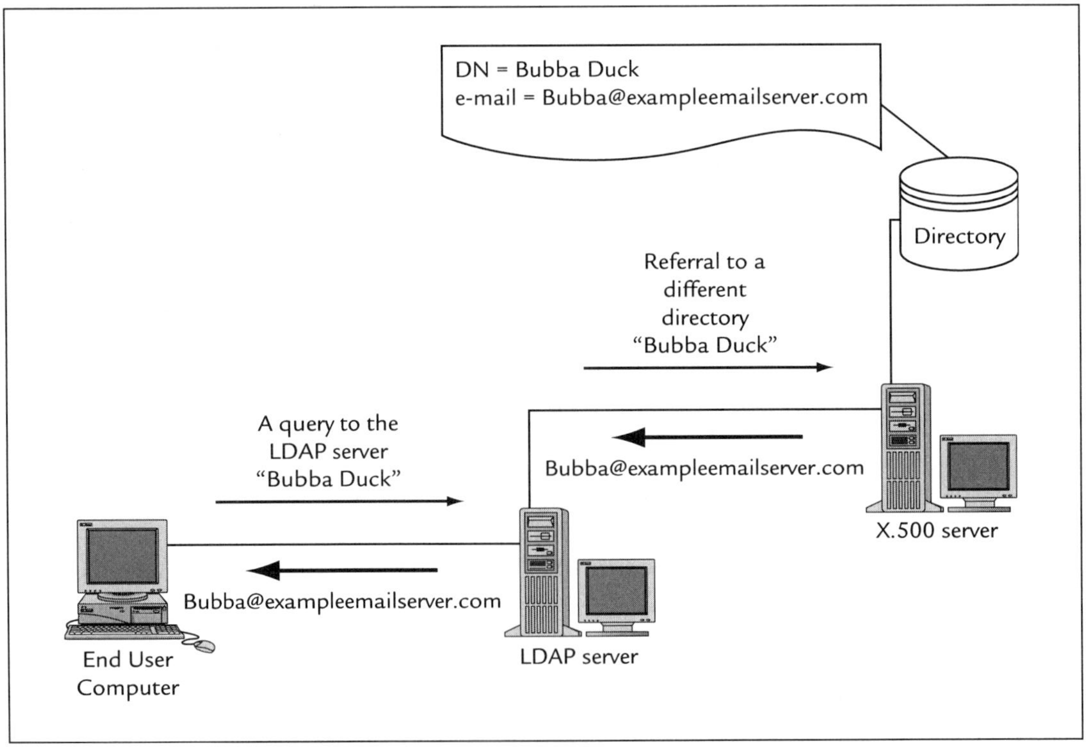

RFC821 address is returned to the LDAP server, and then the address is returned from the LDAP server back to the client.

LDAP servers are also capable of managing transaction logs. This is a process for chronicling additions, changes, and deletions of entries. When using this system, an LDAP server propagates these changes to other LDAP servers. This allows the user to have one LDAP server send the same data to several other LDAP servers.

There also is a method to access LDAP information via a URL (http://www.ietf.org/rfc/rfc1738.txt). A predefined format is listed in RFC 1959 (http://www.ietf.org/rfc/rfc1959.txt). This format is described as a LDAP search operation to retrieve information from a LDAP directory. Figure 1.6 is an extract of the RFC1959 that describes the URL syntax.

LDAP can be used to store X.509 certificates for authentication. The certificates are placed into the directory and then accessed via a Web server, as shown in Figure 1.7. In this example, a user attempts to access a secure page. The Web server returns a status code of 401. Then the users send the query back with their credentials (the user logs in). The Web server looks to see if the information is local. If the information is not local, it performs a

FIGURE 1.6

```
http://www.ietf.org/rfc/rfc1959.txt).
2.  URL Definition
   A LDAP URL begins with the protocol prefix "lap" and is defined by
   The following grammar.
   <ldapurl> ::- "ldap://" [ <hostport> ] "/" <dn> [ "?" <attributes>
               [ "?" <scope> "?" <filter> ] ]
   <hostport> ::= <hostname> [ ":" <portnumber> ]
   <dn> ::= a string as defined in RFC 1485
   <attributes> ::= NULL | <attributelist>
   <attributelist> ::= <attributetype>
                 | <attributetype> [ "," <attributelist> ]
   <attributetype> ::= a string as defined in RFC 1777
   <scope> ::= "base" | "one" | "sub"

   <filter> ::= a string as defined in RFC 1558
Example:
Ldap://ldap.itd.umich.edu/o=University%20of%20Michigan,c=US??sub?
(cn=smith)
```

FIGURE 1.7 *LDAP with Web Server*

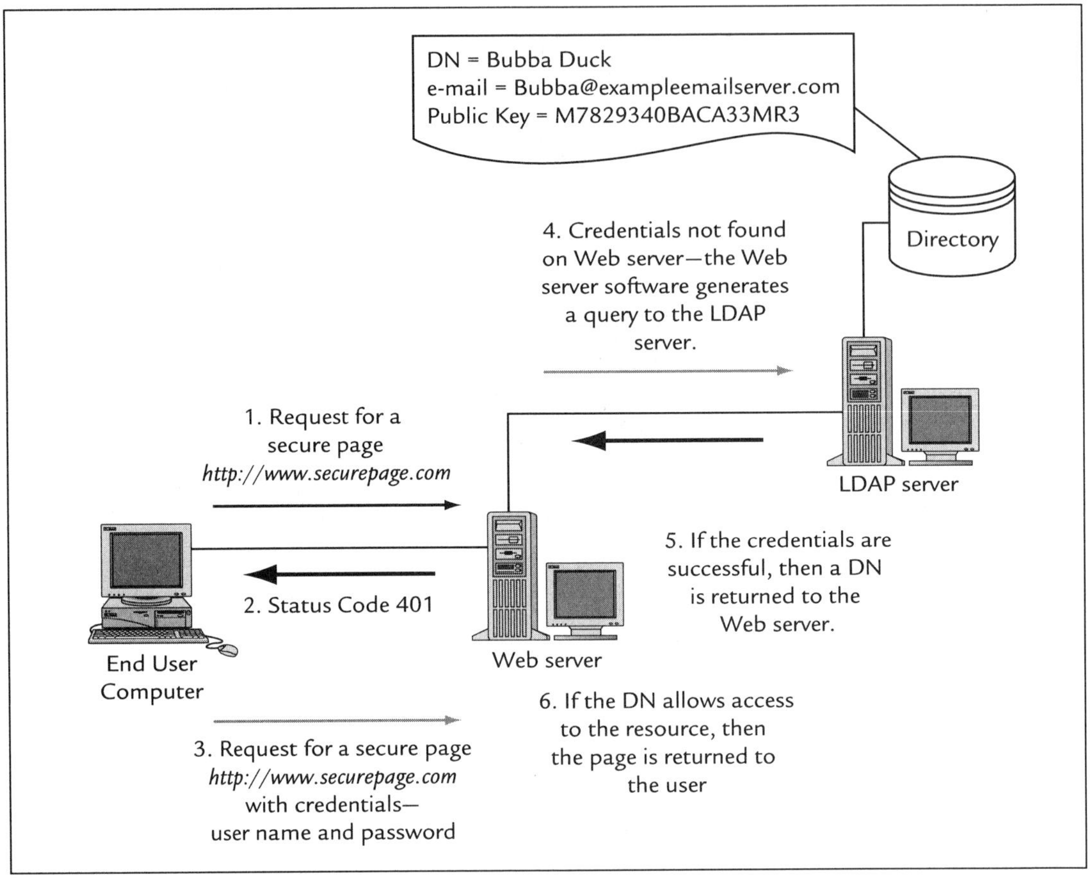

bind operation on the LDAP server and connects to it. Then the Web server sends over a query checking if the credentials are valid. If the credentials are valid, then a DN (you know what this is—*distinguished name*) is returned to the Web server. The Web server then checks to see if that DN has access to the requested resource. Finally, if the request is valid, the page will be returned to the browser.

For more information, see the following Web sites.

http://www.openldap.org/
http://www.umich.edu/~dirsvcs/ldap/
http://www.kingsmountain.com/LDAPRoadmap/Future.html

CHAPTER 2

Directories, Security, and Tigers—Oh, My!

2.1 Directory Types

When we look at directories, we can divide them along functional types (like White Pages) and the purpose they serve or by structural implementation and the way the directory is built (database type, organization, etc.).

In most large organizations, you will find a large number of databases that we can call "directories." In our experience, commercial organizations with 2,500 or more members (employees) will have in excess of 100 directories. Each of these directories was typically designed for a specific single purpose.

These are the "big three" directories.

- E-mail
- Network Operating System (NOS)
- Mainframe Security

The subsidiary directories include human resources, secondary NOSs, applications that store lists of authorized users, router and firewall tables, and organization charts, to name a few.

The primary functions common to the "big three" are storing information about a "user" and providing information that programs and systems can use to access control functions. The Mainframe Security programs, like

RACF and ACF2, exist primarily to provide authentication and to access control functions to programs and applications on mainframe systems.

E-mail was once the traditional use for a directory. The publicly accessible portion of this directory is often called the white pages, after the printed telephone directories. Because we have the data in an electronically accessible format, we can use the typical search and sort functions available in modern databases to look up particular names, addresses (e-mail or physical), and telephone numbers. We can also use these directories for other associative information such as "reports to," "department," or "manages."

Another typical directory is the Yellow Pages. Yellow Pages, also patterned after the printed telephone book, provide information about some business category, typically entities providing a category of goods or services. Examples abound on the Internet portals, where sites like Yahoo provide directory information about businesses.

The directory most familiar to students is the library card catalog. Similar directories on the Internet provide access to various types of electronically published information. Unfortunately, most of the electronically published information is not cataloged as well as the typical library and is thus more difficult to use.

Most organizations currently have multiple directories storing essentially duplicate information that is designed to be used for essentially the same purposes—location, authentication and access control. This has caused some expected results. From the organization's point of view, they contain data of dubious validity that may be out of date, and there can be high administrative costs or errors in implementation of appropriate levels of access. From the user's point of view, they require too many IDs and passwords for handling daily business activities. This situation has led many organizations to explore the concept of an "enterprise" directory.

The function of an enterprise directory is to externalize or abstract the necessary "directory" information and centralize it into a single directory application. Then individuals or applications needing directory data can access and rely on the enterprise directory for the information. The attractions of an enterprise directory are its lower costs for administration (add a user once, and he is added on all required systems) and its higher level of control (we now have one place to look to determine who has access to what data and applications).

The downside is that the great majority of these existing systems (e-mail, applications, networks, etc.) were not originally designed with the idea of externalizing their directory information, and the cost of modifying them or retrofitting them is high. And why fix something that's not broken?

So most organizations have chosen to take a less pandemic approach. They leave "legacy" applications alone and look at implementing a central directory service for new applications. The new applications fall into these two types.

- E-business or browser-based applications
  - Written in house
  - Purchase but designed for browser clients
- Commercial Off-The-Shelf (COTS) applications enabled for external directories

In some cases the off-the-shelf or "shrink-wrapped" applications include proprietary clients, and in others they use browsers for clients. In both cases, the external directory of choice is an LDAP directory or, to be slightly more precise, a directory that can communicate via LDAP (the Lightweight Directory Access Protocol).

As a side note, it should be pointed out that "Lightweight" is in reference to the full X.500 directory implementation and X.400 protocol. Generally, organizations found this implementation too expensive to install, so there are relatively few examples of X.500 directories. Internet application developers found the LDAP protocol using TCP/IP to be an easier and faster solution to implement. The University of Michigan SLAPD program provided working code samples that contained most of the necessary initial functionality. Being functional, available, and inexpensive, it became a de facto standard, which later became a series of formal IETF standards.

Another way to look at directories is in terms of their structure. Harking back to the definition of directories as a database, you can expect that directories are available in the usual database types, including flat file, hierarchical, and relational.

Applications frequently store their internal directory information as a flat file. DNS, or the Domain Name System, is an example of a directory application that uses a simple flat text file for data storage, and a hierarchical structure of associated DNS servers for propagating the information.

LDAP is designed as a hierarchical data structure, and LDAP directories are normally hierarchical. Still, there is no reason that directory information cannot be stored in a relational database, and many directories do in fact use an underlying relational database.

2.2 Directory Uses

Directories store and regurgitate the standard Five Ws.

- Who
- What

- When
- Where
- Why

Directories typically provide information about Who. Who is the user (name, ID, Social Security number, password, etc.)? It is essentially any information needed to identify a user.

Directories typically provide information about What. For people, this means what data they are allowed to see and what they can do with the data they can access. It also includes information about the applications they may be allowed to use.

Directories also contain information about When. Many users have 24-hour access to systems, but many do not. User IDs may have an expiration date. Certificates normally have an expiration period. Almost every directory keeps track of when an entry was initially created and when it was last modified.

Directories also normally contain information about Where. One category of Where is the physical location (street address, postal code, cube or column number, etc.). Another category is where the ID is valid (Global, USA only, only at plant site A, etc.).

Occasionally, directories include information about Why. This is sometimes included in comments or required fields that record information about why particular privileges were granted or whenever an entry is modified. It can also include information about a user class or category. "Administrator" is a typical category that may be noted in a user entry, and it connotes the need to be able to modify entries for other users.

Let's concentrate on the *user* aspect first. E-mail, by nature, is about communication. E-mail directories are designed primarily to provide information about (1) how to route messages and (2) how to identify individual users. They also provide information about how to associate a user with his information. The primary goal here is to determine where a user's files are located (on what server, in what file system, at what location, etc.). Additional information is stored so that the e-mail program knows whether the user stores his messages on a server or locally, what type of client she uses to access the messages, what rights the user has to store or delete messages, and so forth.

It is important to remember that the information e-mail directories store on users is used by two different entities: people and programs.

People (whether the public universe is the whole of an organization's employees or refers to the whole of the Internet community) use the directory to look up an address to insert in the address header of an e-mail. The e-mail program uses the same directory for routing, access control, and internal program functions.

The NOS and Mainframe Security programs keep directories primarily to control access to System or Network resources. RACF™ is an acronym for Remote Access Control Facility, and ACF2™ is an acronym for Access Control Facility Two. In the case of Mainframe Security directories, they typically did *not* have any public access. With their focus both on user access and data security, they didn't provide general users with any querying or viewing ability to the information in the directory. This lack of functionality is a good segue to directory security.

2.3 Directory Security

2.3.1 Why is Directory Security Important?

It may be stating the obvious that directory security is important. What may not be so obvious is the balance between making the data available and keeping it safe.

In a White Pages application, the primary objective is to make the data generally available. You want everybody to be able to look up a phone number or an e-mail address. Security in this case doesn't lie in protecting or limiting access to the data. It may be that you want to limit the ability to change data (only the creator or owner of the data can modify it), or you may want to make it truly public.

On the other hand, if you have an application that controls missile launching systems or nuclear power plant cooling systems, you may not want its access control information to be publicly available.

The concept of an Enterprise Directory makes this balance much more interesting *and* much more difficult. If you exploit the concept of an Enterprise Directory to its logical extreme, all information of the five Ws, including anything necessary to facilitate, allow, or authorize human-to-human, human-to-program, and program-to-program communication, is ensconced in the Enterprise Directory. Now you have all your eggs in one basket. And, in terms of the old saying, you now need to watch your basket very carefully. This can be a disconcerting concept.

This theme can be further explored in relationship to the Internet. In the olden days (circa 1980), a company knew who its users were—they were the employees who had been granted access. These days, with most companies having both outbound and inbound Internet access, a company doesn't limit its users to employees. And even if it does, it doesn't control it in the same way.

A company may put applications on an Internet-accessible server. This server may simply have static pages—"brochure ware"—or it may have actual applications accessible to the user. Should a company employee directory be one of those applications? What data should be available to casual user browsing? Should access to the applications be controlled? If so, how will the user database be populated and controlled? Should the company allow internal employees to access the externally facing applications? If so, should they use the same ID they use internally?

If the externally facing applications link to existing "legacy" applications, where should user ID data be stored (on the existing MainFrame Security system or on the externally available directory)? Should a company allow its RACF™ or ACF2™ system to be used to house its full directory listing of users—both internal (which can be hundreds of thousands) and external (which can be millions or hundreds of millions)?

These are all valid and perplexing questions for those responsible for electronic access and control of an organization's information assets. We hope to shed some light on these questions and their resolution in the following chapters.

At this point, it's a good idea to reemphasize these twin relationships between directories and security. On the one hand, directories need to be secure because they hold confidential data. On the other hand, directories are the primary repository for the base information necessary to secure access to confidential data. They are both subject and object.

2.3.2 Security and Directory

Security is a term that has many meanings. Social Security means money for your old age. Concert security means bouncers with T-shirts. Airport security often means metal detectors, X-rays, guns and badges, and standing in lines. When you put *computer* and *security* in the same sentence, many people, perhaps most, think either "IDs and passwords" or "firewalls."

For those in the profession, security is a blanket term for a basket of services that include the following:

- Identification and authentication
- Access control
- Confidentiality
- Nonrepudiation
- Isolation

We use a variety of security mechanisms to provide these various security services. Each of the mechanisms includes various types of security elements.

We have users and passwords for authentication. We have firewall filter rules for firewalls. The particular products and their capabilities vary over time, but the services generally remain as requirements in an IT structure. The issue is how you provide these required services.

Directories are both consumers and providers of security services. As a consumer of services, directories need identification, access control, and confidentiality services. They also frequently benefit from isolation services. As providers, directories hold (or act as repositories) the information necessary for identification, authentication, access control, and nonrepudiation.

Directories and security have a symbiotic relationship. Because we have substantial amounts of confidential information in directories, we need to be able to protect it. Because we need to protect information assets, we need to use directories to store the elements necessary to provide security.

2.3.3 What Makes a Directory Secure?

Clearly, if the directory holds confidential or valuable information, we need to secure it. That means we need to protect it from unauthorized access and modification. So a directory needs to have all the traditional security services available to it, whether it provides them itself or relies on external agents for these services.

For example, let's take authentication. Directories will need to be able to identify users. Even a public Internet application, openly available to any user, must be able to effectively identify users with administrative access. The directory (as an "application") can rely on some external program for authentication services, or it can provide its own (lifting itself by its own bootstraps).

Closely tied is the issue of access control. Again, the directory (as an "application") can rely on some external program for access control services, or it can provide its own. Confidentiality is normally provided by encryption. Encryption of data can be provided by the directory application or by an external program. Confidentiality may need to be maintained both during the storage and the transmission of data, so some data in the directory may use internal directory encryption while relying on an external service for encryption during transport (SSL or VPNs). (Typically, directory programs encrypt passwords. They do not normally offer the ability to encrypt every data field or attribute.)

Nonrepudiation is a relatively new issue in respect to directories. If you decide to make subclasses of directory users responsible for administering their "branch" or subset of the directory, and then that information is relied on in some way, you may want to ensure that those directory "transactions" (additions, deletions, and modifications) carry the benefits of nonrepudiation.

Isolation will also remain an issue. The best way to protect your data is to isolate it. That way you can protect it so well, no one can use it! Usability requires some compromise. You will always have to determine which data you should isolate and where you should put it. It's unlikely that any directory program or application will provide all the necessary security services internally. One or more will certainly be provided externally.

So back to our question, "What makes a directory secure?" The answer is *you*. You make the directory secure by how and where you provide the directory with the traditional security services.

CHAPTER 3

Directory Architecture

The term *directory architecture* can refer to either the internal or the external design of a directory application/implementation. We prefer to use *architecture* to refer to the design and placement of directory applications in logical designs and in physical (real) instantiations. The internal design of the directory application is normally unavailable to those who work in information technology, but it will be discussed in this and subsequent chapters. It's important to have an understanding of the context for directories.

Directory schema refers to the internal structure of the directory. While we don't have access to a directory application's internal design, we *do* have access to its schema. Directory vendors have provided us with directories that can be customized by modifying the schema.

All directory products ship with a default schema that provides some standard directory elements and some useful vendor-specific elements or elements required by other products in that vendor's line of software offerings. One of the nice things about the default schemas is that they allow the directories to be installed, configured, and used immediately (right out of the box).

3.1 Architecture Defined

A directory architecture is a generalized model (that is, high-level design) that defines a structure that can be used to develop implementations of actual systems. It consists of several elements.

- A set of components
- Interfaces to those components
- Protocols to be used to communicate with those components
- The structure formed by the interrelationships among those components

In addition, the directory architecture addresses the following.

- **Use cases** that validate the appropriateness of the architecture for use with its intended applications.
- **Change cases** that validate the ability of the architecture to accommodate reasonably foreseeable changes
- **Quality attributes** such as performance, scalability, usability, interoperability, simplicity of implementation, portability, and standards compliance

A simple high-level physical design diagram is shown in Figure 3.1.

FIGURE 3.1 *A High-Level Physical Design*

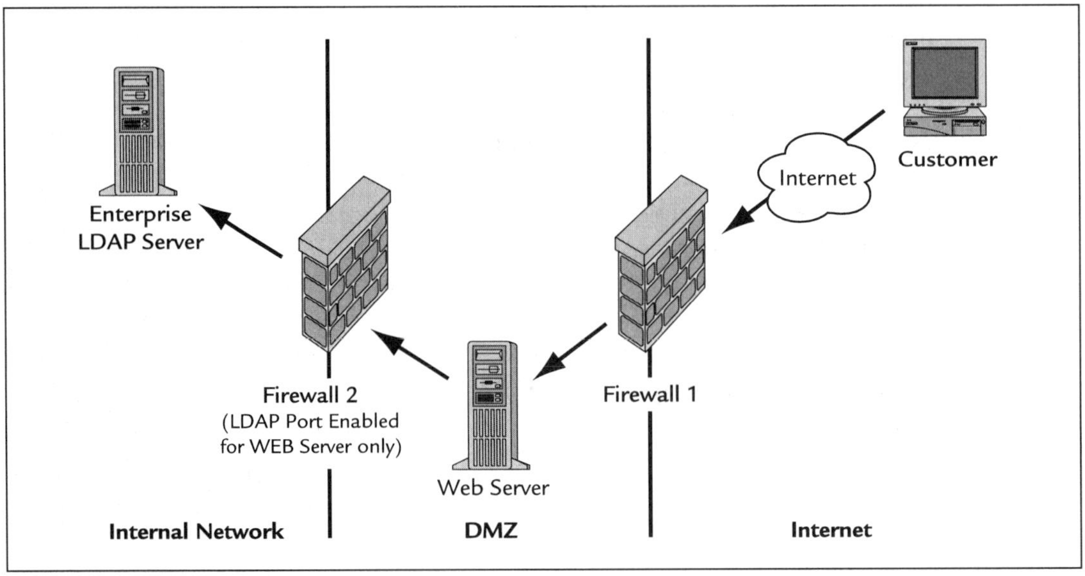

Figure 3.2 separates and identifies directory services, authentication services, and authorization services and the provision of those services to typical clients.

A good approach to beginning an enterprise directory architecture is to view it in terms of services, users, and providers. A simple view of these services is shown in Figure 3.3. In this case we have various types of clients (browsers, e-mail clients), internally developed applications, and external applications that are LDAP enabled, all communicating with an enterprise directory using the LDAP protocol.

We also see that the directory is administered by a browser client using HTTP and that a metadirectory communicates with the directory using LDAP.

FIGURE 3.2 *Architecture*

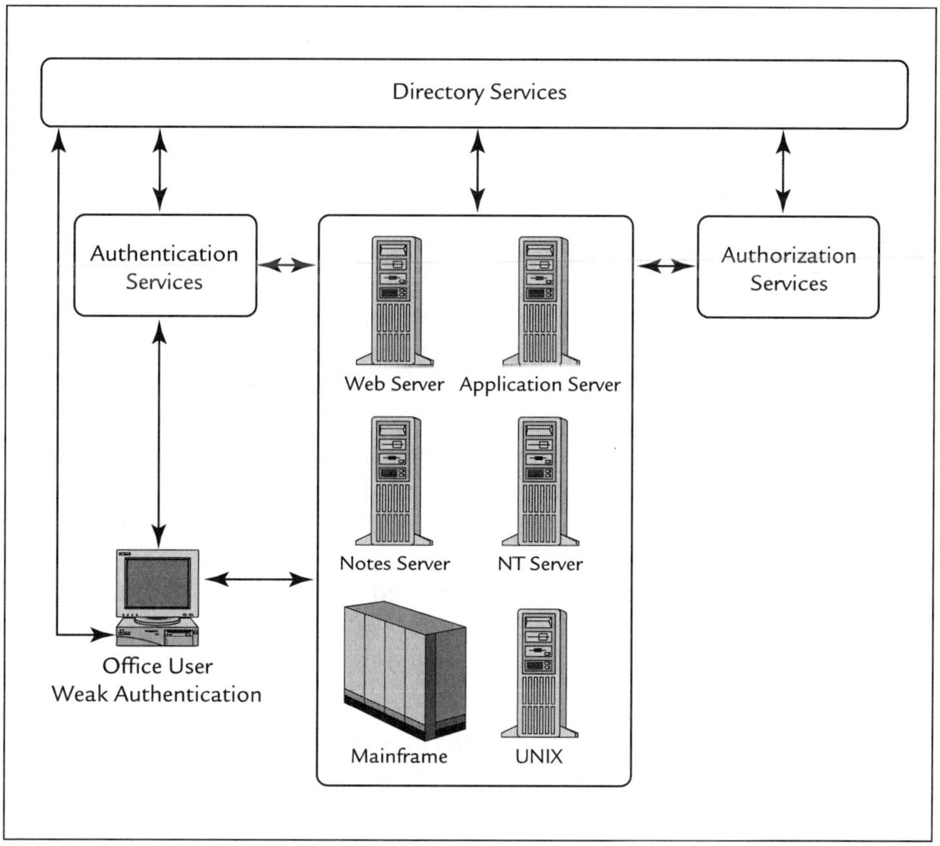

FIGURE 3.3 *Directory Services*

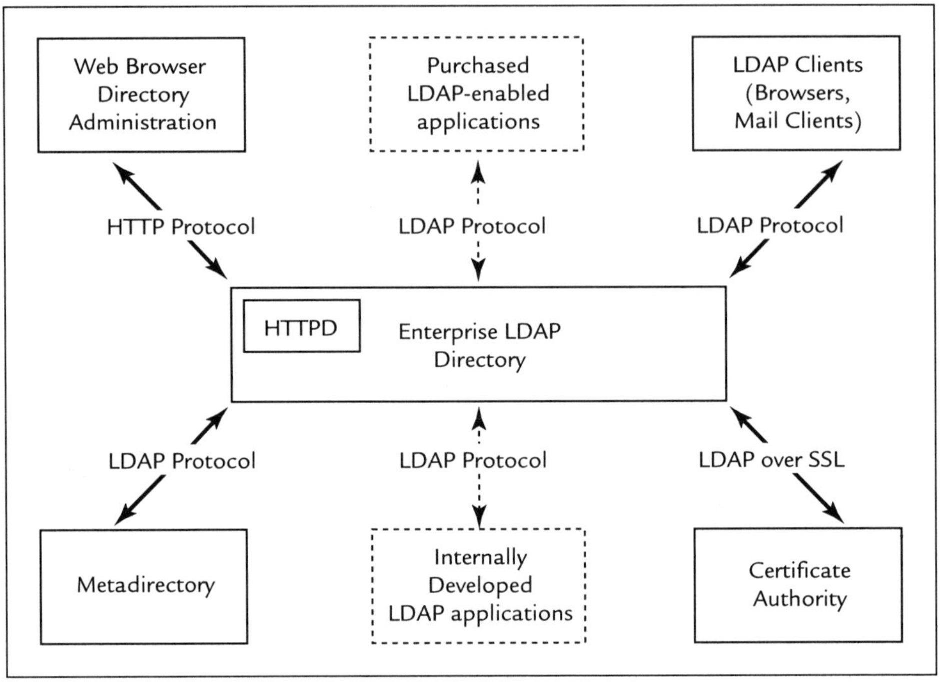

3.2 Critical Elements

As we've said previously, directories are essentially special purpose databases. A directory is simply an ordered listing of information about objects (things) that one has an interest in storing and maintaining data. More precisely, in computer terminology, a directory is a *database* that stores and retrieves typed, ordered information about objects. "Typed" means there is knowledge about what kind of data is stored—for example, numbers or character strings. "Ordered" implies there is some sense of organization about the data.

It is also useful to understand what a directory is not, since on the surface it has many of the characteristics of a traditional database. The following are features of databases that directories do not normally possess.[1]

1. Individual directory vendors may implement some or all of these *database-like* features in their product offerings, and there are also efforts in progress to standardize some of these features.

- Designed to store dynamic (changing) data—directory technology is optimized to read-access, implying they are designed to store relatively static data.
- Designed to store a variety of data types (both simple and complex)—directories store relatively few simple types (numbers, strings, and binary data).
- Designed with powerful interfaces (application programming interfaces—APIs) like SQL—directories typically expose a simple API (see the following LDAP discussion).

3.3 Implementations—Products and Vendors

3.3.1 Purchased LDAP-Enabled Applications

Many LDAP-enabled applications can be purchased off-the-shelf today. Here are some examples.

- Enterprise directory management—Oblix, Intracus
- Human resource systems—PeopleSoft
- Virtual private networks—Red Creek Communications, KyberPASS, Aventail, Checkpoint
- Networking—Cisco, Nortel Networks, Lucent
- Public Key Infrastructure (PKI)—EnTrust, Baltimore
- Firewalls—Check Point Software

3.3.2 LDAP Clients

Here are some examples of LDAP v3 compliant clients.

- Web browsers—both Netscape and Internet Explorer come with LDAP capabilities.
- Microsoft Outlook 2000 mail client
- Lotus Notes client version 5

3.3.3 Internally Developed LDAP Applications

These would be LDAP-enabled applications developed internally by the organization.

3.4 DAP and LDAP

LDAP (Lightweight Directory Access Protocol) is a technology that has evolved in the past few years to become the standard way for a client to access a directory service. LDAP was developed to provide a low overhead (lightweight) alternative to the X.500 Directory Access Protocol (DAP). LDAP runs over TCP/IP (the standard Internet protocol), whereas DAP requires the full ISO communications protocol stack. This full ISO protocol imposes significant resource requirements on the client and has not been well received in the United States. LDAP also simplifies the implementation of directory access in other ways that minimize its resource requirements and complexity while maintaining the majority of the X.500/DAP functionality.

LDAP standardizes the rules for communication between a client and the directory service (in other words, the protocol). It defines the transport and message format to be used by any client to access an *X.500-like* directory. It does not define the API, but that work has been done in individual (nonstandard) efforts by the major vendors effort. All major directory vendors provide a LDAP directory service, or they provide a LDAP interface to their proprietary directory (thereby masking their internal directory implementation and effectively providing for transparent access from an LDAP-enabled client). This is illustrated in Figure 3.4.

FIGURE 3.4 *Domino and LDAP*

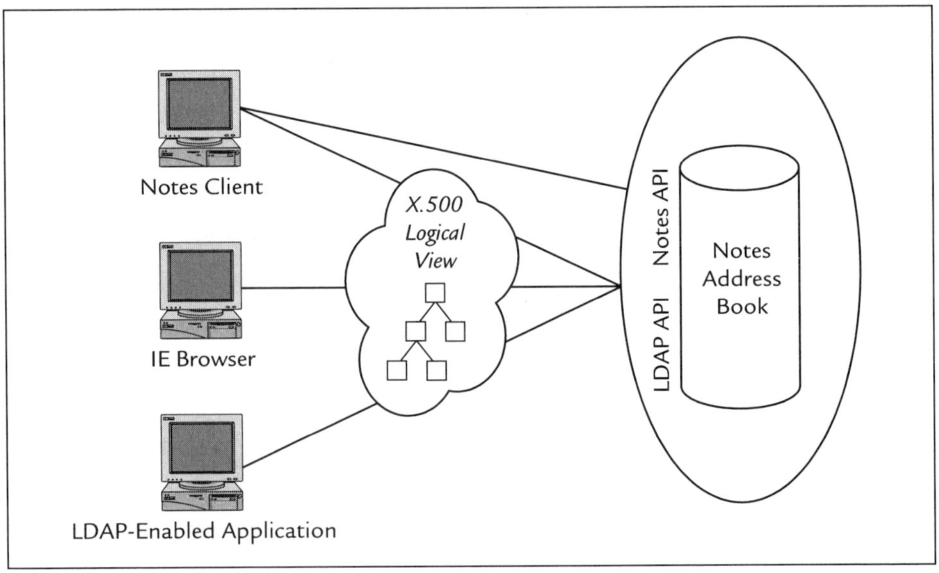

The Notes client can access the directory (Notes/Domino Address Book—NAB in this example) one of two ways: (1) using its proprietary Notes API and following the Notes internal protocols (over TCP) or (2) vis-a-vis LDAP APIs following the LDAP protocol. The Microsoft Internet-Explorer (IE) browser and an example application have been *LDAP-enabled*, and both can therefore access the NAB using the LDAP API.

When accessing the NAB through the LDAP API, all three clients are provided the illusion of an X.500 directory that they read information from and write information into. The API hides the specifics of the internal implementation. Extending this notion to an enterprise level leads to the conclusion that LDAP can be the directory lingua franca. It allows an enterprise to construct a single, unified directory architecture by integrating existing directories, where it makes business sense to retain them, with the new LDAP directory (or directories) it chooses to create.

So, what is a metadirectory? A metadirectory is a join engine that connects various separate directories (see Figure 3.5). Metadirectories don't store the directory data themselves. They store information about where that data is located and how it can be accessed—thus, storing data about data. As we see in Figure 3.5, we can use metadirectories to connect subsidiary directories to the primary enterprise directory. This is a common use of a metadirectory and almost standard implementation.

The need for metadirectories comes from the existence of multiple different directories in an organization. In most cases, these directories must

FIGURE 3.5 *Metadirectory*

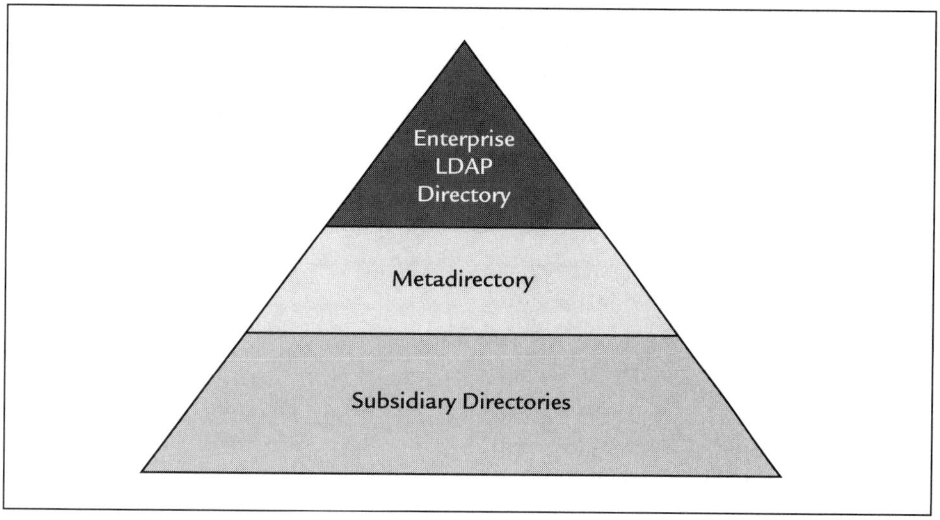

be maintained, and they may not be changed or removed. Generally they are proprietary, non-LDAP-compliant directories. If all the directories "speak" LDAP, there is not a problem. We would just set them up to communicate using the LDAP protocol, and they would share information as required. (Well, *almost* no problem. There are still issues of schema mismatch, authoritative sources, push vs. pull, scheduling of transfers, and so on. It's enough to keep consultants very busy.) In the usual case, these existing directories don't understand LDAP, and we must use a different technology to communicate with them—the metadirectory.

Metadirectories typically have "connectors" that allow the metadirectory (join engine) to connect to multiple existing directories. Some of those connectors are generic and require some substantial effort to configure and use. Others are prebuilt for specific types of product connections (to PeopleSoft™, for example). See Figure 3.6.

In addition to their primary function as join engines, metadirectory products also typically provide functionality in two other areas critical to a real functioning application: data or schema mapping and scheduling. The mapping functions allow the linking of one data element in one directory with another similar data element in a second directory.

This concept of a metadirectory has been recently extended to create the concept of a "virtual" directory. A virtual directory is a directory that uses no data store of its own but relies on the data stores of the sources it connects to create a virtual directory. Such a directory might access some data from a PeopleSoft HR system and other data from an ACF2 system to be able to respond to LDAP formatted requests. However, it would store nothing in a database of its own. Each request would require a connection to and a search against an existing source database.

FIGURE 3.6 *Subsidiary Directories*

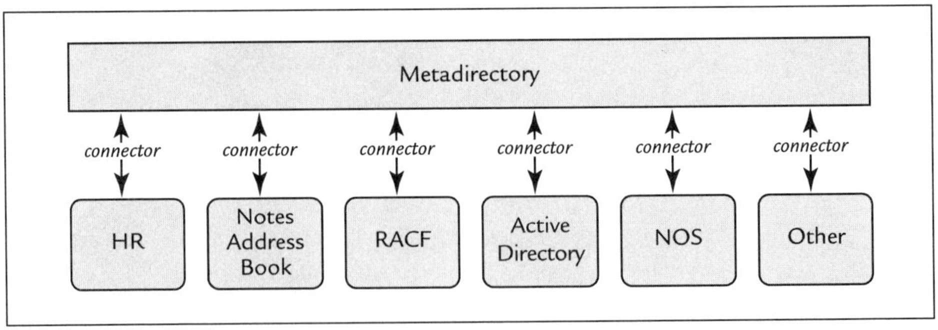

In the case represented in Figure 3.7, we need to map "Person" to "User." We also need to map "Name" to both the "First Name" and "Last Name" objects.

In LDAP terms, "Person" and "User" are directory objects. "Name," "First Name," and "Last Name" are all object attributes. In traditional database terms, "Person" and "User" might be records, and "Name," "First Name," and "Last Name" would all be field names.

Figure 3.8 shows a case where we have a single metadirectory that sits between a single enterprise directory and multiple subsidiary directories. In this case, we are using the metadirectory connectors to aggregate the data in the subsidiary directories and to push it into the enterprise directory via the metadirectory. Once in the enterprise directory, it's available in a single location via the standard LDAP protocol.

In Figure 3.9, we've split the metadirectory into two separate components, each with its own subsidiary directories and feeding a single enterprise directory. This type of directory architecture might be used for performance, security or for network topology considerations.

FIGURE 3.7 *Mapping Directory Trees*

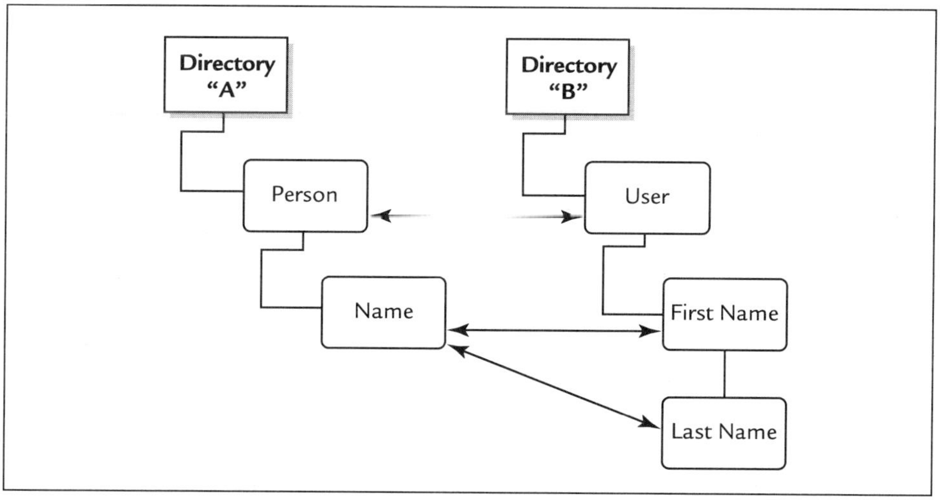

FIGURE 3.8 *Single Metadirectory Join Implementation*

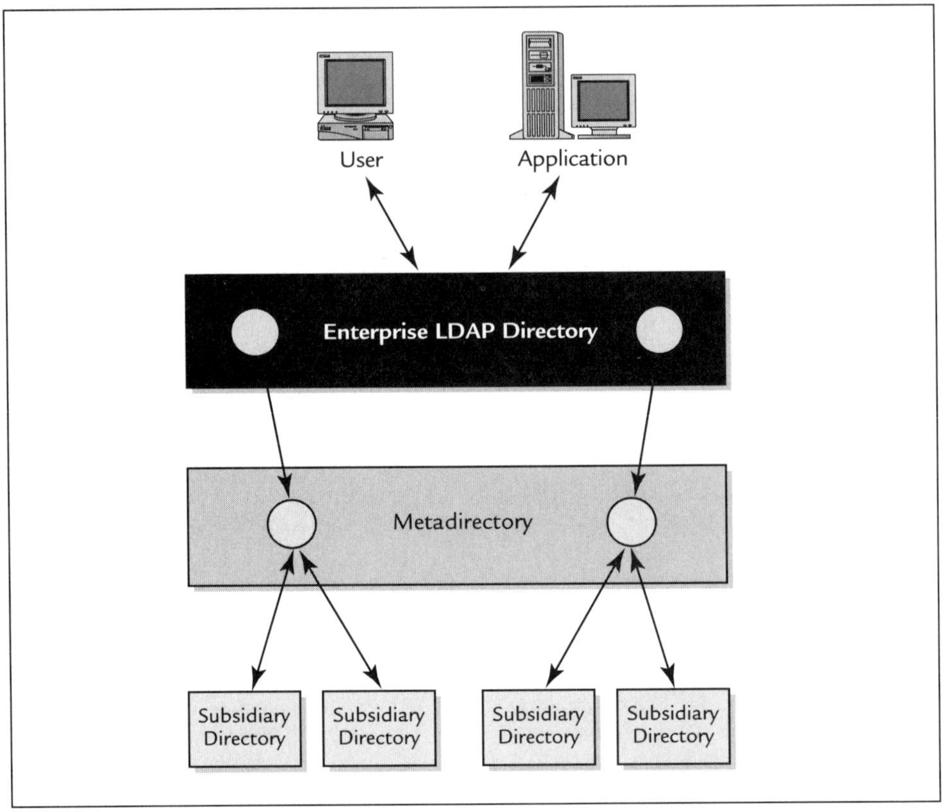

FIGURE 3.9 *Multiple Metadirectory Implementation*

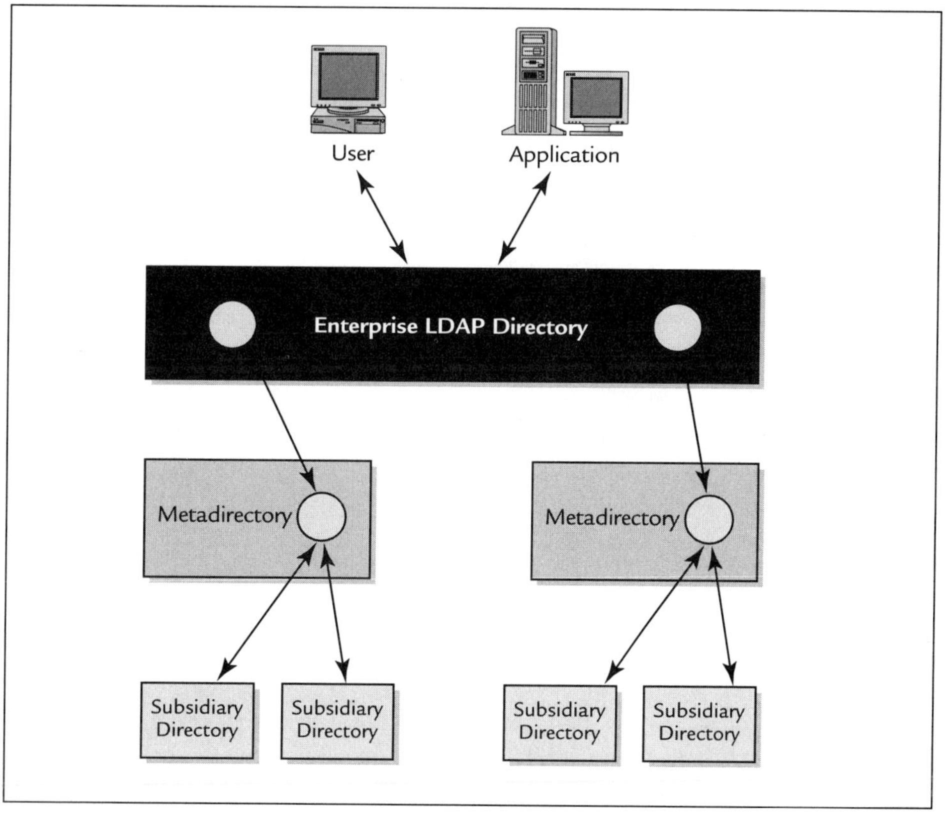

References

http://www.ibm.com/software/network/directory/ [IBM SecureWay Directory (LDAP)]

http://www.kingsmountain.com/ldapRoadmap.shtml [LDAP/X.500 FAQ and roadmap to other directory-related Web sites]

LDAP Programming Directory-Enabled Applications with Lightweight Directory Access Protocol by Timothy A. Howes, Ph.D., and Mark C. Smith. 1997. Macmillan.

Understanding and Deploying LDAP Directory Services by Timothy A. Howes Ph.D., Macmillan Jan-1999.

CHAPTER 4

More on LDAP

LDAP, though simple, has some additional useful characteristics. To use them we need to learn a little more about some standard LDAP features.

4.1 Referrals

In Chapter 3 we saw that the LDAP directory structure was intrinsically hierarchical—a tree-structured database. One of the reasons database designers moved from trees to relational structure was the need to provide a second (or third) method for relating data elements. Relationships between data elements in a hierarchy are defined by their place on the tree. If we have a user branch, and on that branch we have an object (entry or record) for "BUBBA SPEED," with attached branches and limbs with attributes for phone number, address, and shoe size, we know those size 13D sneakers belong to "Bubba" because of *where* they are on the tree. Their relationship is defined by their relative location. So to determine the significance of the data, we have to know its directory context. And in a tree directory, that means its location in the tree.

The primary advantage of the tree structure is that it can be searched quickly. A secondary advantage is that once you have located an object, you can determine its context by backtracking up the tree. In a directory implementation, this seems ideal. We want to be able to optimize our directory for searches, but we also want to define some rudimentary relationships among the data elements, and the tree provides that minimal structure.

Like anything perfect in its simplicity, however, we try to improve upon it, and in doing so, we make it more complicated and less perfect. And this is exactly the case with LDAP when it comes to referrals.

There are times when we want to create a relationship between data on one branch of the tree and data on another branch. For example, we could have an attribute for "SHOE SIZE" and "COLOR" within each person record. However, that might be inconvenient or unwieldy because we have to duplicate a large amount of information. There are not that many shoe colors, and you might have to enter "BLACK" thousands of times. Changes could make it inconvenient, too. For example, marketing might want to change "BLACK" to "MIDNIGHT" because they think it sounds sexier. So we might want to associate "BUBBA, 13D" with a branch for "SHOES," with limbs for "STYLE = WINGTIP" and "COLOR = MIDNIGHT." Thus we have the need for a referral.

A referral is a pointer that creates a relationship between a data element on one branch of the DIT with an element on another branch. Referrals also provide us with the ability to segment the tree into useful subsets. For example, you might want to split up your North American directory into the three subsets "US," "CANADA," and "LATAM." Each subset could be on a separate server located in the local geography. When a search comes in for a name within the local list, it would be resolved on the local server, and an answer would be returned. When a request comes in for a name that is hosted on one of the other directories, the request would be referred to the appropriate directory subset (US, CANADA or LATAM), which would provide the response. Referrals are methods to allow LDAP directories to connect defined relationships outside the DIT structure.

4.2 Authentication and Authorization

One of the most common uses for directories is to store the information necessary to identify or authenticate users and to authorize their access to resources. In the IT security industry, these are called the security services of authentication and authorization. Notice that the directory service simply *stores* the authentication and authorization info. An LDAP directory ALONE does not provide these services—it just stores and serves the information. This bears repeating because it is a common misconception. The LDAP protocol and LDAP directories do not perform authentication or authorization; they just store the data.[1]

Figure 4.1 illustrates how these services relate to the directory and to their normal mutual clients, the servers, and end users of the world. When

FIGURE 4.1 *Authentication and Authorization*

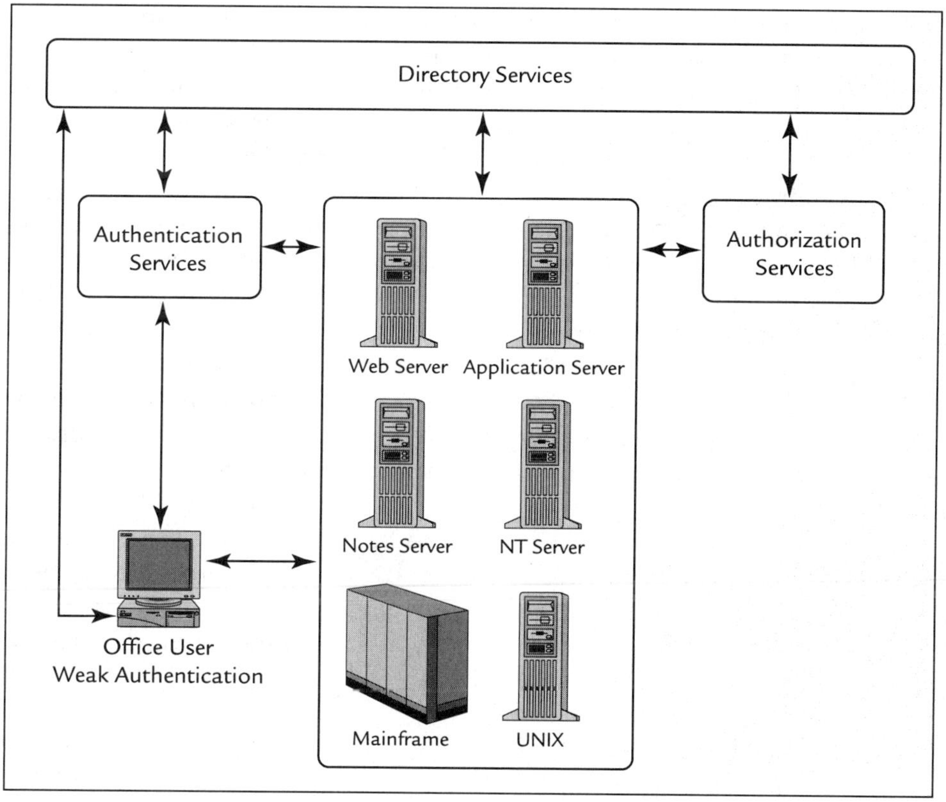

1. This statement generated a lot of comment from my co-authors, so further explanation is in order. Most Directory Service products allow users to authenticate to the product. It is necessary for administrative users and to allow users the potential to update their own entries directly. However this authentication (and the associated access control) is only used for access to the directory itself. Users are not authenticated or granted access controls by the directory product to any other application. For this to happen, the directory product would have to produce some type of credential that could be exported and read or used by those other applications, and directory service products do not produce these credentials. Products like Netegrity's SiteMinder and IBM's Policy Director do produce these exportable credentials, and simply store their information in the directory.

a directory is used to store and serve up identification, authentication, and authorization information, it becomes part of the IT security infrastructure.

A security directory may have very different requirements than a white pages directory providing user names and internal phone numbers for employee convenience. Authentication and authorization services are normally expected to be available at all times—the very definition of 24×7×365. While some amount of unscheduled and scheduled downtime is normally tolerated, the acceptable times may be very short, amounting to only minutes or seconds a year. We'll say more about this later in the chapter.

Authentication and identification refer to some way to identify the user who is requesting system resources. The resources can be Web pages, or a printer, or scheduling a conference room. So how do you know who is asking? Well, you have to ask the requestors to identify themselves before you agree to allow them access to the services. In the real world we ask people for their names. In the virtual world we frequently do the same thing: We ask for a name. Users can respond with something like "BUBBA SPEED" if that's their real name. Frequently, users are given code names or IDs, and they provide these IDs when challenged to give their user names. We use IDs because they are more secure than common names and because they can be unique. We might have more than one "BUBBA" but only in Texas. User IDs are used primarily to provide uniqueness.

Security can be increased further by requiring users to provide both an ID and a password. The ID can be public, whereas the password should be kept secret. In these cases, the IDs and passwords need to be stored somewhere, and the obvious choice is an LDAP enterprise directory. This is one of the more common uses for an LDAP directory today. The normal result would be an entry like this.

```
O=ACME
OU=EASTREGION
PERSON
        FNAME=BUBBA
        LNAME=SPEED
        USERID=SPEEDO
        PASSWORD=**********
```

Here the ID and password are stored as attributes of a person object (record).

LDAP can be used for storage of other identification and authentication systems, including certificates, in which case the record would look something like this.

```
O=ACME
OU=TEXAS
PERSON
        FNAME=BUBBA
        LNAME=SPEED
        USERID=SPEEDO
        PASSWORD=**********
        CERTIFICATE=192834(@985y9485y19845y19485y948y9ry94tryoe
8ryp9q8erhqoiu%rehqpoerhqpeotuhqprprtproht!~qprotqhproiuthqr9t
iqhrpitqhretoqiuerhtqpeoriuhtp#qtpreoheqprtpretpreohtqerohtwpr
oihgewroiugheqoighqeroi;hqoerith;e48tri2847529875-298475709284
75948ht2p94iu5298
```

Notice that the record now includes an ID, a password, and a certificate. Combinations of these can be used to identify the requestor. You can use just the ID, the ID and a password, or the ID and the certificate. Or you could just use the certificate. You can't use just the password because passwords may not be unique across the universe of your users. (I'll bet there's more than one "password," one "pass," one "administrator," and one "admin" in your password files.)

Once you know with whom you are dealing, you then need to decide what you are going to allow them to do. That is the role of the authorization services and authorization components. Again, the authorization and access control information can be stored in an LDAP directory. Unfortunately, while we have current IETF standards for attributes usable for authentication, we don't have comparable standards for access control attributes.

4.3 X.500

The X.500 specification was offered as a standard for creating directories that could interoperate across organizations. It was offered in conjunction with the X.400 mail standard, which is large and comprehensive. One of its requirements is a complete OSI seven level model. This model, while extremely useful conceptually, was frequently more complex than many organizations desired, and it was not widely implemented.

In particular, the widely sold commercial e-mail products and the more widely used open source e-mail and directory products did not implement the full set of X.500 standards. So the market spoke, and it said it did not want to spend the amount of money and effort required to implement a full X.500 directory architecture. Still, we need directories. And directories that are aware of each other and able to communicate in some fashion are more valuable than isolated standalone proprietary directories. So LDAP was offered to fill the vacuum.

4.4 X.509

The X.509 standard refers specifically to certificates. This standard specifies what must be in a certificate, what may be in a certificate, and what format the certificate must take. The advantage, again, is that with such a standard, certificates may be issued and used by different programs, from different authors, developers, or manufacturers.

The practical advantage is that users can accept X.509 certificates issued by companies such as VeriSign, Entrust, or Baltimore, and store them for use by their Netscape or Internet Explorer Web browser. Those same companies sell certificate software (Public Key Infrastructure or PKI) or services that allows organizations to issue their own certificates. And again, because the certs are X.509 compliant certs, they are available and usable by a large variety of programs that need to exchange certificates for the purposes of identification.

4.5 LDIF

LDIF stands for Lightweight Directory Import Format. It is a more or less standard format for LDAP directories and is used for both the export and import of directory data and schema.

LDIF files have a number of common uses. First, they can be used for backup and restore of your directory files. In fact we always recommend that admins and owners of LDAP directories make and keep a periodic backup up their directory data in this format.

Second, LDIF files can be used to populate directories initially. Information from other sources can be put into an LDIF format and then imported into your LDAP directory. Typically, this is much faster than the alternatives of manually inputting or using bulk insertion routines.

Third, LDIF files are typically used during migrations and during upgrades to new LDAP software versions or transfers to LDAP directory software from a different developer.

CHAPTER 5

Directories Within the Enterprise

5.1 Historical Perspective

Directories. Can't live with 'em, can't live without 'em. Directories are widespread throughout organizations. I believe that the first directories were most likely rolls of members, probably for armies in the distant past. When armies became organized enough for payment to the troops, they required a roll. At some point that roll evolved into a directory that identified each soldier and the unit or branch (sound familiar?) to which they were a member. Soldiers had to be on the roll (the pay roll) in order to receive compensation for their service. And as a by-product, the army's generals now had information about how many members and what sort of resources they had at their disposal.

Directories were also used by governments for tracking tax collection. Governments kept track of land and other producing assets so they could exact a tax on the owners of those assets.

Directories took their next big step in London, England, in the 1800s. In order to identify buildings for purposes of fire control, the city authorities decided to put numbers on the buildings so the fire brigades could find their way to the fires without the delays inherent in the directions of the time, which used familiar landmarks and locally known owners' names: "Go down to John's tavern, head out to the blacksmith, then turn up at old man Speed's until you get to the fire." The street numbers and the corresponding street directories were used by the fire brigades to improve service and avoid the devastating fires that had periodically leveled the city.

These first street directories had some of the same issues we still face today. For one thing, they had more than one street with the same name. They resolved this problem in two ways. First, they added a unique suffix (street, avenue, court, way, etc.). Second, they subdivided the city into smaller units so that each section could have the same names—thus, you could have more than one Oak Street.

Another interesting result was a popular revolt. The public didn't believe the government wanted to number the house for fire prevention alone. They didn't trust the government's reasoning and didn't think the government had any right to put a number on their property (home or business). They didn't particularly *want* to be found. Their acquaintances knew where they lived, so they didn't need a number to find them. There was, in fact, a popular opposition that resulted in some demonstrations and small-scale riots. The public was concerned about their privacy, and they realized that even something as simple as a house number could be used by the government to violate their privacy and anonymity. And those concerns are raised about directories to this day.

The next big step for directories came with the advent of electronic communication, especially radio and telephone. Radio was initially used primarily by ships and by land-based stations. Each broadcaster used a call symbol (WXAN, KNOW, etc.) to identify themselves. There was a lot of duplication, which caused lots of confusion. International conventions in 1906 and 1912 standardized radio call signals, and the list of those call signals became a radio directory.

Telephone service had a different problem. Initially, service was provided with operators who individually connected callers. The operators knew the owners of telephones by name, and when a caller asked for a connection, the operators manually connected the wires. Quickly, automated switching equipment was created, but such equipment required the use of dial telephones and numbers. And numbers, while allowing automated switching at local exchanges, created some new problems. While you would certainly know the names of the local drugstore and the pharmacist, you might not know the phone number that the drug store had been assigned by the telephone company. So to expand service, the telephone companies began publishing telephone directories—the white pages.

White pages directories ran into a familiar problem. There was more than one Mr. Smith, so they needed a way to distinguish each Smith. They could have used age, place of birth, mother's maiden name, or a variety of other factors. But they settled on street addresses to make them unique because they knew the address. Fixed wire line service is geographically specific. The phone company ran a wire to your house right to your hall or bedroom and installed a phone. They *knew* where you lived. And addresses are unique (remember London?). So they used that information along with nonunique names and unique phone numbers to publish a directory that would allow anyone to find the phone number of anyone who had a phone as long as you knew their name, city, and street address.

Again, privacy became a concern for some, and the phone companies offered "unlisted" numbers for those whose privacy concerns outweighed the benefits of having their phone number published for all to see.

Multiuser computer systems offered the next set of electronic directory requirements. Multiuser systems (mainframes at that time) allowed various users to perform different functions on the computer at the same time using terminals. Each of these users logged on (identified himself or herself for the system), which then recorded, or "logged," the time in and time out for billing and auditing purposes. Information about these users was stored in primitive directories that kept primarily user name, user ID, and password. Additional data regarding access permissions and manager were often added as the systems became larger.

The spread of network computing, using both local networks, wide area networks, and the Internet, made the need for directories readily apparent. DNS, or Domain Name Service, was a simple hierarchical directory system designed to associate common names with IP addresses. If you know the name, you can find the IP address, in a fashion similar to a telephone white pages. This works pretty well for finding a machine, and it worked satisfactorily when there was only one user per machine. [DNS is designed with a hierarchical referral. Each DNS has an entry for its parent. If it can't resolve an address it forwards the request to its parent—which can forward to its parent—right on up to the root DNS servers for the Internet.

E-mail addressing was (and is) a particularly vexing problem for many people. You know Speedo has an e-mail address, but if you don't remember exactly what it is, you can't send him e-mail. To avoid this problem, we store local directories of e-mail addresses of people we e-mail frequently, or even occasionally.

History does tend to repeat itself. Now many of us have cellular or wireless telephones, and there are no published directories of mobile phone numbers. It's like 1900 all over again! (And no, I'm not going to give you my cell number either.)

5.2 Directories and Privacy

We already brought up the issue of privacy in both the cases of the London residents who opposed to street numbers and early telephone users who requested unlisted telephone numbers.

Directories store information that is directly associated with an individual. Privacy refers to information that can be associated with an individual. The fact that New Orleans has more overweight people than any other city doesn't affect anyone's privacy. That a particular individual in New Orleans weighs 300 pounds *is* private information, only because it can be tied to that particular person. That one resident of New Orleans weighs 300 pounds has no impact on the privacy of all other residents of New Orleans.

Privacy is both a cultural and a legal term. The legal basis for privacy, particularly electronic privacy, is evolving now. Privacy is related to the communication or absence of communication of information about an individual.

Privacy concepts center around this ability to associate data with a particular individual. The fact that a person may be of the male gender may not be private. But if that male is the only male member of a group, then that information is an identifying characteristic, and disclosure of gender might affect a person's privacy.

Directories are, by design, structured to associate data about something or someone with that thing or person. Since privacy only relates to people (inanimate objects and living creatures other than people are not commonly accorded any needs for or rights to any form of privacy), we are only concerned here with directories that contain information about people. When we speak about privacy, we can set aside the issues of directories that only store data about systems. (That doesn't mean that data about machines shouldn't be protected. It should. It's just not a privacy issue but a security issue. Of course, it can become a privacy issue, if it allows access to confidential information about individuals.)

Take, for example, a database that has credit card numbers, credit card payments, and credit card charges. Contrary to general public understanding, that is not private information. If you add the names of the individuals who were assigned those credit card numbers, then the information becomes private. A business might very well want to keep both sets of data confidential, but only the one containing an individual's name is private.

Most of the commonly encountered directories associate information about an individual with that individual: name with password and ID, name with address. These directories exist for e-mail systems, telephone systems, mainframe systems, and local area network systems, and many don't. There are many common e-mail directories that store only IDs and passwords without names or addresses. In essence, these e-mail IDs and addresses are anonymous. While you might be able to link xgh2rxg@anonymousmailserver.com with Bubba Speedo, there is nothing in the directory itself to say Speedo is the same person sending e-mail under the "xgh2rxg" name.

When you are responsible for a directory, you must be aware of privacy issues. You need to know if all the data in the directory is public and if it is not public, is confidential or private. In many business environments, individuals give up many of their rights to privacy to the organizations for whom they work. But some privacy rights are granted by legislation, statute, or finding of law, and they cannot be ceded.

Take phone numbers as a particularly complicated example. Phone numbers are generally listed in phone directories published by the local phone company. As such, telephone numbers might be considered public rather than private information. Additionally, all phone numbers have an address associated with them (even cell phones have a billing address). Now, is it *okay* for a company to publish an internal (available only to other company employees) directory that has home phone numbers and home addresses? (Okay is a trick term.) Culturally, it might be okay to put in phone numbers—but not addresses. In your organization, in your town, it might be acceptable to have both phone numbers and addresses. Legally, due to court decisions, it might make your organization liable for a violation of an individual's privacy, and you could be subject to substantial damages in a lawsuit. Human resources departments are generally very cautious about the publication of any information gathered about employees, including addresses and phone numbers. The fact that your directory has other sources for this data may or may not make it acceptable to publish it.

In the case of the public—whether the general public, customers, or partners—it is wise to be cautious. Collecting information about people who use your systems allows you to personalize their experience and gives you access to your users' behaviors. But you now have the added responsibility of keeping such private information confidential. A detailed discussion of privacy issues and policies is outside the scope of this book, but it is something I suggest you educate yourself about.

5.3 Directories and NOS/OS

Most readers of this book will have the majority of their directory experience with operating systems (OSs) and Network Operating Systems (NOSs). You've certainly used some version of Microsoft Windows or an Apple system (or UNIX, LINUX, CPM, MS-DOS, etc.). You've probably used Novell networks, MS Windows NT networks, or UNIX TCP/IP networks. These systems all have multiple directories.

Most common to users is the file system directory. All of these systems have hierarchical file systems as part of the operating system. Initially the OSs were primarily file systems with file loader capabilities. CPM and MS-DOS are examples of this type of program. These programs were marketed as Operating Systems, when in fact all they did was handle disk and file and I/O and display operations. Their directories were only simple hierarchical file systems. (Remember running out of directories in DOS, anyone?) These directories simply associated a file name with a location, usually on a local storage medium, typically a floppy disk or hard disk.

The LAN network operating systems (like 3Coms 3+ or Novell's Netware) added several features to the directory. These systems had multiple users, multiple printers, and multiple storage locations (local disk and network attached disk). Consequently, they needed more complex directories. Novell "mapped" network drives (actually, network file system locations) to local machine drive numbers as "virtual" drives. A user's "H:" directory was actually a pointer to a file location on a server that was reserved for that particular user.

In similar fashion, printers available on the network were mapped as being shared from a server that was functioning as a print server. Most important, we had multiple users. Now, we had to keep a list of users, their permissions, and their status. The list of users was in terms of users, their user IDs and their passwords. Their permissions included what resources they were allowed to access, what level of access they had to those resources, and the times of access. These OSs also kept two vital pieces of information about user status—whether or not a user was currently active, and whether or not a user was currently valid—or if they were terminated, revoked or suspended.

Although the directory functions required by these OSs and NOSs were much more extensive than the earlier single user systems, the directory functions were still fairly rudimentary. The next major application to drive directory activity was e-mail.

5.4 Directories and Messaging

E-mail was the "Killer App" of the 1980s and 1990s. In the 1980s, e-mail was primarily a Local Area Network (LAN) phenomenon. In the 1990s it was an Internet phenom. In both cases, e-mail drove the need for improved directories and improved directory functionality.

As e-mail is normally implemented, it requires only the simplest of directories. E-mail requires addressing (by the sender) and routing (by the applications that send, handle, and deliver the mail). In the case of a LAN e-mail system, where all mail originates and terminates on the LAN (a self contained system), we normally have a system that is set up with a central post office, or hub. Users in these systems can normally address mail by using an address lookup function in the mail system (point and click). These address lookup functions use a directory. The early LAN e-mail systems used such embedded directories to make life easier for users.

These early systems didn't have to do much, or any, routing. The assumption, or limitation, was that all the e-mail users were on your own (proprietary) system. No routing was required. Sent mail was simply deposited, logically, in the recipient's e-mail inbox. Mail could be sent to Jane Jones because you knew there was only one (unique) Jane Jones, and the only Jane Jones e-mail that existed was the one on your system.

Once these systems became large enough to have multiple mail servers, or multiple physical locations that were geographically separated, routing issues needed to be solved. For example, the Dime Box, Texas office might have a Jane Jones, who wanted to send mail to Billy Bob Beauford in Paris, Texas. This problem is solved in some unique ways in different e-mail implementations, but the normal solution is to tell the mail server engine about other servers with which it is able to communicate. At this point, the mail server knows two things:

1. It knows who its internal users are.
2. It knows other mail servers it can send e-mail to, and receive e-mail from.

If a mail message is addressed to a single person (e.g., speedo) it is assumed to be addressed to another e-mail user on my (home) system. To send it, I just need to compare the recipient name in the To: field to my list of user IDs and deposit the mail in the appropriate user mailbox.

If a mail message is addressed to a person, and the sender has included any additional information (such as BillyBobBeauford@paris.tx, the server compares the @paris.tx to its lists of e-mail servers with which it communicates. If it finds paris.tx, then it routes the e-mail to the paris.tx server. It's important to note what DOESN'T happen. The local (dimebox.tx) server doesn't know anything about Billy Bob Beauford. When it sees that @ sign, it thinks to itself "Oh, this isn't for me and my users." It then sends the mail to paris.tx. The dimbox.tx server has no idea if there really is a user called BillyBobBeauford on the paris.tx server. It just sends the message, and lets the paris.tx server figure out what to do with it.

(The syntax could be different for different mail systems. You could see something like:

- bbbeauford@paris@tx; or
- bbbeauford.paris.tx; or
- bbbeauford/paris/tx

Different mail systems use different syntax.)

If the paris.tx server has a user called BillyBobBeauford, then it deposits the mail in his mailbox. If not, it returns the e-mail back to the dimebox.tx server with a standard message along the lines of "return to sender—user not found."

Now, this scenario can rapidly get more complicated.

Let's say we have three servers instead of two. Our company adds an office in Welfare, Texas so we put up a server there—welfare.tx. The Welfare office is small, but we have a couple of e-mail users there: Pablo Garcia and Ray Smith. When we set this server up, we are told that Pablo and Ray will only need to send mail to Paris and never to Dime Box. So we tell the Welfare server about the paris.tx server, but NOT about the dime.box server. As life would have it, Jane Jones in Dime Box decides to send the company picnic notice to Pablo and Ray. So she addresses the invitation to:

PabloGarcia@welfare.tx, RaySmith@welfare.tx, bbbeauford@paris.tx.

The copies sent to Pablo and Ray are returned with a message like, "undeliverable mail—domain unknown". What happened? Well, the dimebox.tx server didn't know about the welfare.tx server, so it sent the mail back.

At this point the frustrated Jane calls her friendly, and overworked, e-mail admin and asks "What's up?" Our friendly, but unexperienced e-mail admin then replies, "Oh, just address Pablo and Ray like this:

PabloGarcia@welfare.tx@paris.tx
RaySmith@welfare.tx@paris.tx

That'll get it delivered okay."

So what gives? Well, the router component of the dimebox.tx server looks at the To: field, parses (or pulls off) everything to the right of the last @, checks to see if it has a listing for a server called paris.tx. It does, so it sends the mail to the Paris, Texas server. The paris.tx server looks at the To: field, but only the info to the left of the @paris.tx. It parses the entry and sees an @welfare.tx, checks to see if has an entry for welfare.tx, finds that it does and forwards the e-mail to the Welfare server. The welfare.tx server then puts the invitations in Pablo's and Ray's mail boxes.

Now, I'd suggest that the mail admin might want to make an entry for the welfare.tx server. Most users are not happy about figuring out or remembering e-mail routing, and if the admin doesn't improve ease of use, the admin's setting up for a lot of phone calls with frustrated users. (Both those who sent the invitations and those who missed the picnic.)

But the main point here is the routing. Routes can be much more complex than this example, spanning tens of servers. (Typically, the limit is the number of characters allowed in the To: field, which varies by application. You can easily see this if you expand the "reply to" address field of a message received from a remote server.) And the main point about the routing is its distributed nature. Each component only knows about itself, and its immediate neighbor. That's all the info it keeps in the directory, and that minimal info is all it needs to get the mail delivered. That's all assuming . . .

Assuming that the user knows the full and correct address, AND ROUTE, or that the route is one that can be determined via the distributed intelligence of our mail servers and routers. If either of those conditions is broken, the mail will not go through. It should be apparent from the forgoing discussion that depending on your starting point, your address to reach a specific user may vary.

Understanding this level of complication is too much to ask of most users, so users asked for a more comprehensive directory system that would list all of the users on all of the various systems they could send mail to. Initially, this was done by having the admins manually import addresses lists (directories) from other (foreign) mail systems, while adding the appropriate routing information to each entry.

This resolved the usability problem for users, but dramatically increased the workload for administrators, and meant that each mail system had to carry a large directory of information that was duplicated in every location. Every action has unintended consequences.

Imagine that you have a large multinational company with 200,000 e-mail users. Every small office now has to have this huge file with 200,000 entries, and they either have to spend all of their time importing changes (adding new users, and removing old users), or they have to import this new file every day (or week, etc.). This file is so large that it overwhelms their modest mail server, and transmitting changes eats up most of their available bandwidth. Instead of sending and receiving e-mail, their server works full time just getting the latest updates to the directory!

Maybe that "no directory—make the user figure out the address" thing wasn't so bad after all. (Not likely.)

The Internet and Internet mail (including primarily Sendmail and variants) was a big help because it solved many of the routing problems.

Routing was still handled in basically the same way, but Sendmail used the DNS server used by the rest of the Internet to handle the routing.

Without going into great detail, DNS, or Directory Naming Service, is a simple service that performs two functions. One is useful, the other vital. The vital function is to keep a list IP addresses, and to know where those addresses are assigned. The useful function is to keep a list of "domains" associated with an IP address range.

DNS is basically a list of router tables set up in a hierarchical or tree format. When you send an e-mail or a web browser request, it goes first to your local DNS. If it knows the location of that IP address, it sends the request there directly. If not, it forwards the request up one level to the next DNS. This DNS presumably knows more (has information about a broader group of IP address ranges). It may not have any more detail, or more entries, just information about a broader range of addresses. If this DNS server recognizes the IP address of the request, it routes it, otherwise it refers it up one level, etc. Eventually, at the top of the tree we have the "root" DNS servers. The root servers, while they may not carry much detail, do know something about the FULL range of IP addresses and can forward the request down the right chain of DNS servers to the desired address. That's the vital part.

The useful part is to keep a list of the names associated with the IP address. For most humans, it is easier to remember "Yahoo.com" than it is to remember 64.58.76.222. So, our Internet e-mail addressing looks like "MyName@yahoo.com" instead of MyName@64.58.76.222 (which will also work).

What we don't have now, and may never have, is a comprehensive list of all e-mail addresses (the "Mother of all Directories"). We are unlikely to ever have a single directory listing everyone's e-mail address.

The X.500 standard was designed, in part, to compensate for the lack of such a directory. It was envisioned, like DNS, to be distributed with each organization responsible for its own part but able to be shared remotely to provide the information necessary to allow a "foreign" mail system to route mail directly to users in its "domestic" mail system.

CHAPTER 6

Implementation Considerations for the Enterprise Directory

6.1 Directory Content, Design, DIT, and Attributes

As we've just seen, it's highly unlikely that we will ever have a single e-mail directory for reasons of cost, complexity, size, permanence, and privacy. Still, when faced with the proliferation of directories and directory Babel inside their organizations, management quite rightly looks to some sort of consolidation to bring order where there was no order before. They look to the Golden Fleece, the Mecca, the Holy Grail of directories—the *enterprise directory.*

So for many organizations, the first question becomes "What goes in the directory?" And the perennial consultant's answer is "It depends." In the most basic sense, what you put in a directory depends on what you want to get out of it—what you want to use the directory for.

Typically, directories store information about objects—information that can be used to identify, locate, or communicate with those objects. Directories should contain the appropriate information that enables those functions (identification, location, and communication) to be performed. While other (additional) information can be stored in a directory, we do not recommend that you do it. This is not necessarily the majority view, and opinions will definitely vary (as will your mileage).

Let's take a typical case—an e-mail directory that, in addition to name, address, and phone numbers, also includes fields (attributes) for the names of spouses and children. When used as an address book database, this may make sense. When viewed from the directory perspective, it goes against the minimalist credo of only what's necessary to identify, locate, or communicate.

No great harm will come if your directory includes a field (attribute) for spouse's name. And birth dates (and birth counties) are legitimate methods for assisting in identification, so the rules here are not hard and fast. But the direction should be to minimize storage of extraneous information in a directory.

Directories are built on databases, and the tendency is strong to use this database functionality for other purposes. Why not store a record of user access in the directory? We'll add an attribute that logs the time of the last access, the length of time for this session, all Web pages accessed during this session, and the IP address of the session client. As you can see, the possibilities are endless, and they are all better off stored in a general purpose transactional database used by the applications that need that particular data for their applications. This data is not necessary to identify, locate, or communicate, so don't succumb to temptation. Maintain the (general) purity of the directory as a directory!

All kidding aside, your life really will be simpler if you dedicate the directory to only directory functions and resist the temptation to start adding fields and features. Remember that an enterprise directory will serve many users and many purposes across an enterprise (some yet to be imagined). To fill that need elegantly, you need to limit the directory to the common characteristics needed by those many users and avoid the temptation to include data or features needed by only a subset of the users. The idea here is to stay slim and fast, lean and mean. You can't be all things to all users. To be widely useful and serve the greatest number, you have to keep a directory focused on its core purpose.

There are two basic problems with this approach. First, your users and sponsors will resist. They will come to you with a variety of reasons why you should add this or that attribute to your directory—and their reasons will be valid.

Second, if you are trying to consolidate directories and are intent on replacing existing directories, you will be expected to offer a superset of all the data and functions currently stored or offered by the group of directories you will be replacing. This additive set will likely include a lot of application specific data that you must have available to the application but not necessarily in your directory. Unfortunately, the apps have already been designed and coded. So if you want to consolidate directories, you may be forced to include data that you would avoid if you were adhering to our strict directory interpretation. Compromise lies in the way of success in most IT environments. Still, I recommend that you keep the pure and minimalist direction in mind—at least in your own mind and, to some extent, in the minds of others.

As you can imagine, a decision about a directory is seldom a one-time thing. Requests will come to change the directory. New users will want to make additions. Old users will want to make modifications. There will be a near constant stream of attempts to modify your creation.

After you've decided *what* goes in your directory, you have to decide *how* it goes in and *where* it goes. In LDAP terms, we are now speaking of schema and DIT (Directory Information Tree).

The directory, as we remember, is a tree structure—an inverted tree with the roots at the top. We have to decide what structure that tree takes. The inverted tree starts with the root. All LDAP directories start with a root, typically called the "root." (Imaginative it's not, but at least it's descriptive.) All of the rest of the directory entries hang off this root.

Below the root, directory administrators must define additional suffixes to build a tree. The suffixes define the organization and, usually, the country. The first decision one must make when installing a directory is "What suffix will I use?" For descriptions here, we will use a fictional company, RazorSquare. RazorSquare is a small but growing company of 1,000 employees, with eight offices in the United States, two in Europe, one in Asia, and one in Brazil.

In defining our initial directory suffixes we can set the following.

```
O=RazorSquare
C=USA
```

We don't have to set a country, and, since RazorSquare is multinational, we may not want to set a country at this time, but most organizations find it useful.

Next we can define either additional countries, or we can define organizational units (OU). This leads us to a very basic question faced by every directory designer: How do we want to divide our organization? Remember, our directory is hierarchical, not relational, so how we structure it initially will make a difference. We are going to have to live with this decision for a long time.

The usual quandary is whether to organize along functional units or geographical units. Neither is better—they are just different. (We used to offer the advice that geography was more stable than organizations, but we aren't sure that's true anymore. It was recently determined that Pluto is not a planet.) So one option is to use additional countries.

```
C=Japan
C=Germany
C=Great Britain
C=Brazil
```

Another option is to use organizational units.

```
OU=Marketing
OU=Accounting
OU=Manufacturing

OU=AsiaPacific
OU=EuropeMiddleEast
OU=LatinAmerica

OU=NewYork
OU=Chicago
OU=LosAngeles
OU=WestCoast
OU=Central
OU=EastCoast
```

Notice that these OUs can be geographically or functionally oriented.

If RazorSquare has a subsidiary or two, we can use the names of the subsidiary companies as OUs.

```
OU=RazorSphere

OU=TriangleSquared
```

Again, there's no one "best way" to do it, but—Pluto notwithstanding—geography does seem to change more slowly than companies reorganize or change department names. Our current personal preference is to use real or created geographies for OUs.

Part of this decision process is to decide how flat or how deep your tree structure will be. You can create an extremely flat tree by putting every entry under one suffix and one O. This would be a good choice for a small organization of only a few tens or hundreds of members. On the other hand, you could create a very deep tree using multiple Os and OUs in combinations. Even for very large organizations, a flat tree may be adequate and simpler for users to use.

Some available tools that use directories are limited to four or five levels, so there are some reasons to consider a flatter tree structure.

At last, we are ready to create an individual entry in our directory. Well, almost ready. First, we have to choose the object we want to use for our entry. Object refers to the type of entry we want to create. If we want to create an entry for a person, we might want to use a person object. If we want to create an entry for a printer, we might be better off using a printer object. These objects are simply blank templates for an entry. The objects contain "attributes," which are characteristics that help describe or provide information about the particular object.

Let's take a "person" object. A person object may contain the following.

- First name
- Last name
- Middle initial
- Street address
- City
- State or province
- Postal code
- Country
- Telephone number
- Fax number
- Telex number

Each of these things is an attribute that helps describe a particular person. This person object could contain a number of additional attributes such as the following.

- Date of birth
- Social Security number
- Home telephone
- Cellular phone
- Pager
- Department

Most of these items are straightforward. For those of you who don't think globally yet you should remember that not all phone numbers are ten digits and not all postal codes are ZIP codes.

That "department" entry we snuck in is a ringer. Department could be an OU (an object), or it could be an attribute (as it is here). It is easier for a user to change a department code when he or she moves than it is to create a new entry under a new OU. But it's harder to find everyone in a department if you have to search every entry in the whole tree to look for a particular department number.

The IETF has defined a couple of standard objects including: the PERSON object and the INET ORG PERSON object. The INET ORG PERSON object has the same attributes the person object does, but it also includes attributes like EMAIL ADDRESS. (My suspicion is that most of you will be happy using INET ORG PERSON as the object for your person entries.)

But directories aren't limited to holding information about people. Earlier I mentioned a printer object. There are printer objects and objects for other types of information network attached machines (routers, firewalls, servers, etc.), defined as standard objects with appropriate attributes (printer name, IP address, owner, etc.) in many commercial LDAP products.

Whether you choose printers or persons, you are also not limited to the attributes in the standard objects. You can easily add an object, add an attribute to an existing object, or create a new object with a combination of attributes added by you and inherited from an existing object. For example, you could create the following pair of attributes.

```
HairColor
SEX
```

Then you would add them to your PERSON object. Or you could create a new object called RazorSquarePerson that inherits all the characteristics (and attributes) of PERSON and then add these attributes to it. Now we are ready to make some entries to a directory, such as the following.

- O=RazorSquare
- OU=Central
- INET ORG PERSON=
  - First Name = Abraham
  - Last Name = Lincoln
  - Phone Number = 1-512-555-1212
  - E-mail address = Abraham.Lincoln@RazorSquare.com

We don't have to put data in every attribute. Those attributes are simply available for every entry, but they don't need to be filled unless they have been defined as being "REQUIRED."

6.2 Authoritative Sources of the Directory Information

Now that we have a directory and an entry we need to consider how we will keep that information current and correct. In our ideal world, we have only this one directory. In the real world, that's clearly not the case. We have multiple directories, with many sources of information. Birthdays are a good example. Ray's birth date might be stored in both the Human Resources department files and in the department Rolodex.

If the date is 1-1-70 in the Human Resources database and 1-1-75 in the Rolodex, which should be trusted? Is Ray's age 31 or 26? You might decide that the HR data is "better" (better usually means more reliable) because presumably the Human Resources department requires a birth certificate or passport. Or you might decide that the Rolodex was better because it was closer to the source—Ray.

In either case you have to decide how to handle conflicting data. In directories, we do this by specifying the "authoritative source," which might be data that is manually entered (and perhaps documented by a paper form). Other sources may be additional databases or data items that are collected during routine business.

We usually use telephone numbers as examples because we can all relate to phone numbers. Telephone numbers are commonly requested and stored in directories. If someone asks for your phone number and you have only one (lucky you!), you give them that one number. Let's say two months later you are again asked your phone number, and this time the number you give is different because your area code has changed. Now the two systems have different phone numbers for the same person—you. If these two directories are linked in some way, then the data conflicts. In this case, the conflict arises because the data in one system is out of date or "stale."

Other databases may have cell phone and home phone, home phone and business phone, primary line and alternate line, listed number and unlisted number, and so on. A search of multiple directories might turn up a variety of phone numbers. Even "correct" data may be in conflict, so data conflict may arise from many sources.

Going back to our concept of "linked" directories, let's look at an example. Assume we have a Human Resources database that has the following in part.

HR
Name
Home address

Work location
Home phone
Work phone

And let's further assume we have a departmental e-mail system. The system has a directory, used primarily for addressing and routing e-mail, but it is also used by department employees to look up telephone numbers (for those times when an e-mail just won't do). It also has fields in its directory that include the following.

E-MAIL
First name
Last name
E-mail address
Work location
Home phone
Work phone
Alternate phone

And finally, let's say we are setting up a company wide directory, and it has the following.

COMPANY DIRECTORY
First name
Middle initial
Last name
E-mail address
Internet address
Work site
Desk location
Work phone (internal)
Work phone (external)
Home phone
Mobile phone
Alternate phone

Let's further assume that all of the fields in all three of the directories are "single value" fields. That means we have a maximum of one phone number per field. (Multivalue fields could have multiple numbers per field.) Let us also say that *only* Human Resources personnel get to update the HR data, but employees can update their own personal data on the E-mail directory.

Now your job as administrator of the new company directory is to record accurate and timely data and keep it accurate and timely. How do you do that? Human Resources may allow you to pull name, work location, and work telephone number from their system, but they probably won't give you access to a home phone that has been classified as "private."

You have access to the E-mail directory, and you can get information from there. For our hypothetical James Smith, we have the following partial entries.

Human Resources	
Name	James Smith
Home Address	1234 Any Street
	Dallas, TX
Work Location	Downtown Office
Home Phone	940-555-1213
Work Phone	214-555-1212

E-Mail	
First Name	Jim
Last Name	Smith
Work Location	Dallas
Home Phone	940-555-1212
Work Phone	214-555-1212
Alternate Phone	940-444-1313
E-Mail Address	jasmith@xyz.com

If you are going to try to fill as much as possible from existing sources, you get the following.

COMPANY DIRECTORY	
First Name	James
	or
	Jim
Middle Initial	Blank or A
Last Name	Smith
E-Mail Address	James A Smith\Dallas\XYZ
	or
	jasmith@xyz.com
Internet Address	jasmith@xyz.com

(continued)

COMPANY DIRECTORY *(cont.)*	
Work Site	Downtown Office or Dallas
Desk Location	Downtown Office
Work Phone (Internal)	Blank
Work Phone (External)	214-555-1212
Home Phone	940-555-1213 or 940-555-1212
Mobile Phone	Blank
Alternate Phone	940-444-1313

As you can see, we have a variety of conflicts. Is the first name James or Jim? Is the home phone 940-555-1212 or 1213? Is the Work Site "Downtown Office" or "Dallas"?

To resolve these conflicts, we have to declare an authoritative source for the data. We may declare HR to be the authoritative source for a first name. Thus, the conflict is resolved, and Jim becomes James. Or we may resolve conflicts based on some rule. The rule may say that the last data entered is considered most current and, thus, most likely to be correct. The E-mail home phone was entered after the HR home phone field, so in this case the E-mail directory becomes the authoritative source for the home phone number. In practice, the simplest way to deal with this issue is to choose one authoritative source for each data element.

6.3 Uniqueness Criteria

Uniqueness is important to directories. We need to be able to identify a particular entry without ambiguity. In popular detective fiction (and television detective shows) many a case has been solved with a fingerprint, including DNA "fingerprints." In the same way, we want to uniquely identify an individual.

To do that, we have two basic methods. We can either specify a unique data element be assigned to each entry (a key or unique ID) or we can collect a set of elements that in total is unique. Directories use both methods.

The assigning of a unique key is simple enough. At the time of creation, a record has a unique key generated that could be a function of order (sequential numbering of time) or random. The only requirement is that it be unique within its own universe.

In many LDAP implementations, the requirement for uniqueness is accomplished by having a unique DN (distinguished name). For example,

```
DN= (c=US,o=xyz,ou=sales,cn=James Smith)
```

is unique from

```
DN= (c=us,o=xyz,ou=manufacturing,cn=James Smith)
```

So in this name space (this universe) these two James Smiths are unique.

Even if a particular LDAP implementation generates and uses a UID (unique ID), you should implement your name space in such a way as to ensure uniqueness. One of the easiest ways to do this is to include a UID as part of the DN.

```
DN= (c=US,o=xyz,ou=sales,cn=James Smith,uid=jsmith04)
```

Thus, even if your directory implementation maintains uniqueness across DNs only, you will be certain to have unique entries.

6.4 Directory Aggregation

Once you have both uniqueness and authoritative source issues addressed, you can begin the process of directory aggregation. Aggregation is the process of combining data from various directories into one directory.

This aggregated directory can be a real directory or a logical directory. If it is a "directory of directories" (or directory components), we call it a "metadirectory." Such a metadirectory would have pointers or references to the actual directory that stores the necessary information or attribute. The primary value of a metadirectory is that it allows for the least duplication of data. Instead of keeping another copy of a phone number in your enterprise directory, you can store a reference to your e-mail directory where the data (for example, a phone number) is stored.

Ideal data theory may abhor duplication, but practical considerations frequently require it.

CHAPTER 7

Enterprise Security

It's Christmas Eve, and your servers are jammed with hundreds of thousands of e-mails. One of your employees just spilled coffee on a few of the aforementioned servers, and your bandwidth is gone. Everyone around you is screaming in panic, shuffling papers, and typing frantically on their keyboards in a vain attempt to solve the problem. Then the servers crash. A hacker came in amidst the traffic and knocked you out. Nothing works, the business is on the rocks, and the collective screaming of your employees has just reached a deafening pitch. What do you do now?

The fact is, if the situation has reached this point, then you are in serious trouble. But if you had prepared for such a volatile situation, then you wouldn't have had to worry about it getting that far in the first place. This is where security comes in.

There are three types of enterprise security.

1. Bolt-on security
2. Security embedded into a process
3. Security as a competitive asset

Each type of security has its own pros and cons, and one may not be as suitable for your business as another. We'll examine each briefly.

7.1 Bolt-on Security

Bolt-on security is security that is just added on to an existing process or business. For example, say your business has a direct connection to the Internet for SMTP messages with no DMZ, firewalls, or even routers. Now you decide that you should have security installed. This decision could be from either paranoia or common sense, or maybe you just had a security incident. In any case, you decide to install a firewall. With the firewall installed, you can sleep like a baby, but the firewall may not protect you from a messaging virus (such as the "I love you virus"). Yes, it is better than nothing, but you can still be exposed to many different types of attacks. With each type, you can just add another tool or device. The main problem with this approach to security is that the aforementioned afterthought on security can be very expensive over extended periods of time.

7.2 Process Security

Process security is where you add security into a process. This can be a single business process or several processes. This is a step up from just "adding a security component"; this is where a department is being proactive and making sure the department or the process is secure from the ground up. One example of this is where a department is moving an application from a manual process to a Web-enabled process. The following steps should be taken to secure the process.

- Review the old process.
- Analyze the service levels (SLAs).
- Redesign the new process from the ground up—look at exposures and controls.
- Implement the process.

So, you are thinking, this sounds good. The problem here is that the business is looking at security at just the process level. This is a great start, but the business needs to do more.

The next step in our quest for security nirvana is making security a competitive asset. This is where the business, company, and/or the complete enterprise have taken security to the next level. Security is part of every facet of the business, from the CxO (CxO is any officer of the company) to the individual contributor. Security is "top down" and "bottom up."

Everything in a business comes down to the profit and cost (see Figure 7.1). Security costs money like everything else, and if you spend too much

FIGURE 7.1 *Protection and Cost Levels of Each Type of Security*

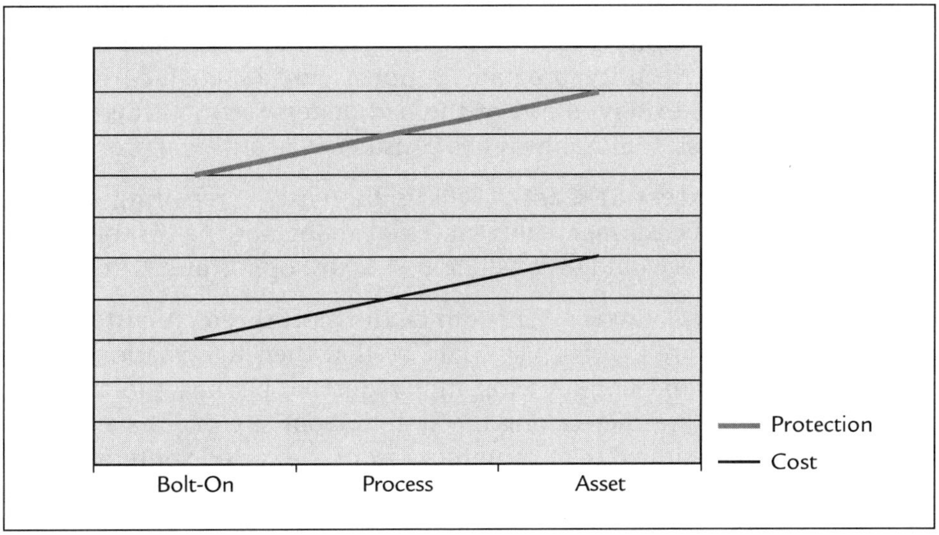

on security, you will not have a profit. This process involves capital expenditures for the hardware and the software. In many cases, a consulting firm may be hired to perform the work and to be available for future upgrades and problems. Personnel must be trained to use the system, and there will be some involved in the constant monitoring such a system requires.

A security computing process is expensive, but if we were talking about a factory that made widgets and the necessity of producing a quality product, you would most likely consider the expense reasonable. The quality product being produced here is a transaction. The quality of the transaction and the value of the transaction to the customer revolve around the safety of the transaction. A quality Internet transaction is a secure one.

If we agree that the expense is a necessary one, what cost do we need to look at and how? Quality costs involve four main items.

1. Prevention costs—Prevention of a security breach
2. Appraisal cost—Ongoing
3. Internal cost—Problem identified before customer is involved
4. External cost—Customer involved, now must fix it

Prevention Costs. This begins with the decision to do something about security. The costs involve planning, information gathering, training, and designing the security system, and then analyzing the system for problems. The planning stage depends on an extensive analysis of the business and its needs.

Appraisal Costs. These involve the constant surveillance measures that the company practices on itself. Reports should be created that list how many security glitches have occurred and where and how they were handled. A security program is not a cure-all; in fact, it requires frequent updates to stay ahead of the bad dudes. Security, therefore, is not a one-time cost. It must always be considered a continual process.

The Internal Cost. This is the cost of repairing a security incident before a customer realizes it. This can include the cost of incident handling. Also, this would involve the cost of lost opportunity.

External Costs. This can be the most severe. A customer or several customers are involved. It could be that their information was compromised or they did not get what they requested because the order was deleted in error somewhere along the system. Your site may have been down for extensive time due to something from the outside entering your system and tying it up. Now the customer can try again to buy from you because you were always reliable in the past, or they can go elsewhere. You may have lost one or possibly more customers. They no longer consider your site reliable. If the Internet is your only place of business, you could end up closing down.

The sad news is that the cost of a secure environment may not decrease much. Things are changing too quickly, and so will your security needs. If you are offering a quality transaction, customers will come to rely on it, and your sales will increase. Forecasting is an integral part of the decisions made regarding the security process. Expense forecasting was considered, but how about forecasting what the consumer will expect from a firm with an Internet presence? The days of the brick and mortar structure are changing; a customer buying on the Internet does not actually interact with a human being. The transaction is conducted on the computer screen without even any paperwork changing hands. If a company wants to conduct business in this environment, future as well as present requirements of the consumer will need to be considered. The forecasting conducted must take into effect daily, weekly, or monthly sales requirements by the consumer. Long-range forecasts that traditionally involve two years or more must also be factored into any decisions about the security requirements for a company. If a company manufactures widgets, there may not be a brick and mortar building where the customer can deal face to face with a service rep. Customers are demanding entities. They require fast, efficient, safe transactions. This does not change, but the customer's definition of what meets or even exceeds these requirements is constantly changing.

Let's look at an example of "The Company." The Company has a reputation for producing the best widgets available. In the past, transactions were mailed in or called in to a person whom the customer knew. With this process there was a delay in processing and shipping (Remember the old "Your order may take up to 6 weeks to process"?) Today, however, the customer enters an order via the Web, and they expect the order to be sent out that same day or the next day. The Company is expected to do all of this processing safely and with little delay. If The Company does not have an up-to-date secure process in place, this transaction may not flow as expected.

The Internet environment is shifting constantly, and therefore appraisal expenses must be ongoing. Installing a security process is not like a hot water heater that will work until it breaks (usually the day after it is over warranty), at which time we replace it with a newer, better model. The security process is just that—a business process—and it must be continually reviewed and updated or there will be problems.

What about the customer's perception? Well, let's assume the customer has been reading stories about transactions being lost or sent to other companies. Now the customer may be worried, and when they access The Company's Web site, they may expect to see certain screens that indicate a secure environment. Some reassurance must be given to the customer, or a sale could be lost. Constant vigilance is required by The Company in order to compete effectively. Security is an extension of the quality of the service provided. It cannot be ignored.

The Web presents a unique set of security issues for the online enterprise. Customers may need to provide personal information, such as credit card numbers, home addresses, and phone numbers. Today's customer will readily hand over a credit card to a waiter or show his or her driver's license number to a stranger behind a counter. But this same customer will get nervous when conducting the same transactions over the Web. Why? Because these Web transactions lack the reassuring physical face-to-face interaction with salespeople. In summary, the ultimate cost may be the loss of customer confidence. If the customer thinks that your site is not secure, then you will not have that customer.

So what is the cost of security? *CIO* magazine reported the following.

> Worldwide IT security breaches cost companies about $15 billion each year, but spending on security measures was an estimated $8.7 billion in 2000. That figure will rise to $30.3 billion in 2005, showing 28% growth year on year. . . . Global investments in public key infrastructure (PKI) will reach $2.6 billion, and spending on virtual private

networks will hit $3.9 billion by 2005. Spending on e-security services will nearly triple from $4.3 billion in 2000 to $11.9 billion in 2005.

7.3 Competitive Asset

How do we reach the nirvana of having security as a competitive asset? The answer is both simple and complex. You must start at the top of the organization and at the bottom of the organization at the same time. Much like a virus that attacks the body, you need to inoculate the system. In this case, you need to inoculate every subsystem in the body.

The Internet Security Guidebook by Juanita Ellis and Tim Speed presents the following formula that describes security.

$$SE = (P^2 + T) * C$$

SE (Secure Environment) =
P^2 (Policy and Procedures) + T (Tools) * C (Commitment)

As you can see, every part of the formula is important. **P**olicy is what drives the security of your business. **T**ools can help implement the security decisions from Policy. **C**ommitment is required to make it all work. Without commitment nothing works! So looking closely at the math, the formula shows that if the organization creates the best policy in the world and then buys the best tools but has zero commitment, the security for the business environment will fail—guaranteed.

7.3.1 Commitment

So let's start with the most important factor—commitment. The organization needs to integrate security into every facet of the business—the "top down and bottom up approach." First, you need management to drive the importance of security. Security is started from the top of the organization down to the individual contributor. Security is not an added-on burden that needs to be reviewed once a year in the budget process. Security must be part of every process and part of every subsystem because, just as security will not work without commitment, your business will not work without security.

Security is implemented from the bottom of the organization up to the CxO. (The CxO is any officer of the organization: CEO, CIO, CFO, etc.) One of the biggest mistakes Internet-facing enterprises make is looking at Internet security as a necessary evil. Internet security *should* be considered a competitive asset. How you conduct business says a lot about your company, including security. You want your customers to feel comfortable and secure doing business on your site, which is a competitive advantage.

7.3.2 Policy and Procedures

A security policy is the driving force that dictates what security is needed and where. The policies should drive the procedures and tools that need to be identified and created. The process of creating these policies will take into account the business requirements, the business risks, the Internet risks, and the cost of protecting the various components of the business. The policies could also be defined as the following.

- A company's requirements for the proper protection of information
- A company's procedures for preventing and responding to security incidents
- The strategic requirements to securely conduct business for the e-enterprise
- A living document that does not collect dust on the shelf

The security procedures define the precise steps you must take to protect your enterprise. Security procedures are "implementable" and "practical." The procedures will include the actual steps to implement your security policies: processes, standards, and guidelines.

Standards are requirements that are designed to support a specific policy. Typically they are mandatory actions or steps as part of a process. Guidelines provide—you guessed it—guidance! But they also support a policy. User training will be part of the security procedures.

7.3.3 Tools

Finally, we get to the tools. This includes the software and/or hardware used to implement the dictates of a policy. This can include, but is not limited to, virus scanning software, firewalls, application signing software, network scanners, admin hacking tools (to acquire passwords), and event O/S security review tools.

7.3.4 Internet Fraud

At this point you are probably saying, "We have a firewall, and our customers use SSL. We are committed to making sure that all of this works and

FIGURE 7.2 *Internet Fraud*

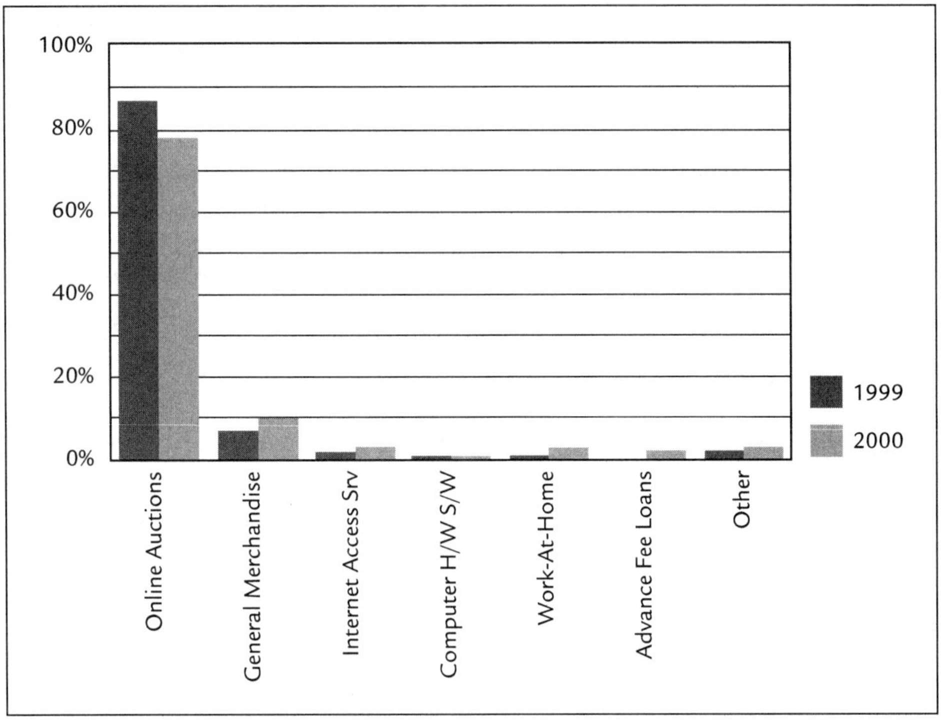

Source: http://www.fraud.org/internet/lt00totstats.htm.

stays online." Will SSL and security protect you and your customers from Internet fraud?

Let's look at some other security related issues.

- Virus—Desktop and e-mail
- Laptop theft—Do you have a policy for data encryption on your laptop? Do you need one?
- Employee theft of proprietary information
- External or internal denial of service attacks
- Do you have a method to quantify your financial losses in the event of a security incident?
- Do most of your attacks come from the inside of the organization or outside? Check out the computer security survey from www.gocsi.com. You will see some scary statistics.
- Is your company under some type of legal requirement for security—like HIPPA?

- What about employee abuse of the company resources? What policies do you have?
- What if one of your employees sends an attachment to your competitor? Is that attachment a virus? How would you like that one to hit the newspapers?
- Do you track your security incidents?
- Do you have an incident response team?
- Here is a good one. Your CEO takes his PC home. Now the PC at work is behind the DMZ and is protected from the outside world, but at his house he plugs it into the cable modem with no protection. Now what do you do?

Will a firewall, DMZ, and SSL solve these preceding problems?

Back in 1992, there was a movie, *Sneakers,* that was about security and computers. In 1992, the Web was just starting to give birth to the early Web application servers. SLAC, the Stanford Linear Accelerator Center, in California, became the first Web server in the United States. And in 1992, we had this movie about computer security and glamorous hackers saving the world from the bad dudes. In the movies, the good guy always wins, but in reality, the good hacker wins. Remember the Los Alamos incidents in March 1999? United States Energy Secretary Bill Richardson confirmed there was a "serious breach" of security at the Los Alamos laboratory (see http://www.financialexpress.com/ie/daily/19990324/ige24021.html). As you can see, security is important to both governments as well as private companies. Was *Sneakers* a harbinger of the future? Despite the best intentions of security officers and the regular employees, complete security isn't possible when you're connected to the Internet. Exposing your business on the Internet opens one up to security issues that brick and mortars are often able to deter as a matter of routine.

Let's start with the security policy. An effective security policy must address the goals of the business. The policy has three parts.

1. **The policy must match the company's business goals and objectives.** What are the business goals? Somewhere there should be some type of corporate charter that defines "why you are in business" (FYI not every business exists for a profit). After you have answered this question, look at what it takes to protect your business as it expands on the Internet. You may even need to revise your charter. One big mistake that companies make at this time is that they go into "secure everything" mode. This is where risk analysis is used and then balanced with the needs of the company.

2. **Management must drive the policy.**
   You may need to do some selling. Use these steps to convince management of the importance of systemic security.

   - Determine the requirement before you show the cost.
   - Show the statistics.
   - Make it legal.
   - KISS.
   - Communicate the policy

   - ***Determine the requirement before you show the cost.*** At this point, I would hope that a team has been established in your company. This team will be the drivers of security. (We'll see more on this in a later chapter.) The team should have performed the business justification for the security needed to protect your business. Have the requirements and costs been listed and ready for discussion? One important point: Be sure to include every facet for the organization, from the CXO to the individual contributor.
   - ***Show the statistics.*** Get the number from the http://www.gosci.com Web site. This will scare anyone. Also, try to get any existing numbers on security incidents from your IT organization. Unfortunately, until an incident response team has been put into place, your organization may not track the numbers.
   - ***Make it legal.*** In most companies the CXOs have some type of fiduciary responsibility to detect and protect areas where their information assets might be exposed. Ultimately, the cost of security is small in comparison to the cost of a downtime and not being able to support your customers.
   - ***KISS.*** Keep it simple, Sam (or stupid, if you like that better). This is where the strength of your procedures comes into play. Tools alone will ***not*** solve the problem. Your employees, vendors, and, yes, even your customers can do their part. Finally, the cost of doing nothing. This is where the rubber meets the road. Take a few minutes to outline a few disaster scenarios. Here is one.

     > In early January 2001, a well-known company with a significant presence on the Internet reported that they had a breach of security and that customers' credit cards were compromised. Okay, this is bad, but at least the company told the truth. At the same time, the company lost a competitive asset—security. Now customers would not be confident in using that company for future transactions. Over time, the company ***should*** be able to recover from this, and customers should eventually be *willing*

> to purchase products over the Internet. Unfortunately, things got worse. A few weeks later, the company announced that the credit card numbers may ***not*** have been compromised.

This is beyond bad. This is stupid. This announcement was a message to the world that "We have no idea how to secure our site." Where was the incident response team? Were they trained properly? You can see how things can go terribly wrong.

3. **The policy must be communicated to all parts of the organization.** Here is what you need to do: build a factory to produce widgets. In that factory you need to hire about 5,000 employees. Now make sure you ***don't*** train the employees. Here is the riddle: Without trained employees, how many widgets will you be able to produce a month? You are probably saying, "It does not take a genius to answer that question." And it doesn't take a genius to figure out that if you don't arm your employees with security awareness, then you will not have a secure enterprise. A well-known security consultant once said, "Training employees on security awareness does not work. In fact, most people can't be trained." In the end, the message he was giving was that the only way to secure your organization was with tools. Sorry, Charlie, this is not the answer. Tools alone cannot (and will not) keep your enterprise secure. Employee training is part of a holistic approach.

   So where do we go from here?

The Discovery Process

Information in many organizations is the organization. If this information is compromised or destroyed, then the company cannot continue its business. Your business needs to conduct a complete analysis of your corporate assets. At the end of this process, you will know what you are trying to protect. Also, a part of this process is to generate a threat analysis. List all of the potential threats and the probability of each threat.

Analyze the Consequences and Countermeasures

Do you want to spend $10,000 to protect $1,000 worth of data? This is where the security teams will analyze the tools and the cost of the tools in relation to the security needs of the enterprise. The cost of beefing up security may be a tough sell at any time. However, any company that fails to manage its security may not be around long enough to learn from its mistakes. The true cost of a security breach is not the time your emergency response (cert) team takes to repair a problem—it is the loss of confidence from your customer base.

Create and Plan an Implementation Strategy

Careful planning is critical to any successful project. The same is true of your enterprise security. Now we'll look at the issues that must be considered.

7.4 Physical Security Policy

A physical security policy will be required for most enterprise companies. This is where network systems administrators and end users need to take precautions to prevent physical security breaches. Physical security can include access to the servers, routers, wiring closets, specific departments, or any place where someone can just walk up to a system and access the information or data. This should also include control access of software passwords and even the use of methods to "lock" systems when a user is away from the computer. Physical security includes the steps taken to protect the actual machines used to store and process sensitive or valuable data. One of the basic standards of physical security is that the computer system must be protected as any valuable equipment would be. This normally involves placing the computer in an environment that is locked and out of bounds to unauthorized users. The following sections cover some of the basic issues that should be covered with a physical security policy document.

7.4.1 Access Zones

To start, your company should define access zones. These zones will define areas for access from the general public to the "secret formula" area. Figure 7.3 shows an example.

Zone A: Areas open to the public.

Zone B: Areas not open to the public; open to employees.

Zone C: Protected areas; only accessible with identification, card keys, or biometrics. Visitors not allowed.

Each company's requirements will be different. A company with ten people can easily be trained to ask strangers what they are doing in the building, but a company with 10,000 employees cannot distinguish a visitor from an employee.

7.4.2 Server Room Access

Server rooms must be locked, if possible, with electronic or scan card access. By using biometrics and electronic cards, you can control and audit access. Even in the server room, you may add additional security as needed. The

FIGURE 7.3 *Sample Access Zone Layout*

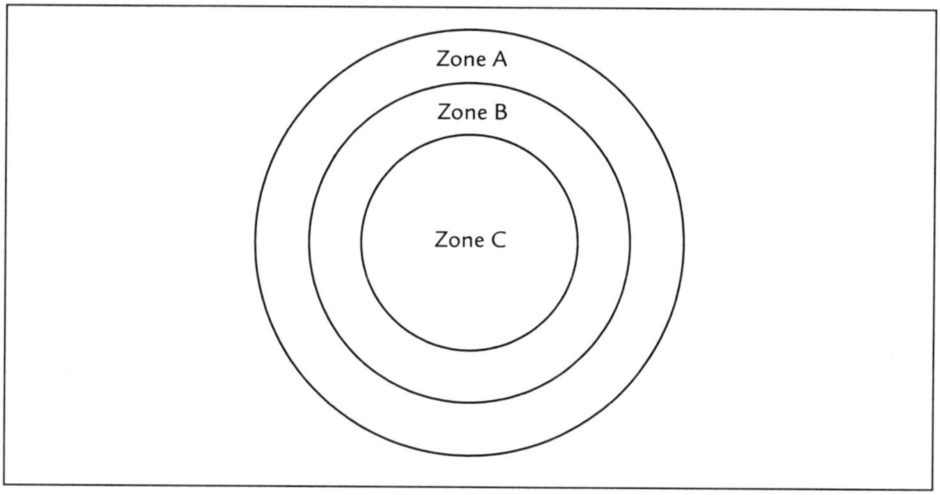

use of locked cabinets can limit administrators' access systems from other departments.

7.4.3 Backups

Backups are an integral part of any computing system. This can also be linked into disaster recovery. In any case, you will need to make some type of backups. Just a quick reminder: Be sure to test your restores from time to time. With that said, let's review some of the issues. Backup media can be stolen and then taken to another computer and restored. This can be a big problem. Make sure that you protect the location of your media. You may even want to encrypt your backups and/or put a password on the backups. Since files must be accessed to be backed up and written to be restored, backup privileges should be limited to administrators and backup operators. Here are some of the issues that should be reviewed for backup management.

- Backup media should be stored in locked areas or locked rooms.
- Regular backups should be placed off-site. In a small company, this could be as simple as taking a copy of the backup home and putting it in the basement (not the best place, but better than nothing).
- If you need to use an off-site storage from an external vendor, then review their policy and get your legal department involved.
- Have your backup tested on a regular basis.

If you use an off-site service, then look for some of the following services/features.

- Environmental monitoring and maintenance to minimize media degradation
- 24 × 7 staffing to work with your schedule
- A fleet of specially equipped vehicles to pick up and deliver your media
- Bonded
- Customer reference list
- Use of a hardened facility to withstand various disasters
- Professionally trained couriers and librarians

Here is a list of questions that you can use to determine if the off-site company you are looking at is right for you.

- Can the facility offer 24-hour service?
- Is the off-site facility close by?
- Does the facility provide specialized media transport canisters that are well insulated?
- What physical security does the facility have?
- Is the facility's name on the premises so that it can be easily identified? This is not a good thing if the facility can be identified. Make sure the address of the site is not listed on the Web or the phone book.
- Is the facility able to offer more than one off site? In the event of the facility losing its own site, does it have a backup site, and how long will your service be interrupted if the facility has a disaster?
- What is the response time of the service from the facility? Make sure you have some SLA—service level agreements—in place.
- Will the facility participate in a 'test' run to see if they can meet the SLAs?

7.4.4 Media

Floppies, CDs, tapes, and removable disks are often an entry to the trusted network for viruses. These various medias may be also used to illegally copy confidential data and take it off site and then to be read and/or redistributed. More and more companies are removing floppies from the desktop. Consider carefully if the general public should have this type of removable media accessible to the desktop.

7.4.5 Computers

There are several different steps that can be taken here. Consider some of the following items for security of your computer systems.

- Policy-based systems management. Microsoft NT has several features that can implement this.
- State a policy on the use of password and locking your computer. Example: Screen saver password should be set for five minutes in the event a computer is not being used.
- Laptops should be locked into their docking stations with a key lock.
- Encrypt laptop data for sensitive files.
- Virus software must be installed.

7.5 Network Security Policy

Create your network security policy reviewing the network infrastructure that supports your computing environment. Again, as with all of the steps, you need to make sure that the network is there to service the business. I have seen networks so locked down that they are almost useless. At the same time, most of the networks that I have worked on have little security. If possible, you will need to build the network with security integrated before you build the network. Yes, I know: You have a network, and you have connections all over the place. With that said, we would need to bolt on the security, but we can still make this work. Here are the steps.

7.5.1 Do a Business Review of What You Need

This is where the security committee will help determine what networks may be needed to meet the business needs. Figure 7.4 shows an example of how a network may be implemented. This figure shows that a DMZ is being used to filter access to the Internet (the untrusted network). But if you look closely, you will see there is a rough access point to the Internet. This could be just a single PC with a dial-up line, or it could be a T1 via an ISP.

So, since we have been talking about how to deal with mergers, how could we connect the two new networks safely? Figure 7.5 shows an example.

Place a DMZ between the companies, at least until you get the network normalized and secure. Some public utilities have divisions that are treated this way in case they need to spin off one of the divisions quickly.

FIGURE 7.4 *Sample Network*

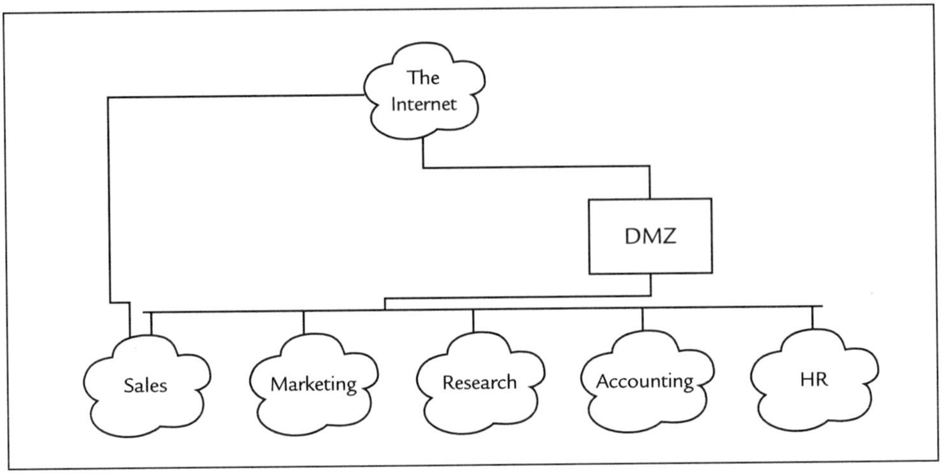

Another example is a company that has zones of access set up via the network infrastructure. In this case, you cannot access another part of the network unless you have access. Figure 7.6 shows an example. In this case there are several DMZs. Each DMZ controls access to and from the Internet, based on the various rules of each network. At the same time, accounting, sales, and marketing will be able to access each other's internal systems as needed. But due to the DMZ rules, accounting will *not* be able to access the Internet via sales or marketing DMZ. Also, there is another DMZ that

FIGURE 7.5 *Connecting Two Networks*

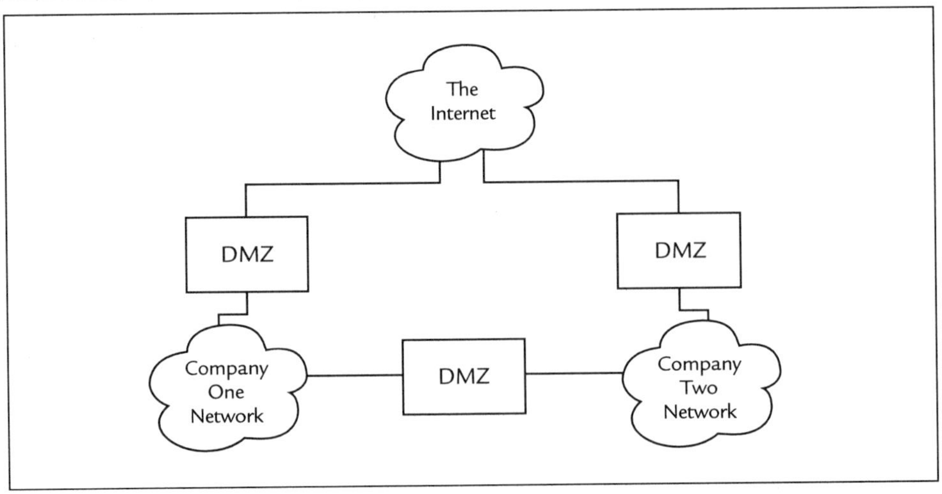

FIGURE 7.6 *Access Zones*

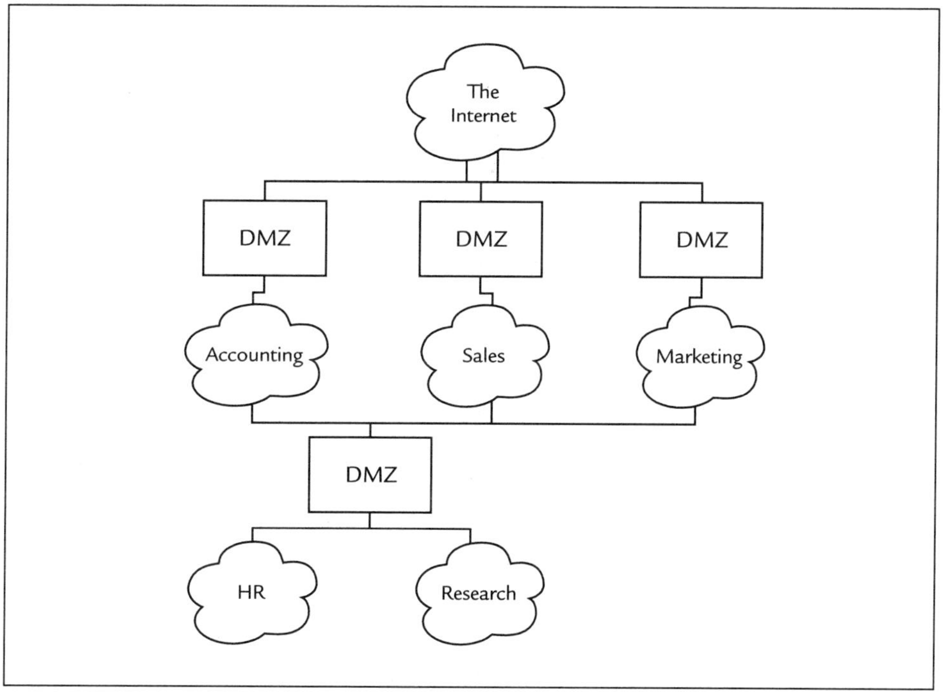

restricts access to human resources and research networks. These networks contain data that is very sensitive and must be kept from unauthorized users. Again, the users on HR and research can get to the Internet but only under the rules of each DMZ.

Design the network to meet the business requirements and security requirements at the same time. This will give you the service levels required as well as the security needed. Create the policy based on these requirements, not the other way around. Some companies have a firewall and/or a DMZ, but many of them will not have a network policy that supports the needs or requirements for this type of architecture.

7.5.2 Determine the Protection Needed on a Particular Network

Your corporate information exists in two states in the computing environment. It can reside on physical storage media, like a hard drive, or it can exist in process across one of the corporate networks or the Internet. We have discussed the security around physical access to media. Now we will discuss network attacks. The following are two common methods of attack that can compromise your network and its data.

IP Spoofing. Remember that we discussed TCP/IP and that network routing is accomplished via an IP address. The IP spoof attack is where someone outside the network attempts to impersonate a computer from the trusted network. If a hacker can access your network, then this is not hard to do. They need only determine the class range of the address and then set up their workstation to match a computer in that range.

Network Packet Sniffers. Network packets are sent between computers. These packets can be intercepted via listening devices. If the packets are not encrypted, then they can be read and understood by any sniffer application that can pick them up off the network. A packet sniffer is a software application that uses a network adapter card in a special configuration. This is known as "promiscuous mode." This mode enables the network card to capture the network packets that are sent across that particular network. If you are in the right place, you can pick up almost any packet that is transmitted across the network. Many applications will send data across the network in clear text or encoded. In either case, the messages are readable. Did you catch that: I said *encoded,* not encrypted. So these sniffers can pick up data as well as usernames and passwords.

Based on the analysis of your environment, you may decide that you need several different defenses. (See Chapter 11 for details on firewalls.)

- Packet filters
- Circuit level firewall
- Application layer firewall
- Proxy servers

7.5.3 Determine the Physical Access Points to the Network

Your network can have many different access points; the wiring closet is one of many sources for the network. Once a company had a power outage of the network on the ninth floor at about 5 P.M. The network analyst started to diagnose the problem, and after about 20 minutes, he discovered that the hub in the wiring closet on the ninth floor had no power. The cleaning lady had unplugged the power to run the vacuum cleaner. This incident also falls under physical security. What is important, as part of this policy, is to identify all of the access points. Not only can you have an outage, but it can also be a point of access to an unauthorized part of the network.

7.5.4 Determine the Monitoring Tools Required to Watch the Network

As part of the process to secure your network you need some type of network monitoring tools. The purpose of these tools is to alert you to any issues that may need attention on the network. These tools must have the following features.

- Graphical display of components being monitored and their status. This should include some type of mapping component.
- Monitoring of a wide range of network elements, including hosts, servers, workstations, bridges, routers, hubs, LAN concentrators, and printers
- Monitoring of multiple predefined services
  - — SMTP
  - — POP3
  - — LDAP
  - — FTP
  - — HTTP
  - — Telnet, and others
- Indication of a network problem displayed via visual and audible alarms
- Ability to notify via pager, cell phone, and e-mail
- Reporting
- Web monitoring

7.6 Acceptable Use Policy

An acceptable use policy is a critical part of any company's security implementation. The following issues should be covered in an acceptable use policy.

7.6.1 Policy Overview

The policy overview is the introduction section of the policy document. This should include a statement of corporate goals in its use of technology and some initial definitions. This section of the document will need to focus on the company's information and computing assets.

7.6.2 Scope

Define the scope of the acceptable use policies and documents:

- Company employees
- Temporary workers
- Contractors
- Vendors

Discuss how this scope can impact each group and their basic responsibilities.

7.6.3 Procedures

The procedures section is where you will need to describe the principles to follow when using these documents. Here are some example statements.

- The [employees, contractors, vendors] will need to adhere to The Company's Corporate Policies as outlined in this policy.
- The [employees, contractors, vendors] will only use services that they have authorization to use.
- The [employees, contractors, vendors] will comply with applicable licensing agreements and copyrights of any software that is being used at The Company.
- The Company employees and temporary workers are given access to The Company's computing resources in order perform their jobs. These resources must be maintained by the standards as set in the policy.
- Any data or information that has been classified by The Company's classification systems must be handled as specified in the data classification policy. Any data marked "Secret" must not be stored on any network outside of Zone B.
- If you receive another company's classified data, you must comply with that company's requirements for protecting the data.

7.6.4 Business Use

In most companies there will be some type of policies that discuss business conduct. You may want to put this section in that document. The business use section should cover the following topics.

- Unauthorized use of the network for any purpose other than company business, such as the following.
  - Running your own business
  - Playing games
  - Using the network as a "test bed"
  - Hosting a personal Web site
  - Hosting a Usenet group
- Unauthorized use of any services on the network, such as the following.
  - Accessing pornography
  - Storage of personal materials on any company storage device
  - Sending personal messages to or from the Internet

7.6.5 Computer Workstations

This is one of those areas where companies do a good job on paper but in practice fall flat. I have been in many companies where the administrator to a critical system leaves their workstation unprotected while they go to lunch or even go home for the day. I could walk up to the workstation and access sensitive data if I wanted to. Here are a few rules to consider when you make this part of the acceptable use document.

- Always use power-on and keyboard lock passwords, including a timeout.
- Employees must password-lock their workstation when away from their desk.
- Computers in public areas will not have access to sensitive data.
- Workstations and laptops will have physical locks installed.
- All laptops will encrypt sensitive data in the event the laptop is stolen.
- When traveling, you must keep portable computers in your possession. Do not leave them exposed in hotel rooms or rental cars. Use the hotel safe if you need to leave your laptop.
- Do make any network changes to your laptop configuration without first obtaining permission.
- Never leave a modem on your workstation set in an auto-answer mode.

7.6.6 Virus Management

Virus management is a critical part of a company's security defense. You may have virus software installed on your workstations. The problem is that users can turn off the virus software. Use of policy-based workstation software can keep this from happening. But if you don't use policy-based software, then you will need to enforce the use of the virus software on the user's system. Also, there is the issue of software downloads and even floppies (or any media) being brought into the site. Your acceptable use policies should include a section on virus management. Here are some examples of what you may need in your documentation.

- All users must use the The Company approved virus software. For configuration settings see The Company document "Virus123.doc."
- Users must report any viruses discovered to the Virus Help Desk at ext: 12345.
- Users are not to send the virus to other users or outside of the company.
- Users are not to send "warning messages" about a virus to anyone. Some virus warnings are hoaxes. If you think there may be a danger from a virus, call the Virus Help Desk at ext: 12345.
- Check for virus updates at www.TheCompanyInternalWebsite.com/virus.

7.6.7 Network

An acceptable use document on "Networks" can be a very large and broad document. Take the time to scope out and focus on the important messages that can impact your network. Here are a few examples.

- Do not use monitoring or sniffer devices on the network.
- If you need to share a file via a network share, then create the share, share the file, then delete the network share.
- Do not set up unauthorized servers on the network.
- Do not connect networks together or bridge any networks together.
- Do not add devices to the network, such as printers, workstations. If you need to add a device to the network, then call the Network Help Desk at ext: 54321.

7.6.8 The Internet

This is another big document. You may need to create several documents and/or place references between documents. Areas that need to be discussed include the following.

- Access to the Internet
- Internet content/browsing

- Internet file downloads
- Messaging over the Internet

Here are a few examples of what you can put into your documentation.

- Only access the Internet via the company's firewall or DMZ.
- If you must download a file, then you must virus scan it before using it.
- Do not store or send unencrypted The Company confidential information on the Internet.
- Use of the Internet is for business use only.
- Do not send or forward The Company internal proprietary information through the Internet.
- Set the security control options in your browser to prevent execution of applets or JavaScript.

CHAPTER 8

The Security Strategy

The Internet is like the American West of the nineteenth century. It was explored by a handful of brave souls, and a few dubious cartographers even published unreliable maps of it for unfortunate travelers. In the end, though, it was only what they made it. In the Old West, some made it their graves, succumbing to starvation in the harsh mountain winters or attacks by unlawfuls. Others made it their wealth and future, digging for gold in California or creating financial empires selling unclaimed land.

You make the same choice today as those adventurous souls did then: You decide whether the Internet will be your grave or your gold mine by developing and maintaining policies, procedures, standards, and guidelines that will help you navigate through this unruly terrain. One of the first questions you must ask is "Who will write and maintain these policies?" The answer is both simple and complex.

The simple part of this answer is that you need to have a central focus so that everyone is looking at the problems and their solutions from the same perspective. The complex part of the solution is that every department in your organization will need to be involved in developing the questions and the answers for implementation of the security system. Confusing, isn't it? Simple. Complex. Good grief! Give me something I can use! All right, here you go.

8.1 The Security Committee

Regardless of who is responsible for leading your security implementation, you should form a security committee. This committee will help you determine what should be included in your company's enterprise security implementation and will be the overseers of the security for the company. This will include initial direction, feedback, and auditing. The committee must include representatives from each department within the enterprise. Using this approach, the policies created will meet the needs of the entire company. Additionally, this creates buy-in from all departments.

So the next question is "Where does the security committee fit within our organization?" The answer is quite simple.

- A corporate reporting structure
- A security reporting structure

Figure 8.1 shows an example of a corporate reporting structure that highlights the security part of the organization.

FIGURE 8.1 *Corporate Report Structure*

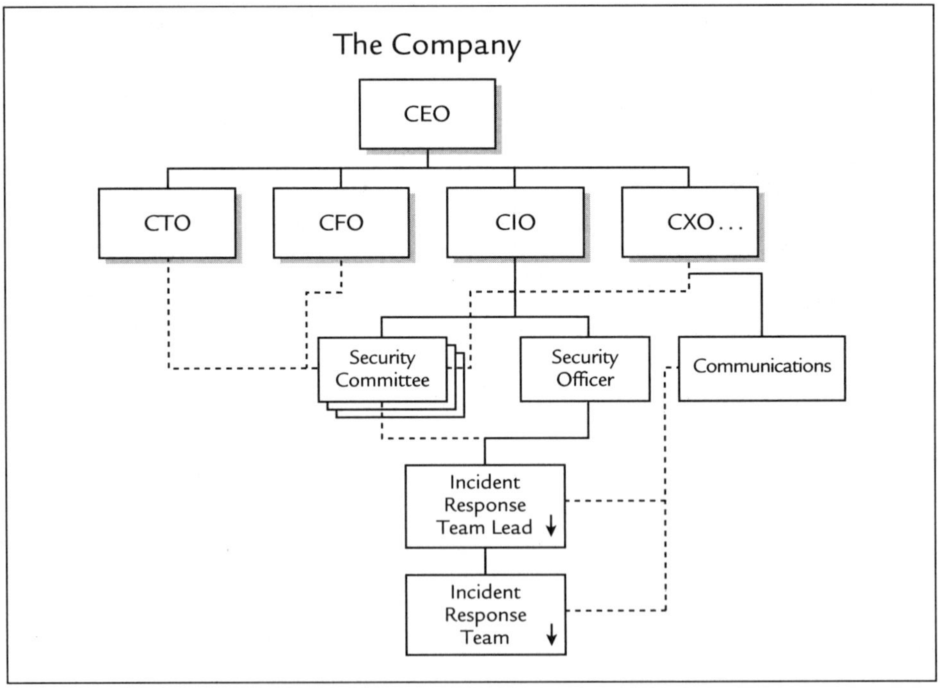

In this top-down report structure, the security committee reports to the CIO along with the security officer. The security committee and the security office have dotted line reporting to all other top-tier executives. The incident response team has a dotted line report to the security committee, but it is a direct report to the security officer. This reporting structure is needed for day-to-day operations, reviews, and HR-type status. This structure supports the organization from the human perspective. If someone needs vacation, sick leave, or a leave of absence, then this structure can accommodate this need. This is not the structure for managing and implementing security. In the case of the security, the committee rules.

The security committee is a collection of existing resources with an organization. A hierarchal structure is required in order to facility the business of security. Actual human resource reporting is not covered by this organization chart (figure 8.1). Per figure 8.1 you see a reporting structure for the Security committee. The Security committee, led by the security officer, will provide analysis and status to the CxOs. Figure 8.2 shows the basic representation that makes up the security committee.

Table 8.1 lists the team members the committee should have. Depending on the size of the company, this will be adjusted accordingly.

FIGURE 8.2 *Security Committee*

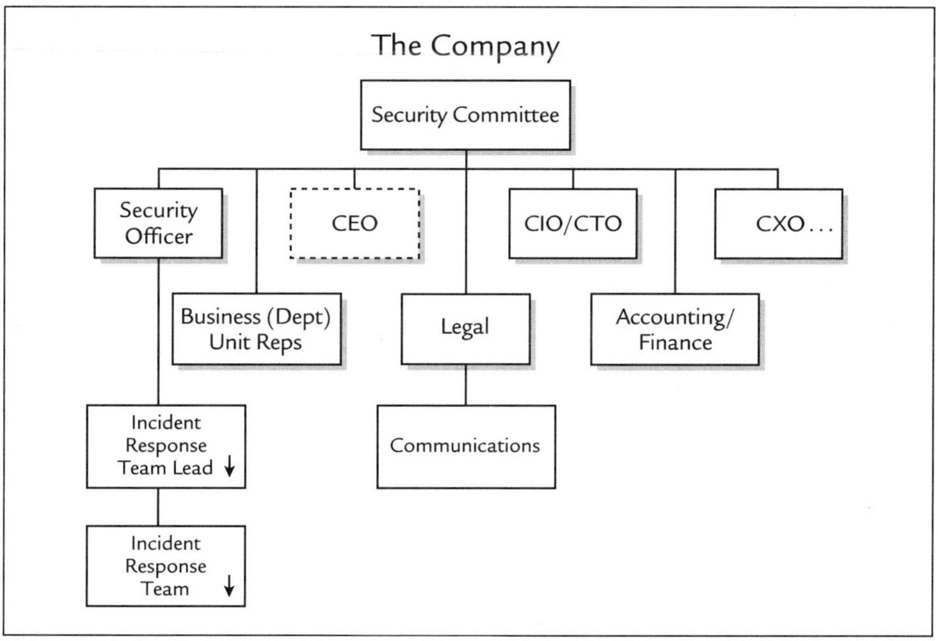

TABLE 8.1 *Security Team Personnel*

Role	Responsibility
CEO	The CEO must be a virtual member of the team. Security must flow from the both the top-down and the bottom-up.
CIO / CTO	All of the technology officers need to be members of the team. It is okay for these members to delegate their role to someone else as long as they have the authority to make decisions.
Security Officer	Obvious choice. This will be the driver of security in the organization.
Representatives from Each Functional Department	These representations must have decision-making authority.
Accounting	They will provide the information for the risk analysis.
HR / Training	Need to assist with user training and information. Also can impact the type of information that needs to be secure.
Documentation Experts / Technical Writers	Need someone to create the documents.
IT Department	Need members who can translate the technology into business needs and requirements.
Legal	Need to keep up with the latest laws. May need an expert in Internet law.
Member from the Incident Response Team	This team will handle incidents that are not covered via implemented security.
Communication Specialists	In many enterprise companies, there is a communication team. Communication to the end users about security is critical.

In larger companies, the security committee will actually be two groups: an executive committee and an operation committee. In any case, the committee is the driving force for security decisions in the company. Overall, the committee's primary responsibility is to create security policy and guide security activities. One important "member" who is not listed is the individual user. Normally, the representatives from the functional departments fill the role of representing the individual user. Generally, the representatives from each functional department have the responsibility for covering this.

At the same time, you need to perform two steps for your users. First, communicate to the end users the message that security is critical. Without this very important step, your security system will fail. Technology alone will not keep your organization secure. The second step should be conducting a survey on your company's users to find out what level of enterprise security they expect and what assets they feel should be protected. Try an anonymous survey; this is a great way to discover security issues that users may not be willing to express openly.

The committee will own security for the enterprise. One big problem that exists with large international enterprises is that individual business units will either ignore security requirements or will make their own. The corporate policy may state that there will be a single presence to the Internet, but the "tools" division in Malaysia has installed a T1 to a local services provider. There are many consequences from this action, one being that a potential hacker could access the trusted network without having to attack the corporate DMZ.

One question that is often asked is "How often should the security committee meet ?" The answer is "It depends." Here is an example. The executive security committee should meet at least once a year. The working security committee should meet every quarter. Individual security groups, new projects, and new processes should meet as needed.

8.2 The Corporate Security Policy Document

So where do we start? The corporate security committee will need to create a Corporate Security Policy Document (CSPD). This will be the first document that will need to be created. The CSPD will include policy and direction that support the enterprise mission by providing guidance to protect corporate resources. The CSPD should establish uniform policies, responsibilities, and authorities for carrying out the corporate security program. This document will make reference to other required documents. These should include acceptable computing use, network, Internet, messaging, and specialized applications and services (see Figure 8.3).

The scope of this document should include all of the enterprise companies, vendors, communities, and customers. One of the biggest mistakes companies make is to overlook the security issues when bringing a new company into a corporation via a merger. This also works in reverse fashion when a company is spun off. All of these issues need to be considered when looking at security for your enterprise. The CSPD should make specific statements about how acquisition and spin-offs will be handled and managed from a security perspective. The hardware and software components

FIGURE 8.3 *Corporate Security Policy Document*

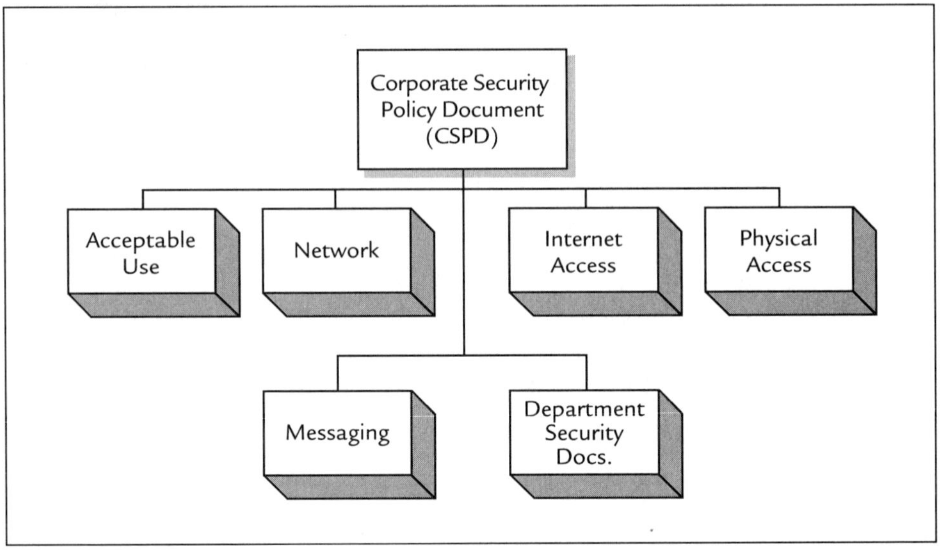

that constitute the enterprise's assets represent a sizable monetary investment that must be protected. The same is true for the information stored in its legacy systems, some of which may have taken huge resources to generate and some of which can never be reproduced.

8.2.1 Mission Statement

The CSPD must also have a mission statement that discusses the specific goals the company will accomplish and methods it will use on its security quest. The following points should be included in a high-level mission statement.

- The security design and implementation
- Explanation of the need for security
- Security safeguards
- The security responsibilities for the various roles in which each member of the company may function
- Appropriate levels of security through standards and guidelines
- Security classifications
- Legal consideration
- Incident handling
- Auditing

FIGURE 8.4 *A High-Level Mission Statement*

The Company's Security infrastructure can be defined as "the state of being free from unacceptable risk, all the while keeping the business running as an Internet-facing enterprise."

The Company will maintain business continuity via the following categories.

- Confidentiality of information
- Integrity of data
- Efficient and appropriate use of assets
- System availability

Integrity refers to the accuracy of data. Loss of data integrity may be gross and evident, as when an IT system fails. The assets that must be protected include the following.

- Computer and peripheral equipment
- Communications equipment
- Computing and communications premises
- Power, water, environmental control, and communications utilities
- Supplies and data storage media
- System computer programs and documentation
- Application computer programs and documentation

The mission statement (see Figure 8.4) should be created by the executive security committee and executed by the security committee into the complete enterprise.

The next section of the CSPD deals with general policy statements for the enterprise. The following points should be considered at a high level.

- The oversight of the security officer and the security department
- Risk analysis
- Threat analysis
- Cost of security, including the forecasting of security costs

8.2.2 Roles and Responsibilities

Roles and responsibilities (R&R) should also be discussed in the CPSD. This document is not the place for a detailed analysis. Each department will have its own R&R implementation. Again, at a high level, the following R&R's should be described.

- CEO—Approves security strategy from security committee
- Security committee
- Security officer—Leader of the security committee
- Department heads—Members of security committee
- Team
- Legal
- Communications
- Human resources
- Accounting
- All other officers of the company

The security officer is a critical part of any organization. If possible, the security officer should be a permanent employee and not a contractor, a consultant, or a temporary employee. The security officer has several roles.

- A member of the executive security committee
- A member and consultant to the standing security committee
- A consultant to business units on security needs and requirements
- Primary lead of the incident response team
- Primary owner and implementer of corporate security policies

The security officer is not the author of corporate policies. This is where many companies have made a mistake. The security officer is a consultant and a police person. The security committee, along with any specific business unit requirements, creates the actual security policy. The security officer implements the policy and enforces the policy.

Although it is preferable for the security officer to be a permanent employee, smaller companies may not be able to afford a full-time security officer. Here are some alternatives.

1. The company should still assign a single person in the company to own corporate security. This must be a permanent employee.
2. Bring in a consultant to act as your security officer, even if this person is part time. Make sure you have your lawyers involved and/or use a company that is bonded. You can check out security services at http://www-3.ibm.com/security/.

3. Don't turn over 100 percent of your security to a single individual or company or vendor.
4. If you do use external vendors or ISPs, make sure you define the service levels. The levels can be as simple as "Vendor A will provide firewall services to block hackers from access ports."

Here are just a few more things to keep in mind if you are considering using a consultant to act as a security officer.

- Full time employees will care more for your company than any contractor. The contractor will work for the length of his or her contract and then leave. The full-time employee is there every day.
- A full-time (permanent) employee must have final ownership of the enterprise security.
- External vendors have experience that an internal employee cannot obtain.
- Not every company can afford to have a full-time security officer.
- Remember—the security of your company needs to be a competitive asset.

8.2.3 Security Life Cycle

The next section in CSPD is the security life cycle, which documents the identification of activities and implementation of the security needs for the enterprise, thus ensuring that all systems conform to a confident approach to security. The following topics are included.

- **Security planning**—Security planning activities will be the responsibility of the appropriate department and or process owner. The security department and the CSPD security officer will oversee these activities.
- **Security oversight**—The security officer conducts policy-related security oversight activities for ongoing day-to-day operations.
- **Budget and forecasting**—This is the process to ensure that the proper funds have been budgeted for the security analysis and implementation. This also includes the necessary approvals for budget processes.
- **Security education, training, and awareness**—These activities are ongoing and apply to all personnel, users, vendors, and members of the business communities.

- **Security testing**—All security processes need to be piloted and tested.
- **Backup operations**—High-level description of the backup and restore plans and the testing of those plans.
- **Risk management**—The processes for performing risk analysis. Risk management is the total process of identifying, controlling, and eliminating or reducing risks that may affect the computing enterprise. This should include some of the following.
  - Risk analysis
  - Threat analysis
  - Cost of the risk, including the cost of doing nothing
  - Definitions of the responsible parties that will carry out the risk analysis
- **Incident handling**—Include the requirements for incident handling.
- **Disaster recovery and contingency operations planning**—Yes, this is different from incident handling. Each essential mission-critical-sensitive process/application should have a viable and logical disaster recovery and contingency operations plan. This document should only specify the basic high-level requirements for that plan.
  - Emergency response plans and procedures as appropriate to keep the business running.
  - The plan should cover fire, flood, natural disaster, bomb threat, or other incidents or activity where lives, property, or the capability to perform essential business functions are threatened or seriously impacted.
  - Also, the plan should cover high-level, backup operations plans, procedures, and responsibilities to ensure that essential mission-critical operations will continue if normal processing or data communications are interrupted for an unacceptable period.

Many companies will implement a security certification process. This process is a comprehensive evaluation of the technical and nontechnical security features of a particular technology, application, or service. The certification process will establish the extent to which a particular technology's design and/or implementation meets a specified set of security requirements. Specific business processes would also be reviewed under this certification scheme. The certification process would also be linked into the change control systems. Here are some examples.

- **In-house developed applications**—Application design reviews and systems tests should be performed and a certification of the results reviewed for any potential exposures.
- **Commercial-off-the-shelf software (COTS)**—Off-the-shelf software should be reviewed for any exposures, as it would be installed in its default configuration. Then the software should be reviewed for any potential configuration settings that could lend itself to an exposure. For example, if a Web server is set up to default as Anonymous, this may not be desirable in many cases.
- **New business processes**—Each new business process will need to be reviewed for security exposures. One simple example would be a registration system. In this case, users register before they are allowed to see a white paper or other documents. If the information that the user is inputting is compromised, then the user's privacy may be violated. This could involve legal issues as well as loss of customer confidence.

8.2.4 Training

The next section of the Corporate Security Policy Document is user education and training. As we have stated many times, security is the responsibility of every individual in the enterprise, including the CEO. It is everyone's job to ensure security. With that said, we must now tell everyone what they need to do.

Periodic training in computer security awareness and accepted computer security practices of all employees, vendors, and users is an ongoing process. The training of employees and vendors is one thing, but how do you train the customers that use your Web page? Look at your own software vendors from whom you purchase products. You may see the following on their Web sites.

- A message about security
- A message about privacy
- Instructions for using SSL (a secure page or a secure transaction)
- A link with information about the security of the site
- A number to call if the users have any questions

This is where you will see the real value of security as a competitive asset.

Training can take many different forms. You can use training as a mechanism to grant access. If a user has been to a certain class, then they can have access to certain materials or sites. Training can be conducted in a classroom or even via a shared video network session. In each case, the appropriate document(s) should be provided with each training session. If you train someone, always give him or her something to take away. It is not enough to just supply them with a URL and expect the training to be complete. Experience tells us that people want to have something they can look at, especially during the first wave of training. Refresher courses can be done paperless. Put the URLs in the training documents, but always give them something to take back to their workstations. It works! The training must be tailored to what a user will need to use the system securely. Try not to cram everything into one single training manual. For example, don't mix administration-level training with user-level training.

Above and beyond specific process or application security training, you will need generic security awareness training to provide a broad overview of topics and general guidelines and requirements. These should include the following.

Common threats, vulnerabilities, and risks—This should include virus systems, media handling, and the use of laptops. One big problem that many companies are facing now is the cable modem. Employees use a laptop on the secure network at the office, and all is well. Then they go home and hook up the laptop to the cable modem. The modem has no firewall or protection, and the user may have open shares. The employees now have compromised their data and may even bring a virus back to work.

Information accessibility—This should include data categorization and how to handle information as it is labeled. For example, if the company policy states that if data is marked "Secret," it cannot be sent to another person unless it is encrypted.

Physical protection considerations—This section should include instructions about access sensitive areas. The corporate policy may state that if you enter the computer room, you must scan in and out via your access card.

Security incident reporting—This would cover the aspects of reporting a security incident. This could include restrictions about reporting an incident. Here are two examples.

1. If you, as an end user, received a report of a virus, then you are not allowed to send messages to others warning of the virus. The policy would state that you contact the virus help desk—*http://TheCompany VirusHelpDesk.com.*
2. Next and most important, if you know of a security incident then you must report it to the correct department. Also, you cannot disclose the incident to anyone, including the media. The problem here is that if

the media got the word about an incident, then it could publish the information and hurt the company. *Note:* We are not saying, "Don't report the incident." We are saying, "Report the incident only to the proper systemic channels in your company." The message here to CEOs and security officers is to meet with your legal department and discuss the impact of reported incidents. Everyone has the responsibility to report new attacks so others can thwart the attack. If you are in a sensitive business, then work with CERT to discuss mechanisms to anonymously report incidents.

Facility requirements need to be addressed by the Corporate Security Policy Document. Facility security addresses the requirements to provide physical and environmental controls based on the level of risk to the computing systems supported in a facility as identified by a risk analysis. Physical security is concerned with the countermeasures designed to prevent unauthorized physical access to equipment, facilities, knowledge, data, information, and documents. For example, you may have a Certification Practice Statement (CPS) in place. The CPS may state that CA root certificates are to be placed in a secure location to which very few administrators have access. This could be a locked room or cabinet—or both.

The Corporate Security Policy Document should also address high-level security background checks for specific individuals. This could be very important for the handling of certificates. The CPS should detail these types of requirements.

The Corporate Security Policy Document should also contain a section on auditing. The company should define the auditing requirements, methods, and timing of the audits. As part of this process, controlled system vulnerability testing (also known as "ethical hacking") should be performed. Ethical hacking would show if the systems could be accessed via known attacks. These types of vulnerability testing procedures should be controlled to prevent disruptions in daily business.

The Corporate Security Policy Document should have a section dedicated to data classification requirements. This is where the company needs to identify the data from a security perspective. Not all data is public; employee data with Social Security numbers should be kept private from other employees as well as from the general public. The secret formula needs to be kept in a secret place and encrypted. At the same time, the list of items for sale on Web sites needs to be available to the public—in read-only mode. The CSPD must state the data categorization required and may even state a few policies that must be followed. But it is each division or department that will make the assignment of the classifications to the data.

The CSPD must consider the issues of personal computers or handheld devices. Remember we talked about the risk of home-based access equipment, like cable modems. This exposure is not limited to cable modems; this is an exposure for anyone who accesses the Internet via an ISP where there are no protections against hacking. The cable modem is now becoming the easy target for hackers. As we mentioned, this is a problem for the person who takes his or her computer home and then back to work. This can even be worse for the person who takes a personally owned computer to work. Many companies will have a standard supported desktop environment that could include many different features.

- Virus scanning when the desktop software is loaded
- A mechanism to automatically check for the latest virus signature files from the vendor
- Virus can be checked when the users log into the system

You may think there is no risk of spreading a virus when a user brings his or her laptop from home because you cannot log in to the network without scanning. This is a nice line of reasoning, but it is not always true. DHCP (Dynamic Host Configuration Protocol) is a mechanism that will assign an IP address to a computer. Many times in a corporate enterprise network, you can get a DHCP address without logging in. This is a problem because now TCP/IP is functional and you can access corporate TCP/IP services. If each of these services has an individual login or any systems that will allow you to log on, then you will be able to access those resources. If you can access those resources, then you will be able to infect those resources with viruses. So what is the message here? The message is *not* that users should not bring their home laptops into work. The message is that you must be aware of the risks and have a policy to deal with these risks. The CSPD is the place to document that risk, and it is the responsibility of the Computer Users Policy Document to detail that risk and to list the control factors for that risk.

The Corporate Security Policy Document should have a section dedicated to network definitions, both trusted and nontrusted. Again, this is a high-level definition of the corporate policies. The details will need to be in the Network Policy Document. A high-level discussion of Internet services will need to be mentioned here. The Network Policy Document may house the details, but more and more we have seen companies that do not have an Internet Policy Document. One very important item that should be covered in the CSPD is the fact that users cannot and must not connect networks together. The CSPD is not the place to define a firewall. The CSPD will state that adequate network protection will be required, but that is it. The Network Policy Document will define the requirements needed for the DMZ and/or firewalls.

8.2.5 Messaging Policy Document

Messaging is a very critical area that the Corporate Security Policy Document must address. You will need a Messaging Policy Document. The basics should be covered in the CSPD. The CSPD should state the corporate policy for messaging. Here are some examples.

- The messaging infrastructure is to be used for business purposes.
- Sensitive messages are to be encrypted (the type of encryption will be defined in the Messaging Policy Document).
- Virus scanning must be used on the messaging infrastructure.

Once again, the details do not belong in the CSPD but will be placed in the Messaging Policy Document—for example, the type of virus software that will be used.

The next section for the Corporate Security Policy Document is security incident handling. A security incident is an unplanned and unexpected event that causes impact to the security infrastructure. These incidents can range from a premeditated attack to an unwitting user/administrator. At a high level, the CSPD should discuss incident handling; the Incident Handling Document will cover the details.

The CSPD should also have a section that deals with ethical conduct. This section should discuss the consequences of not following the policies and outline disciplinary action that will be taken. Some companies will have a separate Ethical Policy document, and many will put the information into applicable Human Resources documents.

A basic policy document should contain the following.

Policy Goals and Objectives. Define what you are trying to accomplish with your policies. The objective defines your approach to Internet security. These approaches could include the use of tools, systems, and employee/user training.

Scope. The scope specifies the assets that will be protected by the security policy. The scope could define a specific policy or a body of policies. The scope should include who is impacted by the policy: end-users, employees, customers, vendors, and so on.

Responsibilities. The responsibilities section of the policy document describes how the individuals defined in the scope section will be responsible for the security of your environment. Detail the security responsibilities as needed by region, department, or groups. Depending on the company size, responsibility may be assigned to the following personnel.

- Executives—The top directors, the CXO's, are responsible for high-level security strategy and must make the necessary resources available to combat security threats to the business.
- Security officer—The security officer/manager is responsible for the entire enterprise security. The security manager defines the enterprise security policies and procedures. The security manager will work with the business managers to implement the initial risk analyses as well as the individual process risk analysis. Also included in this job responsibility is the implementation of each facet of security.
  - Secure network
  - Security applications
  - Auditing
  - Incident handling
  - Facilitate legal reviews of the various security issues
- Process owner—The process owner is directly responsible for a particular business process. The process owner can be a department manager, a lead engineer, a specification custodian, or any employee tasked with accountability for a business system. The process owner will work with the security manager to analyze risks and recommend the countermeasures for each process. The process owner may not have extensive experience with security, so the recommendation may be at a business level only. For example, the process owner may say, "We need to limit access to this application to a single group." The security manager hears, "Access control will need to be set up and implemented for applicable personnel in the process group via the corporate policies and procedures."
- Legal—The legal department needs to be involved with the design of the security policies and procedures from day one. Make sure the following issues/items are covered within each policy.
  - Guidelines for acceptable use
  - Ethics—users and administrators
  - Access by customers—liability and damages, performance, and compliance
  - Risk and exposures in the event that business data is compromised

- — Analysis of communications sent to customers in the event of a security event—hackers, data compromised
- — Auditing and use of logs for evidence
- — Copyright issues
- — Use of electronic signatures and encryption
- — Management of unauthorized access
- — Review of any agreements with extranet vendors, customers, and ISPs
- — Interpretation of the Uniform Commercial code in relation to business use of the Web for your particular business. [http://gopher.law.cornell.edu]

- Developers—Define the responsibilities of the application developers. Security needs to be built into the application from day one of the development cycle.
- Users—The users are responsible for security in the enterprise as much as the CXOs. Every user needs to be trained on the company security policy, data categorization, and system procedures, and understand what the consequences of their actions are and how to act accordingly.
- Auditors—The auditors should be familiar with, but independent of, the activities performed by the organization or group being audited. The auditors will perform audits specific to requirements in the security policies and procedures.

Physical security. Physical security measures must provide for the protection and access to the physical assets of the business (such as servers and applications). The physical security document will describe how the various assets are to be protected (such as locked server rooms, card readers with limited access, logging systems to track who has access to each type of server).

Network Security. The network security document describes how you will protect assets stored on the network. This document could include security steps on the following.

- Network access
- Use of sniffers
- Access to Internet services
- Methods of DoS attacks

Data Classification (Data Categorization). Every business possesses data that is owned by someone. The value of this data can vary from one application to another, from one business to another, and even from one competitor to another. Business data should be classified based on the security requirements of that data.

A data classification policy document should be created to describe the requirements to classify the data. Do not confuse the classification of data and the service level of that data. You can make the data open to the public, but if the public cannot read the data due to a DoS attack, then that data is useless, no matter what your classification is.

Here are some example of data classifications.

- Public—This data/information is available to the public. Access to this data by competitors is acceptable and does not represent a threat to the business.
- Vendor restricted—This data is available only to approved vendors and/or business partners. Access to this data by competitors can pose a risk to the business. Access to this data must be logged and restricted.
- Internal information (proprietary)—External access to this data is restricted. Access to this data by competitors or the general public could put the business at risk or cause embarrassment. Access to data is restricted to internal employees only, and access will be logged.
- Confidential information (limited)—This data is confidential within the company and protected from external access. Access to this data can give competitors an advantage in the marketplace. Access will be limited to select employees and groups. All access will be logged. Backup tapes will be controlled.
- Secret information—This data will not be placed onto any networked systems. Access is limited to very select individuals, and all access is logged and monitored. If this data is compromised, the business can be highly at risk.

Access Control. Depending on the application and the data, users may need to be authorized. Define your requirements in this section of the document. Additionally, define the access to the authoritative directory for this authentication. Finally, include the following access control features as needed:

- Users should be prevented from deleting other users' files in shared directories.
- Users should be able to manage the privileges of data elements that they own.
- Access control should be linked into data classifications.

Note: Not all authentications will necessarily be from an authoritative directory.

Password Change and Enforcement Policies and Procedures. Be careful with this section of the document. Not all applications or operating systems have the same password management systems or rules. You may need several documents to cover each type of password management. Also, consider using a single sign-on system. This can help manage passwords and the password rules. Additionally, consider the following examples when setting up your policy document.

- Set up password rules so "crackable" passwords cannot be created.
  - — Require a mixture of numbers, uppercase and lowercase letters, punctuation, and so on.
  - — Ability to remember without the need to write it down.
  - — Use of minimum password lengths.
- Create some guidelines for users on how to manage their passwords.
  - — Do not share or give out passwords to others. Do not allow others to tailgate into applications using your password.
  - — Do not write the password down or send it to someone via e-mail.
  - — Do not create a single administration username and password that will be shared between several administrators (compromises the ability to audit).
  - — If possible, set up an administration account and password separate from the administrator's personal account. For example, your messaging administrator is named Joe Smith. Joe will be assigned two accounts: "Joe Smith" and "Joe SmithAdmin." The "Joe Smith" account will have a different password from the "Joe SmithAdmin" account. Additionally, the privileges will not be the same. The "Joe Smith" account will have the standard user access privileges that a typical user will have. The administrator will send all e-mail via this account as well as accessing any applications. If the administrator needs to make any changes to the environment, he would then use the "Joe SmithAdmin" account. This account will provide the needed level of access to administer the environment. Joe will not use the "Joe SmithAdmin" account to send e-mail or use any applications.
  - — Educate users about the dangers of password hacking/cracking.
  - — Passwords must be encrypted within the directory.

— Define the age expiration limit of the passwords and management and tracking of password history
— Define the encryption strength.
— Define the mechanism and systems to track and stop directory attacks.
— Define the use of smart cards, tokens, and biometrics.

Incident Handling Procedures. An incident is an unplanned, unexpected event that requires immediate action to prevent a loss of business, assets, or public confidence. All policies *must* have an incident handling component plus a feedback component. The feedback loop is the mechanism that will keep the policies current and updated. Why is an incident handling process so important? It permits continuity of important business processes in the event of an incident and allows the business to function. Service levels will be needed to determine what level of handling is needed based on each incident type. An incident where the Web site is down and the business cannot conduct electronic transactions will generate a different response than a situation where a user may have lost an e-mail message.

The response team should include representation from the following.

- Management
- Technical personnel
- Legal counsel
- Team coordinators
- Communication specialists

Be sure and define the basic procedures for handling an incident. In case of an incident, each of the following points should be implemented.

- Preparation: The team should have a charter.
- Incident detection—Have the processes and tools in place to detect an incident.
- Immediate action—This needs to be prioritized based on a scale of importance (more in Chapter 11).
- Communications—Critical to handling of an incident.
- Detailed situation analysis—Observe and report what happened.
- Recovery—Get the business running again.
- Feedback—How can we keep this from happening again?

Here are some general guidelines to help you set up and manage your incident response team.

- Take a look at http://www.cert.org/nav/recovering.htm and http://www.first.org.
- Create a hardcopy list of contact names, telephone numbers, and e-mail addresses.
- Test the processing on a regular basis.
- Test your backups.
- Test your communication process.

Acceptable Use Policies. The acceptable use policy section states how users will be allowed to use network resources. There should be several policies created.

- Acceptable use for e-mail
- Acceptable use for network access
- Acceptable use for data disclosures

Change Control. Some people may argue that change control is not a security concern. But without adequate change control, a site can crash without warning. Hence, our future discussions will address change control as a security concern. Just a simple change can impact the infrastructure and/or application. One of the best checks for this is "Does the site have a change control system and/or policy in place?"

Training. User training is critical. A very important element of a successful security program is user training, which helps ensure that users take an active part in implementing the company's security measures. You should conduct classes, present videos or other training methods to ensure that users follow your company's security measures. An educated user is an important weapon in keeping your environment secure.

Compliance. The compliance section details how your company will enforce the various security policies. This section should state the methods that will be used to investigate breaches of the policy.

We began this chapter by recalling the Wild West. The Internet is somewhat like the lawlessness of those days, and your best protection from this insanity will be processes, tools, skills, and commitment.

CHAPTER 9

PKCS, PKIX, and LDAP

9.1 The Public-Private Key

Today's Internet offers incredible opportunities for delivering services, products, and information to a global marketplace. The challenge we face is in securely managing these business transactions. The issue involved in daily transactions is *trust.* How can you trust that your transaction is safe and secure over the Internet? One mechanism that can be used to develop trust is using server and user certificates. These (digital) certificates are based on a public-private key technology. These keys can be thought of as a secret handshake by which the user and recipient recognize each other. There are basically two types of key-based algorithms: symmetric (secret-key) and asymmetric (public-key). The difference between them is that the symmetric keys use the same algorithms for encryption and decryption. The asymmetric algorithm uses two different keys, one for encoding and creating the ciphertext, and another for decoding, or translating the ciphertext into readable text. You may have heard of the term *public-private key;* this is the technique that current encryption systems use within today's Internet environment. The public-private key system is based on a technique patented by Diffie-Helman in 1974 and formatted into architecture by Rivest, Shamir, and Adelman (RSA). Take a look at http://www.rsa.com and http://www.verisign.com for more information.

Figure 9.1 shows how a public-private encryption system works. A computer system will generate a key pair for an assigned user. One public key and one private key are generated. These keys are mathematically related so that the private key can decrypt any messages that are encrypted by the public key. The following is an example of the steps used to encrypt a message.

1. The public-private key pair is created.
2. The public key is placed into a public directory. (LDAP directories are commonly used to house the public keys.) A directory (see Chapter 1) is a storage facility that can house usernames and information about the users (such as e-mail address, phone numbers, and the public key).
3. The private key is stored in an area that only the designated user can access, such as his or her local PC or laptop. *Note:* This example does not address roaming users and the management of keys. Print out the private key and eat it (Just joking).
4. Now see Figure 9.2. You can now send an encrypted message. From the directory you select the intended recipient's username. (This is managed via a software program.)
5. The message is encrypted using the targeted user's public key.

FIGURE 9.1 *The Public-Private Encryption System*

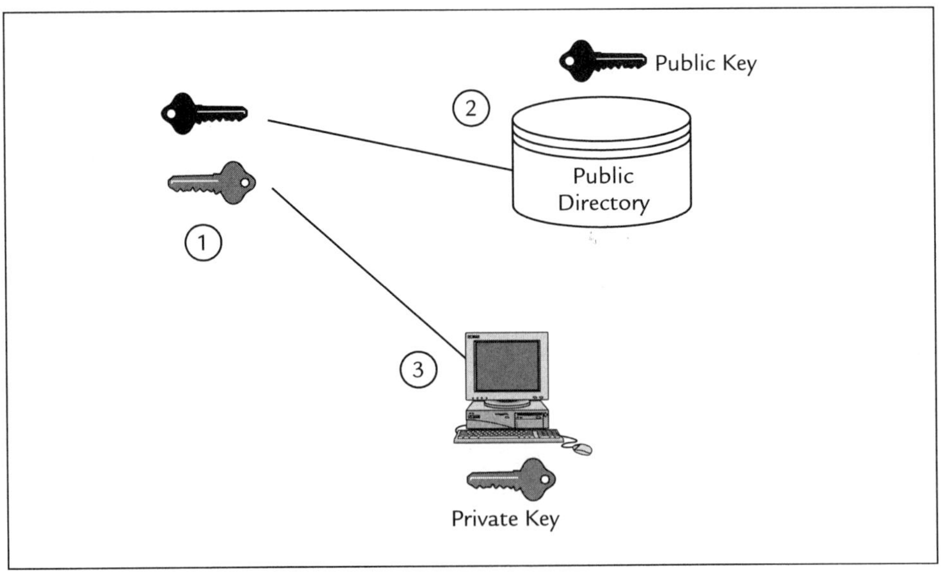

FIGURE 9.2 *Encrypted Message*

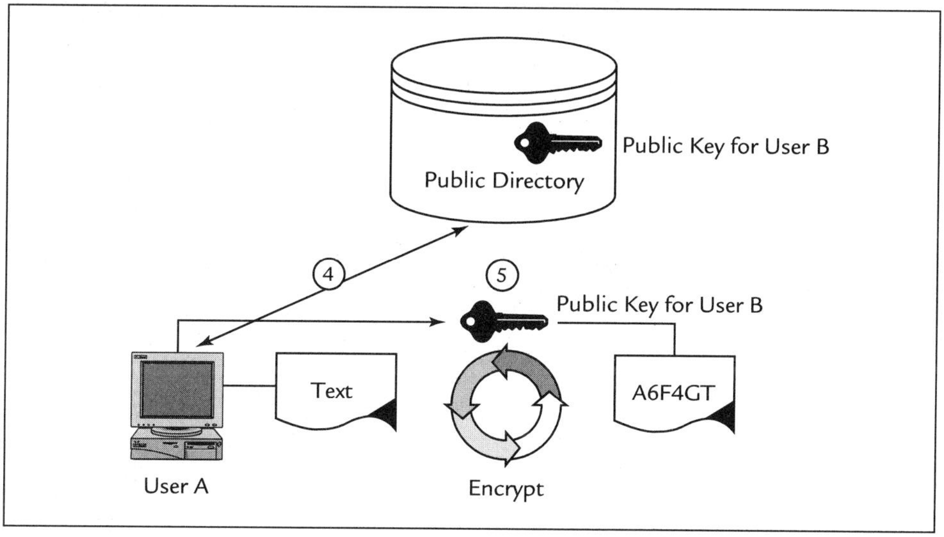

6. The data is now transferred between systems (see Figure 9.3), applications, or e-mail as ciphertext. You now have an encrypted message that is difficult to read by a third party.

Okay, but how can we read the message? This is where the private key is used (see Figure 9.4).

7. The user then retrieves the message and decrypts it with their private key. The private key may be locked with a password that only the user knows. The message is now readable by the targeted user.

There are several methods to encrypt messages. One standard is S/MIME. There are also secret key systems and other systems to encrypt data as it travels from one location to another. There is a process that can

FIGURE 9.3 *Message Transfer*

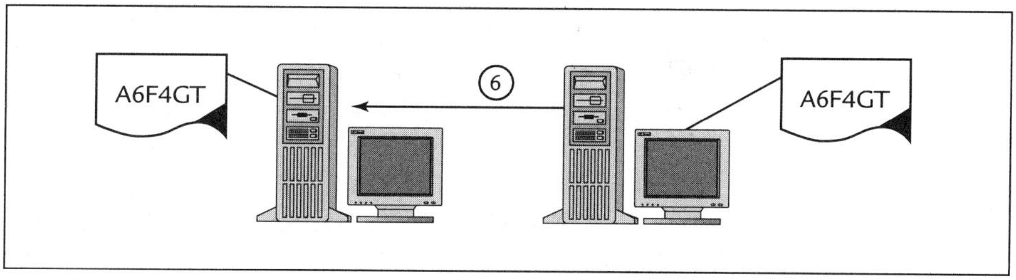

FIGURE 9.4 *Using the Private Key*

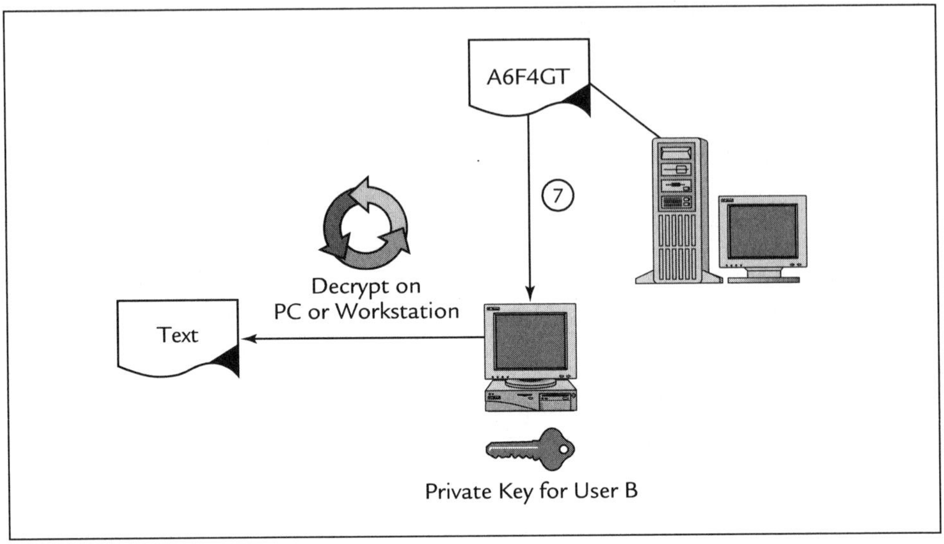

be used from a by-product of public-private keys that is known as "digital signatures." Digital signatures can be used to authenticate messages and prevent forgeries and/or tampering. You can get more information at http://www.cylink.com/library2/white/digitalsig.htm.

Here are some encryption techniques with which you should be familiar.

- DES is the U.S. Government's Data Encryption Standard, a cipher that operates on 64-bit blocks of data using a 56-bit key. IBM developed DES under contract to NIST (National Institute of Standards and Technology).
- Triple DES (http://www.cylink.com/library2/white/thefuss.htm) is a cipher-like DES that operates on 64-bit data blocks; the difference is that Triple DES uses the basic DES cipher three times.
- RC2 is a variable-key-size symmetric block cipher and can serve as a replacement for DES.
- RC4 is a variable-key-size symmetric stream cipher known for being faster than DES.
- S/MIME (Secure/Multipurpose Internet Mail Extensions) provides a method to send and receive secure MIME messages. S/MIME is included in the latest versions of various Web browsers from Netscape and Microsoft. S/MIME is based on the RSA Public-Key Cryptography systems. See Request for Comments 2311 and 2312 for more information on S/MIME.

- MD2, MD4, and MD5 (MD stands for Message Digest). A digest is a computed value known as a hash. A hash creates a fixed-length string from a block of data. The hash is created based on the content of the message. Using a hash or message digest, a user will digitally sign a message. This process will identify the person who sent and/or created the message. MD2, MD4, and MD5 are hash functions created by Ron Rivest of RSA, Inc. Each one will create a 128-bit digest. The MD2 digest is the slowest, while the MD4 digest is the fastest. At the time of this writing, the MD5 algorithm is the de facto hashing standard for digests. See Internet RFC's 1319, 1320, and 1321 for more information.
- SHA-1 (secure hashing algorithm) is an NIST sponsored hashing system that has been adopted by the U.S. government. SHA-1 produces a 160-bit hash, which is larger than the 128-bit hash and is slower than MD5. One fact about all computed digests (ask hash) is that they are very difficult to duplicate. For example, if you change one bit in message for an existing MD5 digest, then up to half of the digest will change.

PKI is the use of public key cryptography via some type of network (for our discussion the Internet). In most cases, a standard public-private key system will be used. This PKI will includes several components.

- Certificate Authority (CA). The CA issues, verifies, renews, and revokes digital certificates. A certificate includes the public key or information about the public key and may even offer a directory to store the public key.
- The Management System. There are many different implementations of PKI in the market place. Many of these systems are shipped with a Web server or are offered as a standalone program. The keys are typically created simultaneously using the same algorithm by a certificate authority (CA—see the preceding paragraph). First we'll discuss some of the features we'll see when using a PKI.

Certification. Remember we talked about binding a user to a certificate? This is certification; certification is the process of binding a public-key value to a person or system.

Authentication. Again, we already talked about this. This is the process of allowing access into a system based on a set of credentials. This does not guarantee authorization. Once we know who you are, then we can authorize you. Do you see the relationship between the certificate and binding? We bind you to a certificate via certification and then we authorize into the subsystem and then you are authorized to perform a function (access, read, write, etc.).

Validation and expiration is the process of verifying that a certificate is valid. We used the analogy of a driver's license that has an expiration date. The CA and the "stamps" that have been placed on the certificate by the CA verify the certificate.

Nonrepudiation. This is where there is a scheme in which there is proof of who sent a message and the recipient can show this proof to a third party, who can then independently verify the source.

Digital Signatures. When a public-private key is issued, the CA generates two separate pairs of public and private keys for each user or server. One pair is used for encrypting and decrypting information, and the other is used by client applications to create a digital signature on a document or transmission.

Encryption of E-mail. Using PKI we can encrypt documents, files, and e-mail. You can use S/MIME to send encrypted e-mail.

One of the most widely used standards for defining digital certificates is X.509. This standard focuses on defining a mechanism by which information can be made available in a secure way to a third party, and it supports the authentication of the entries in an X.500 directory. Every X.509 certificate will be "signed" by a certificate authority, or a CA. The main purpose of a CA is to bind a public key to the name contained in the certificate, which will provide assurance to third parties that some measure of care was taken to ensure that this binding is valid. Here are the features of an X.509v2 certificate. (See Table 9.1)

Version. This identifies which version of the X.509 standard applies to this certificate. This impacts what information can be specified in it.

Serial Number. A unique number assigned to the certificate by its issuing CA. This information can be used in several ways—for example, when a certificate is revoked, its serial number is placed in a certificate revocation list, or CRL. We will be discussing the CRL later.

Signature Algorithm Identifier. This identifies the algorithm used by the CA to sign the certificate.

Issuer Name. This is the name of the entity that signed the certificate. This is typically the CA.

Validity Period. This is a pair of dates/times for which the certificate is considered valid. Each certificate is valid only for a limited amount of time. A start date and an end date describe this time period.

Subject Name. The subject name uses the X.500 standard, so it is would be unique across the directory or DIB. The entry will be in the format of a distinguished name (DN) of the entity—for example, "CN = Bill/OU = Dallas/OU = Texas/OU = The Company/C = US." (Each of these refers to the subject's common name, organizational unit, organization, and country.)

TABLE 9.1 *Elements of an X.509v2 Certificate*

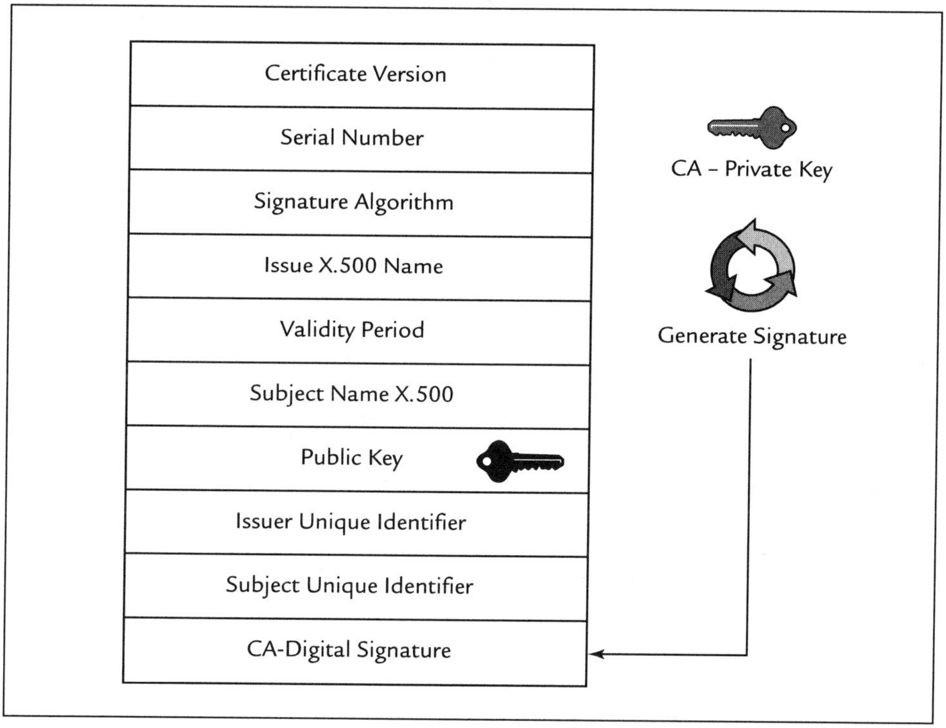

Public Key. The content value of the public key along with an algorithm identifier, which specifies which public key cryptography system this key belongs to.

Issuer Unique Identifier. This is an optional bit that is used to make the issuing certification authority name unambiguous in the event that the same name has been reassigned to a different entity. This field is not widely used, since they have turned out to be difficult to manage and are ignored or omitted in most implementations.

Subject Unique Identifier. This is an optional bit string used to make the X.500 name of the subject unambiguous.

Now you have seen what an X.509v2 certificate looks like. More information can be gained by reviewing http://www.ietf.org/html.charters/pkix-charter.html.

Now let's look at an X.509v3 certificate. (See Table 9.2) Extensions are new fields that have been added to X.509v3. These are significant changes to the X.509 standard. One of the fundamental changes was to make the certificate and CRL formats flexible. These extensions are fully described in RFC2459.

TABLE 9.2 *Elements of an X.509v3 Certificate*

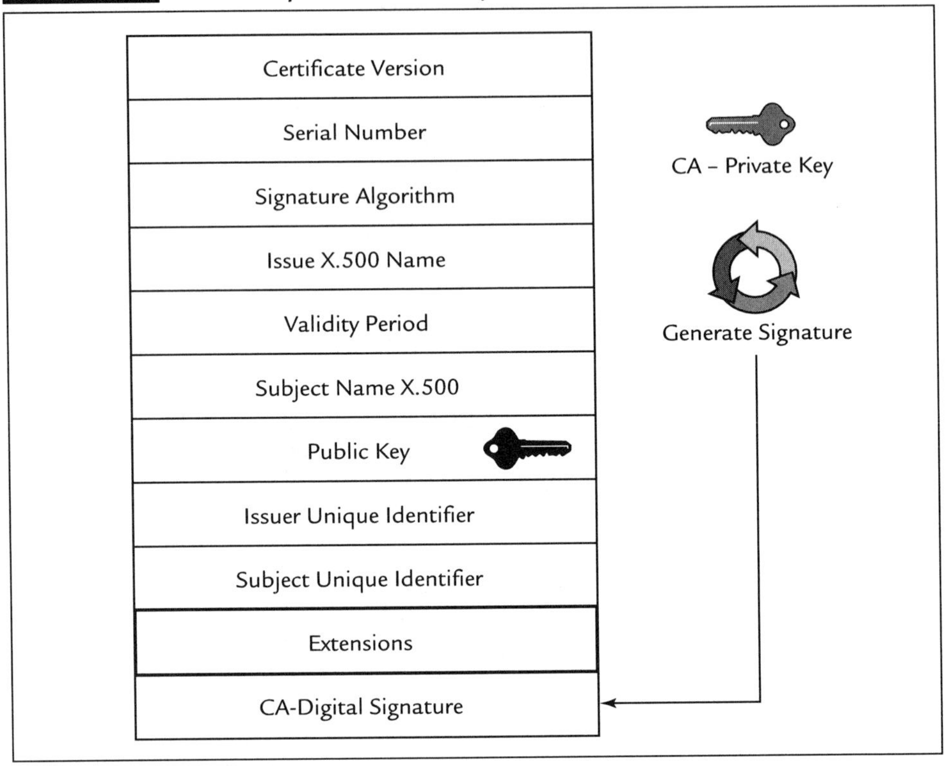

Key Usage. This field indicates the purpose for the key—for example, digital signature, certificates signing, CRL. This is becoming very important in the maintenance of keys because keys that encrypt data may need to be recoverable, and keys for nonrepudiation may be defined as "nonrecoverable."

Certificate Policies. X.509v3 gives the CA the authority to include with the certificate a list of policies that were followed in creating the certificate. These policies are intended to help users decide if a certificate is usable for a particular application.

Alternative Names. This field contains one or more alternative, unambiguous names.

Certification Path Constraints. These extensions help different organizations link their PKI infrastructures together. These fields include the following.

1. The **basic constraints** indicate whether the certificate may act as a certification authority or is an end-entity certificate.

2. The **name constraints** can be used to restrict a name-space that will be considered acceptable in subsequent certificates via this certificate.
3. The **policy constraint** will specify a set of constraints with respect to explicit certificate policy identification and policy mapping.

For the most part, there are two basic systems in use for issuing certificates: a closed system (private hierarchy) and an open system (public hierarchy). The closed system will have a certificate authority as part of one entity. In theory, you could have several organizations and organizational units. Also, in theory, you could distribute the responsibility of supporting and maintaining those organization certifiers. With a closed system, your company is in the business of being a CA. There are many reasons to do this. One example would be that you have several bank branches and that you want to encrypt data between each branch. In that case you would be the CA and issue the certificates. In reality, you would place the certifier under lock and key and may even put a guard (an actual person) in charge of handing out the key via a very controlled mechanism. You might have a multinational company with several CAs, or, in the same example, you might have a multinational company and have only one CA.

These are the advantages of a closed system.

- You are the CA; you control the certificates.
- You also control the binding of the user to the certificate; in theory, you could physically look at each person and then issue the certificate.
- You manage the certificate structure, naming, validation, and expiration.
- You have control of your own destiny.
- No one else can use certificates or impersonate yours. (Well, hang on for a second on this one.)

These are the disadvantages of a closed system.

- You are the CA; you control the certificates. Why is this a disadvantage? Now you need a support structure to accommodate this mess.
- You will need the proper software and/or hardware to implement the solution.
- You will need to have a support staff to manage the certificates. Remember that certificates expire. Guess what? People may need to change their names (such as in the case of marriages). You will need to figure that out also.
- How will you handle issues about people quitting? (CRL—later)

- Now, in theory, if you are your own CA, then you control that CA, and no one else will have it. This is true, but it can also be very false. The issue is that in order to create a certificate, someone or something will need to "touch" the CA—act as a certifier. The CA certifier is a physical entity that exists somewhere (in a document, file, hard drive, floppy, etc.). So as a result, you can lose control of the CA. Even if the CA file has a password, you can still lose control of it. Administrators do quit and move on to other companies. So if you do become your own CA, then work with your software vendor and determine methods to protect the CA certificate.

Now let's talk about open public systems. A public system is one where an individual or a company can go to another entity for certificates. This public CA is typically an independent entity that provides the service of issuing certificates. In some cases this CA is known as a third-party CA.

These are the advantages of an open public system.

- Even though you are not the CA, you can set up a service via a public CA to provide certificates on your behalf. You still control the certificates, but you do *not* control the root certificate.
- Again, you can control the binding of the user to the certificate. In theory, you could physically look at each person and then issue the certificate. (This does not scale very well.) Many vendors have automated systems that can register users and issue certificates. (The automated systems scale very well.)
- Again, using a service from a public CA, you manage the certificate structure, naming, validation, and expiration, but as we mentioned, you cannot control the root certificate.
- Cost—Overall the cost of an open public system can be less expensive than a closed system. This is due to the fact of an existing infrastructure and people to support the system.
- Reliability of infrastructure—Most "known" public systems have a proven track record. We have never heard of a case where a public infrastructure had an outage.

These are the disadvantages of an open public system.

In this case you would not be able to own the root certificate. So in theory, someone at the service could create an unauthorized certificate. Here we need to balance some of these issues. We would hope that if your company does any business with any type of service provider, you would look at the following:

- Service levels
- Legal liability
- Legal responsibility
- Code of ethics

Each of these will need to be reviewed and agreed on. Also, define the consequences for breaches of any of the listed issues. In the end, you should have a Service Provider agreement. These agreements define the rights and obligations of the service provider and the company requesting or purchasing the services. The end story here—consult your legal department before using a public CA.

Which system is better—a closed private system or a public system? The "consulting" answer is "It depends." You know the saying, "Ready—Aim—Fire." Please don't select the technology before understanding the business problem that you are trying to solve. Here are the issues that you should review before making your decision.

- What are the business requirements? (As always, what is the need, what is being supported?)
- What are the user requirements?
- What is the cost?
- What is the cost of doing nothing? (This is very important.)
- Are there other options? Is PKI really the answer?
- What are the support requirements?
- What user issues need to be addressed?
    - Number of users
    - Location of users
    - User types—office, roaming, remote
    - Bandwidth
    - Language
- Based on the business requirements, can we use a public service provider?
- What options does the public service provide to manage our users?
- What are the training requirements?
    - Users
    - Administrators
    - Help desk

- Who owns this project? Is there a person who can make decisions if the project gets stalled?
- What is the cost if we need to be our own CA?
- What happens if the root certificate CA is compromised? (This question needs to be asked for both public and private systems.)
- Based on our decision, what is the per-user cost?
- Can the technology be used on other applications or business services?
- Will this be offered to the general public? What services are available for the general public from a public CA?
- What service levels are required? This question is for both public and private CAs.
- Depending on the solution, what processes will be used to bind the user to the certificate?

Now you have an idea of how important the CA is. If the CA certificate(s) fall into the hands of the Bad Dude, then they can create certificates that can impersonate a valid member of your organization. With that said, let's delve into what it really means to us and what the true risks are.

Let's start with Figure 9.5, which shows an extract of a certificate that was taken from a browser. *Note:* Serial numbers are 128 bits in length. The serial number shown below is an example only.

FIGURE 9.5 *Example of a CA Certificate*

This certificate belongs to:
Bubba Duck
Bubba@testmeduck.com
The Duck
Texas, US

This certificate was issued by:
The Big Cert CA for BUBBA
The Company
Texas, US

Serial Number: 38:90:5F:C1
This certificate is valid from Wed Jan 26, 2000 to Sat Jan 29, 2000
Certificate Finger Print:
4E:1A:07:E7:EA:DC:82:D9:4E:1A:07:E7:EA:DC:82:D9

In Figure 9.5 the CA is "The Big Cert CA for BUBBA." Let's assume that a Bad Dude has obtained a copy of this cert. What can he do with it? Let's also assume that it provides open access to a directory source that would house public keys and that it is available in read mode. Here is what the Bad Dude could do.

- First, he could create a bogus user using the stolen CA.
- Then, with access to the public directory, he could send encrypted messages to those users. In those encrypted messages, he could request actions or items be sent back to him via e-mail.
- He could also sign messages. Now, there is a hitch in this one. If the targeted user's software validates the signature via the public directory, then this could generate an alert condition to the targeted user. So signing may not work. But guess what? You could send a message to a remote user that may not have direct access to the public directory. Again if the user were trained, then they would know to check the fingerprint. Using the fingerprint, you can check for a signed message from the "real Bubba" instead of the "fake Bubba." The targeted user could just call the real Bubba and say, "I just got this request from you for a billion dollars, and you want it sent to Cuba. Please read me your fingerprint for validation of this transaction."
- The Bad Dude could possibly authenticate into your Web servers with illegally obtained certificates. How? Easy—if all you do is check for a root certificate in common, then they can access your servers. Then the Bad Dude would be able to access any resource or database that does not have any restrictions (a.k.a. anonymous). If you have access restrictions, then the Bad Dude will not be able to access those resources due to the following reasons.
  - The bogus name is Bubba Duck.
  - The access list is David Smith and Maria Jones.

Authorization to the resource is controlled via the public keys of each user name. Remember that in this example the Bad Dude did not have write access to the directory source. So the Bad Dude cannot get the needed public keys into the directory to gain access to an authorized resource.

So what are the rules? (By the way, it is not practical for an outsider to pull this off. Most likely it would be an insider or former insider who has had access into critical systems such as PKI and/or e-mail.)

1. Don't lose control of your CA(s).
2. Don't grant write access to your directory resource, or at least control it and audit it.

We have seen the importance of a CA. What we need to discuss now is the recognition of the services that the CA provides. This can be for both open and closed systems. We need to look at the practices of the CA, including the actual services itself, the legality of the CA, and the trustworthiness of the CA. The concept that drives this is the Certification Practice Statement, or CPS. This term originated in the American Bar Association Digital Signature Guidelines (http://www.abanet.org/scitech/home.html).

The purpose of the CPS is best described in the following statement.

> This document presents a framework to assist the writers of certificate policies or certification practice statements for certification authorities and public key infrastructures. In particular, the framework provides a comprehensive list of topics that potentially (at the writer's discretion) need to be covered in a certificate policy definition or a certification practice statement. (http://www.ietf.org/rfc/rfc2527.txt)

A CPS is valuable for most any or all CAs. You can see the importance of having one for a public CA. Using the CPS from a public CA, your company could review the practices and then determine if you trust the CA to manage your PKI. The CPS should also dictate legal responsibilities, roles, policies, and procedures. Here is what should be included in most CPSs.

Introduction. The introduction should include the scope and basic responsibilities of the document.

What Is a Certification Practice Statement (or What Is a CPS in Our Organization)? Overall we have described it here in this book. What this section needs is a definition of what it means to your organization. Or if you are using a service provider, make sure that they have a documented definition.

Legal Obligations—the company and the CA's. This section needs to define the rights and duties and expectations of each party.

Detailed Practice Specifications. This refers to various actions taken by the CA to validate the certificate applicants' identities and confirm the information they provide during the application process. The type, scope, and extent of confirmation depends on the class of certificate, the type of applicant, and other factors. This also includes processes to manage expired certificates.

Privacy. This section determines the privacy information and how to deal with each customer or user. Also, what directories are the public keys placed in?

Confidence and Reliability (Including Nonrepudiation). One of the most important factors of PKI is nonrepudiation. This is can be used in various applications, including but not limited to messaging. The recipient of an electronic message needs to be confident of a sender's integrity. Nonrepudiation is concerned with binding the sender to the message. The sender should not be able to deny having sent the communication if it was in fact sent.

Statement Regarding Trustworthiness. The reliability of any PKI system has much to do with the security and authentication practices of each party involved. These practices establish the "trustworthiness" of the system, which is based on good security practices. A very important factor in the trustworthiness of any public key infrastructure is the trust in a "trusted third party" or the CA. The CA will need to provide a trustworthy infrastructure. This definition of trustworthiness should include (1) administrative personnel, (2) employees, and (3) systems and networks.

Statement Regarding Audits. Audits should be defined and scheduled. Also, the systems for reporting the audits should be defined. *Note:* Keep in mind that your CPS may become a public document. In that case you cannot provide details about the internal workings of the organization. Most CPS statements are not this granular regarding auditing, so be careful in providing too much information that could be used in security penetration.

Statement Regarding Root Key Certificate. The following items should be considered for this section.

- Root certificate and public-private key pair creation—The procedure for root certificate and public-private keys.
- Private key security—Describe how the CA will protect access to the private keys after they have been generated.
- Physical security—Describe the security of the environment and access to the environment, including (1) card key access—if any, (2) network firewalls, and (3) physical access audit logs.
- Backup and storage facilities—Describe the mechanism that will provide backup and recovery of the root keys.
- Root key compromise—Describe the steps taken to keep the root keys from being compromised. Also include the plan in the event a compromise occurs.

Statement Regarding Identification and Authentication Practices. The identification and authentication process requires that the certificate applicant provide specific information in order to receive certificates. This could include the following (or be a combination of several identifications).

- A PIN assigned by an external entity
- A driver's license
- Passport
- Employee ID
- Other type of recognized ID

Statement Regarding Certificate Revocation. This is the process of publishing and managing a Certificate Revocation List (CRL). We will be discussing the CRL in the next section.

Management of the Certificate Life Cycle. The life cycle of a certificate will in most cases follow the diagram in Figure 9.6.

FIGURE 9.6 *Certificate Life Cycle*

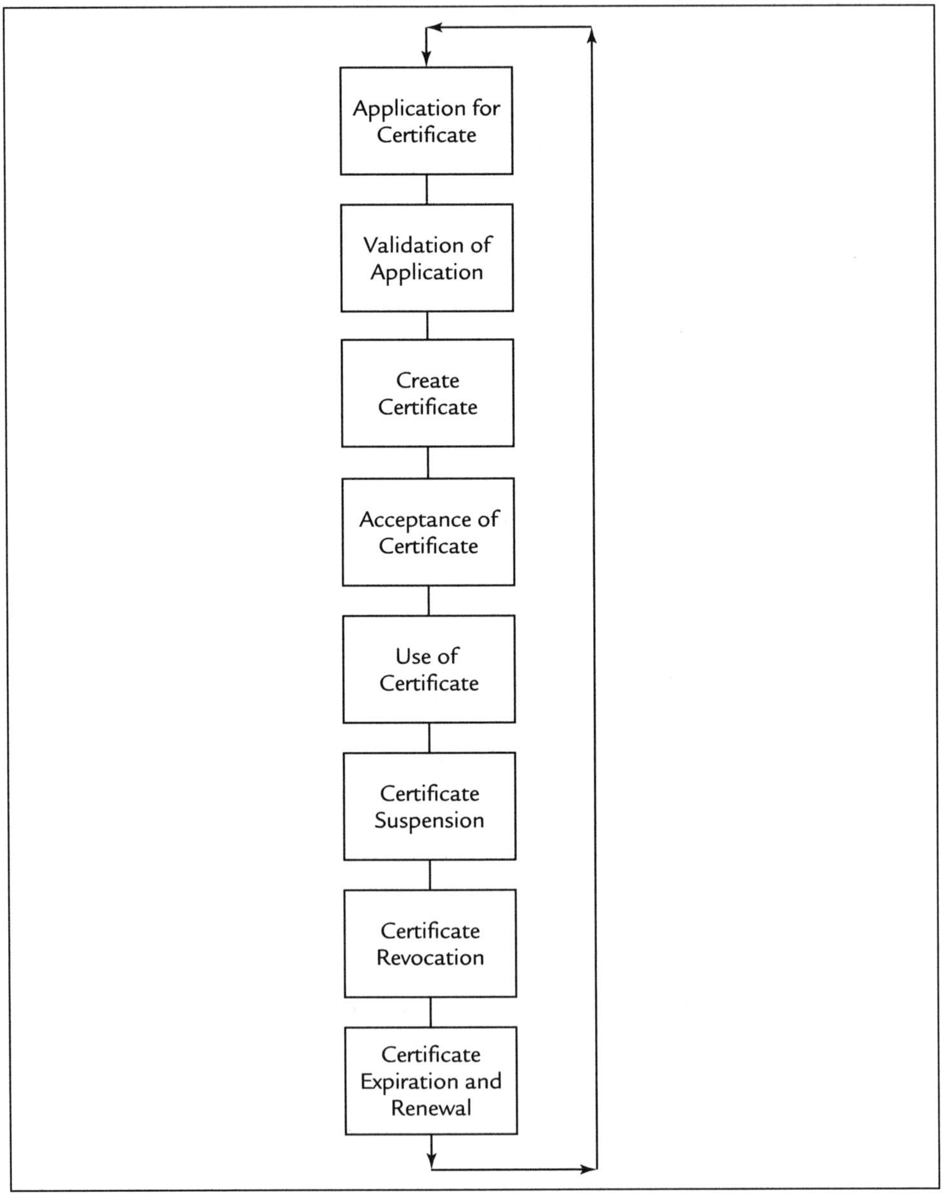

9.2 The CRL

At long last, we finally get to the CRL. So what is this magical thing called the CRL? (You can find one answer at http://www.ietf.org/rfc/rfc2459.txt.) The CRL is a certificate revocation list. When a certificate is issued to an end-user or system, it is expected to be in use for the period that it is valid. So far so good. But there are circumstances where you may want to revoke that certificate.

- An employee quits. If an employee leaves your organization, you will want to invalidate the certificates that this employee has been using. The CRL will accomplish this.
- You suspect that the certificate has been compromised. This actually is an old problem, notably with passwords. "Here, use my password while I am gone. It is okay, but don't tell anyone." In many browsers you can export a certificate and import it into another browser. The next thing you know, someone has submitted a purchase order for a billion dollars in chewing tobacco. So in this example, you place the old certificate into the CRL and issue a new one.
- A person changes his or her name. In this case, the old certificate is placed into the CRL and a new one is issued.

Overall the CRL is a list of revoked certificates that is signed by a CA. One of the biggest issues with a CRL is the time difference between when a certificate has been identified as required to be in the CRL and when it actually gets put into the CRL. PKI systems have actually been around for several years, and as a result, there are many bad habits that have been noticed by most organizations.

- Taking days or even weeks before a certificate has been placed into the CRL (in some implementations this is also known as the termination list).
- Not putting the certificate into the CRL at all.
- Not having a CRL!

As you can imagine, this is bad. So make sure you put processes in place to manage certificates that need to be removed from your organization. Another bit of concern is the huge size that the CRL can become. Think about a large enterprise organization. The CA can be expected to certify thousands or even hundreds of thousands of entities. Over time the CRL can get really big. In itself, this could be a problem. Some PKI systems have software that can help manage this. Check with your vendor.

There are a variety of "key recovery," "key escrow," and "trusted third party" encryption requirements that have been suggested in recent years by government agencies. All key recovery systems require the existence of a highly sensitive and highly available secure secret key system. Key recovery is sometimes called "key escrow." The term "key recovery" is used as a generic term for these systems, encompassing the various "key escrow," "trusted third party," and "key recovery" encryption systems introduced in recent years. Although there are some differences between these systems, the distinctions are not critical for our purposes. A CA can exist without any form of key recovery, and a key recovery infrastructure can exist completely independently of any CA infrastructure. More and more businesses understand the importance of having a key backup, since they must be able to retrieve encrypted data when users lose their decryption keys, forget their passwords, or leave the organization.

Why do we need a key recovery mechanism? Users can lose the keys, in which case you may need to declare the keys "compromised." Why is this a problem? If a user loses a certificate, then he or she will not be able to read any encrypted mail. So the data can be lost. Having a key escrowed (or in a backup) will allow you to access that data. But this is also a problem. Who will have access to the backups (a.k.a. escrows)? This is a big problem, and a problem that each company will need to deal with. We cannot recommend that all companies have an escrow. In some cases this could be a violation of the Policies and Procedures of that company. What we do recommend is that you review the business needs in relation to the security requirements and then make your own decision. Also, you may issue two keys: one for encryption and one for signatures. The encryption key will be escrowed, and the signature certificate will not be escrowed. Why do this? The reason is nonrepudiation. If you back up the signature keys, then someone could access the keys and use them illicitly. So somebody in your company could access the backup, or safe storage, and then use one of the certificates to purchase one billion dollars' worth of chewing tobacco. What are the considerations for having one or more keys and using escrows?

- Business requirements
- Support requirements
- Nonrepudiation requirements
- Encryption requirements
- Roaming users (in some cases, the certificate with the private key is stored in some type of encrypted directory—don't lose control of this!)
- Cost
- If an escrow is implemented in your company, how will it be protected?

9.3 The LDAP

The Lightweight Directory Access Protocol, or LDAP, is a directory protocol (http://www.ietf.org/rfc/rfc1777.txt). LDAP defines a simple mechanism for directory clients to query and manage a database of hierarchical entries. Overall, LDAP is a simplification of the X.500 directory access protocol that we discussed in the first part of this chapter. If you delve into the LDAP protocol, you will see that it is a subset of the X.500 access protocol. As a result, LDAP can access X.500 directories, and LDAP and X.500 servers can interoperate within the same environment. LDAP runs directly over TCP, eliminating the need for the complicated OSI (Open Systems Interconnection) stack.

The LDAP directory service model is based on specific and unique entries. An entry is a single collection of attributes with a single key (key in this definition is that of a parameter that can be used to look up something and not a key for encryption). In each entry there will be a name. As you may recall, we have discussed DNs, or distinguished names. The DN is used as a unique value that represents each collection, or entry. Much like the X.500, each of the entry's attributes has a type and one or more values. Again, like our X.500 example, the LDAP directory entries are arranged in a hierarchical, treelike structure. This structure can reflect political, geographic, or organizational boundaries.

The LDAP directory service is based on a client-server model. An LDAP server will offer the directory data via TCP/IP port 389 and SSL encrypted port 636. Clients will access the LDAP server via a set of queries. The results of these queries can be used in messaging, applications, and authentication. One feature that is built into the protocol is that of a referral. If in the process of a query an answer is not available on the local server, if configured to do so, the LDAP server will attempt to connect to another server. If that server can service the request, then the result of the query will be returned to the client. One example of this could be name resolution. You may have a person's name but not his or her RFC821 Internet address. (This is an address like Bubba@exampleemailserver.com.)

See Figure 9.7. The client sends a request for "Bubba Duck." The first server performs a lookup and does not find the entry in its local database. The server then sends a referral to the X.500 server, and the entry is found. A lookup is performed for "Bubba Duck," and the RFC821 address is returned to the LDAP server and then from the LDAP server back to the client.

LDAP servers are also capable of managing transaction logs. This is a process for chronicling adds, changes, and deletions of entries. Using this system, an LDAP server can send this list of changes to other LDAP servers.

FIGURE 9.7 *LDAP Server*

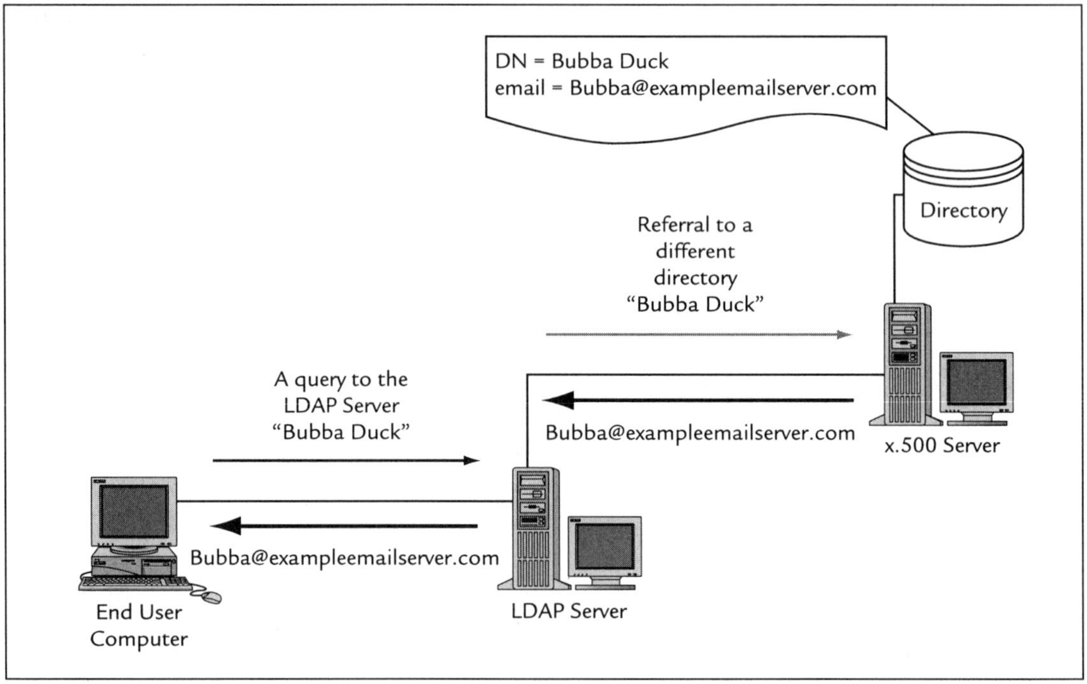

This way you can have one LDAP server send the same data to several other LDAP servers.

There also is a method to access LDAP information via a URL (http://www.ietf.org/rfc/rfc1738.txt). A predefined format is listed in RFC 1959 (http://www.ietf.org/rfc/rfc1959.txt). This format is described as an LDAP search operation to retrieve information from an LDAP directory. Figure 9.8 shows an extract of the RFC 1959 that describes the URL syntax.

LDAP can be used to store X.509 certificates for authentication. The certificates are placed into the directory and then accessed via a Web server. See Figure 9.9. In this example a user attempts to access a secure page. The Web server returns a status code of 401. Then the user sends the query back with his or her credentials (the user logs in). The Web server looks to see if the information is local. If the information is not local, then it performs a bind operation on the LDAP server and connects to it. Then the Web server sends over a query checking for validity of the credentials. If the credentials are valid, then a DN is returned back to the Web server. The Web server then checks to see if that DN has access to the resource being requested. If the request is valid, then the page is returned to the browser.

FIGURE 9.8 *RFC 1959 Extract*

```
(http://www.ietf.org/rfc/rfc1959.txt).
2.  URL Definition
   An LDAP URL begins with the protocol prefix "ldap" and
is defined by
   the following grammar.
    <ldapurl> ::= "ldap://" [ <hostport> ] "/" <dn>
    [ "?" <attributes>
                        [ "?" <scope> "?" <filter> ] ]
    <hostport> ::= <hostname> [ ":" <portnumber> ]
    <dn> ::= a string as defined in RFC 1485
    <attributes> ::= NULL | <attributelist>
    <attributelist> ::= <attributetype>
                        | <attributetype> [ ","
<attributelist> ]
    <attributetype> ::= a string as defined in RFC 1777
    <scope> ::= "base" | "one" | "sub"

    <filter> ::= a string as defined in RFC 1558
Example:
ldap://ldap.itd.umich.edu/o=University%20of%20Michigan,c=US
??sub?(cn=smith)
```

FIGURE 9.9 *Accessing a Page*

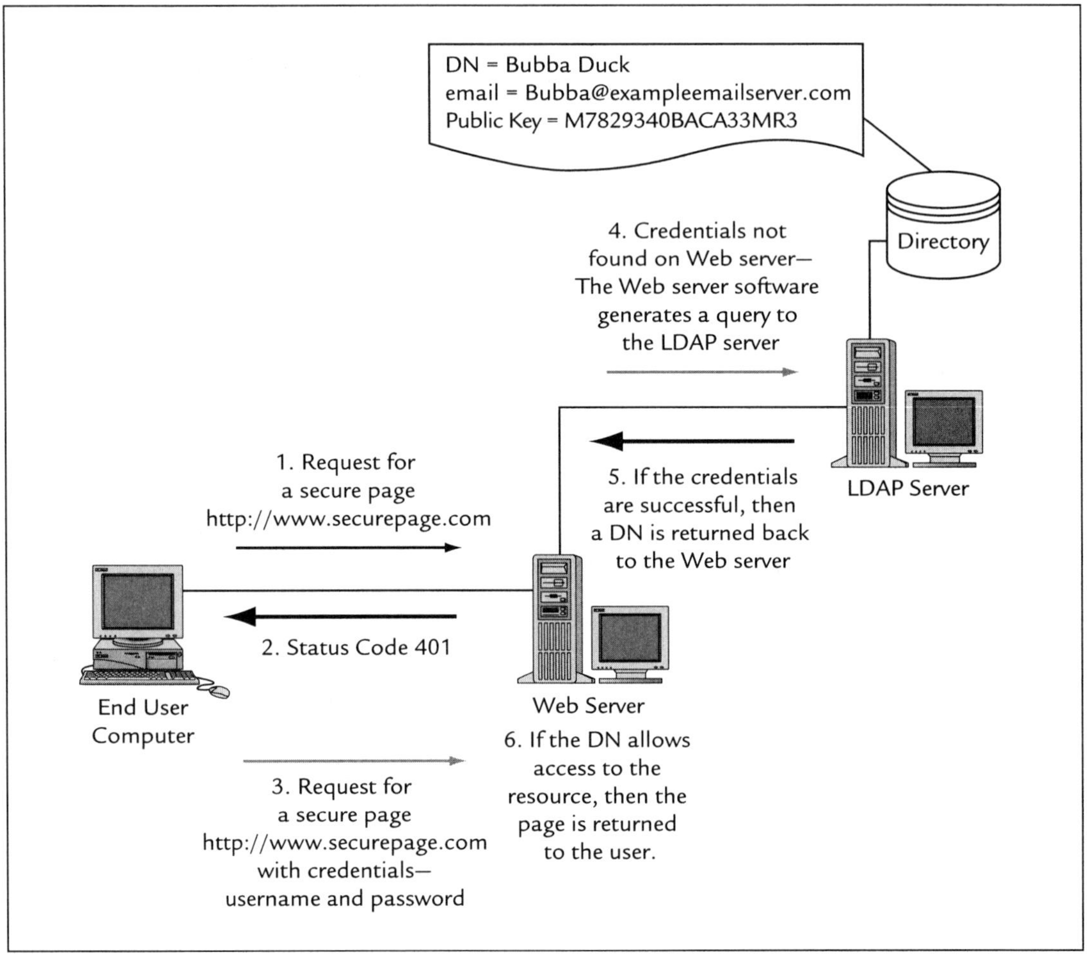

9.4 Public-Key Cryptography Standards

We are now going to review the Public-Key Cryptography Standards, or PKCS. These are specifications that have been produced by RSA. They were first published in 1991 from various groups and early adopters of PKI technology. Currently there are 15 standards (though some of the following have been combined) that are defined by RSA.

Abstract Syntax Notation number one, or ASN.1, is a standard that defines a formal notation for the specification of abstract data types. ASN.1 is a formal notation used for describing data transmitted by telecommunications

PKCS #1: RSA Cryptography Standard	PKCS #1 describes rsaEncryption and syntax for RSA public keys and private keys. Also defines three signature algorithms.
PKCS #2	PKCS #2 has been incorporated into PKCS #1.
PKCS #3: Diffie-Hellman Key Agreement Standard	PKCS #3 describes a method for implementing Diffie-Hellman key agreement.
PKCS #4	PKCS #4 has been incorporated into PKCS #1.
PKCS #5: Password-Based Cryptography Standard	PKCS #5 describes a method for encryption with a secret key derived from a password.
PKCS #6: Extended-Certificate Syntax Standard	PKCS #6 describes syntax for extended certificates.
PKCS #7: Cryptographic Message Syntax Standard	PKCS #7 describes syntax for data that may have cryptography applied to it. PKCS #7 is compatible with privacy-enhanced mail (PEM). See RFCs 1421-1424.
PKCS #8: Private-Key Information Syntax Standard	PKCS #8 describes syntax for private-key information. Private-key information includes a private-key and public-key algorithm.
PKCS #9: Selected Attribute Types	PKCS #9 defines attribute types for use in PKCS #6 extended certificates, PKCS #7 digitally signed messages, and PKCS #8 private-key information.
PKCS #10: Certification Request Syntax Standard	PKCS #10 describes syntax for certification requests. A certification request consists of a distinguished name, a public key, and optionally, a set of attributes.

(*continued*)

PKCS #11: Cryptographic Token Interface Standard	PKCS #11 specifies an API to devices, that hold cryptographic information and implement cryptographic functions.
PKCS #12: Personal Information Exchange Syntax Standard	Specifies a portable format for storing and/or transporting a user's private keys and certificates.
PKCS #13: Elliptic Curve Cryptography Standard	This standard is still under development.
PKCS #14: Pseudorandom Number Generation Standard	This standard is still under development.
PKCS #15: Cryptographic Token Information Format Standard	This standard is targeted at establishing a standard, which ensures that users will be able to use cryptographic tokens to identify themselves to multiple standards-aware applications.

protocols. Also ASN.1 covers the structural aspects of information. One of the main reasons for the success of ASN.1 is that this notation is linked with several standardized encoding rules such as the BER (basic encoding rules) and the PER (packed encoding rules). ASN.1 has been used in PKCS documents, including PKCS #5 v2.0, PKCS #12 v1.0, and PKCS #15v1.0.

One topic that we have not previously discussed is where X.509 came from and what organizations support it.

The International Telecommunication Union (ITU) is an organization formerly known as Consultative Committee on International Telephone and Telegraphy (CCITT). The ITU provides telecommunications standards as well as the "X." standards such as X.500 (directory services) and X.509 (secure directory services). (See http://www.itu.int/.)

The Internet Engineering Task Force (IETF) is an open international community of network designers, vendors, and researchers focused on the evolution of the Internet architecture and the operation of the Internet. (See http://www.ietf.org/.) The IETF has recognized the X.509 standards to be used in the Internet technologies. To understand the IETF you should look at a document that they created (see Figure 9.10).

In order to generate some methods and standards to deal with encryption, the IETF formed the Public-Key Infrastructure (X.509) (pkix) (http://www.ietf.org) working group. The main drive of this working group was to

FIGURE 9.10 *IETF Document*

> The Internet Engineering Task Force is a loosely self-organized group of people who make technical and other contributions to the engineering and evolution of the Internet and its technologies. It is the principal body engaged in the development of new Internet standard specifications. Its mission includes:
>
> Identifying, and proposing solutions to, pressing operational and technical problems in the Internet;
>
> Specifying the development or usage of protocols and the near-term architecture to solve such technical problems for the Internet;
>
> Making recommendations to the Internet Engineering Steering Group (IESG) regarding the standardization of protocols and protocol usage in the Internet;
>
> Facilitating technology transfer from the Internet Research Task Force (IRTF) to the wider Internet community;
>
> and providing a forum for the exchange of information within the Internet community between vendors, users, researchers, agency contractors and network managers.
>
> The IETF meeting is not a conference, although there are technical presentations. The IETF is not a traditional standards organization, although many specifications are produced that become standards. The IETF is made up of volunteers who meet three times a year to fulfill the IETF mission
>
> There is no membership in the IETF. Anyone may register for and attend any meeting. The closest thing there is to being an IETF member is being on the IETF or working group mailing lists (see the IETF Mailing Lists section). This is where the best information about current IETF activities and focus can be found.
>
> (Extract from http://www.ietf.org/tao.html)

develop the Internet standards needed to support an X.509-based PKI. One of the goals of this PKI is to facilitate the use of X.509 certificates in various applications that reside on the Internet. As part of this process, the working group was looking to promote interoperability between many vendor implementations. The result of this work was to provide a PKI framework based on X.509 (http://www.ietf.org/html.charters/pkix-charter.html).

So how do we get a working group to generate a standard? Here is a high-level overview. (For a detailed understanding of this, go to the source: http://www.ietf.org/tao.html.)

Overall we start with a description that will solve some type of technological problem. A team of Smart Dudes will get together and generate a draft document of their solution. We call these draft documents "Internet-drafts"—somewhat of a catchy phrase there. When submitted to the IETF, the "draft" documents are valid for six months. These drafts then go though a process of review and development, which can consist of several revisions, each of which would be reviewed by the Internet community. If all goes well and the "draft" is accepted, then it will become a Request for Comments (RFC) document. If a specification has been adopted as an Internet standard, it is given the additional label "STD," but it keeps its RFC number.

For more information about this process check out these RFCs.

Bradner, Scott O. "The Internet Standards process." *RFC 2026.* http://www.ietf.org. 1996.

Cerf, Vinton. "The Internet Activities Board" *RFC 1160.* http://www.ietf.org. 1990.

Postel, Jon. "Request for Comments on Request for Comments." *RFC 1111.* http://www.ietf.org. 1989.

Postel, Jon. "Introduction to the STD Notes." *RFC 1311.* http://www.ietf.org. 1992.

The following lists the various PKIX standards and RFCs.

Adams, Carlisle and Stephen Farrell. "Internet X.509 Public Key Infrastructure: Certificate Management Protocols." *RFC 2510.* http://www.ietf.org. 1999.

Adams, Carlisle et al. "Internet X.509 Public Key Infrastructure Data Validation and Certification Server Protocols." *RFC 3029.* http://www.ietf.org. 2001.

Adams, Carlisle et al. "Internet X.509 Public Key Infrastructure Time-Stamp Protocol (TSP)." *RFC 3161.* http://www.ietf.org. 2001.

Boeyen, Sharon, Tim Howes, and Patrick Richard. "Internet X.509 Public Key Infrastructure: Operational Protocols—LDAPv2." *RFC 2559.* http://www.ietf.org. 1999.

Boeyen, Sharon, Tim Howes, and Patrick Richard. "Internet X.509 Public Key Infrastructure: LDAPv2 Schema." *RFC 2587.* http://www.ietf.org. 1999.

Chokhani, Santosh. "Internet X.509 Public Key Infrastructure Certificate Policy and Certification Practices Framework.' *RFC 2527.* http://www.ietf.org. 1999.

Housley, Russell, et. al. "Internet X.509 Public Key Infrastructure: Certificate and CRL Profile." *RFC 2459*. http://www.ietf.org. 1999.

Housley, Russell and Paul Hoffman. "Internet X.509 Public Key Infrastructure: Operational Protocols: FTP and HTTP." *RFC 2585*. http://www.ietf.org. 1999.

Housley, Russell and Tim Polk. "Internet X.509 Public Key Infrastructure: Representation of Key Exchange Algorithm (KEA) Keys in Internet X.509 Public Key Infrastructure Certificates." *RFC 2528*. http://www.ietf.org. 1999.

Myers, Michael et al. "Internet X.509 Certificate Request Message Format." *RFC 2511*. http://www.ietf.org. 1999.

Myers, Michael et al. "X.509 Internet Public Key Infrastructure: Online Certificate Status Protocol—OCSP." *RFC 2560*. http://www.ietf.org. 1999.

Myers, Michael, Xiaoyi Liu, and Jim Schaad. "Certificate Management Messages over CMS." *RFC 2797*. http://www.ietf.org. 2000.

Prafullchandra, Hemma and Jim Schaad. "Diffie-Hellman Proof-of-Possession Algorithms." *RFC 2875*. http://www.ietf.org. 2000.

Santesson, Stefan et al. "Internet X.509 Public Key Infrastructure Qualified Certificates Profile." *RFC 3039*. http://www.ietf.org. 2001.

The following were IETF Internet Draft documents at the time of this writing.

Arsenault, Alfred W. and Sean Turner. "Internet X.509 Public Key Infrastructure: Roadmap." *Internet Draft*. http://www.ietf.org. January 2002.

Farrell, Stephen and Russell Housley. "An Internet Attribute Certificate Profile for Authorization." *Internet Draft*. http://www.ietf.org. June 2001.

Kapoor, Amit and Ronald Tschalär. "Transport Protocols for CMP." *Internet Draft*. http://www.ietf.org. November 2000.

Malpani, Ambarish, Russell Housley, and Trevor Freeman. "Simple Certificate Validaton Protocol (SCVP)." *Internet Draft*. http://www.ietf.org. March 2002.

Pinkas, Denis and Thomas Gindin. "Internet X.509 Public Key Infrastructure Permanent Identifier." *Internet Draft*. http://www.ietf.org. August 2002.

The following lists references for LDAP.

Howes, Tim. "A String Representation of LDAP Search Filters." *RFC 1960.* http://www.ietf.org. 1996.

Howes, Tim and Mark Smith. "The LDAP Application Program Interface." *RFC 1823.* http://www.ietf.org. 1995.

Howes, Tim and Mark Smith. "An LDAP URL Format." *RFC 1959.* http://www.ietf.org. 1996.

Howes, Tim and Mark Smith. "The LDAP URL Format." *RFC 2255.* http://www.ietf.org. 1997.

Kille, Steve. "Use of an X.500/LDAP Directory to Support MIXER Address Mapping." *RFC 2164.* http://www.ietf.org. 1998.

Wahl, Mark et al. "Lightweight Directory Access Protocol (v3): Attribute Syntax Definitions." *RFC 2252.* http://www.ietf.org. 1997.

Wahl, Mark, Tim Howes, and Steve Kille. "Lightweight Directory Access Protocol (v3)." *RFC 2251.* http://www.ietf.org. 1997.

Wahl, Mark, Tim Howes, and Steve Kille. "Lightweight Directory Access Protocol (v3): UTF-8 String Representation of Distinguished Names." *RFC 2253.* http://www.ietf.org. 1997.

Yeong, Wengyik, Tim Howes, and Steve Kille. "Lightweight Directory Access Protocol." *RFC 1777.* http://www.ietf.org. 1995.

9.5 Cylink

Cylink™ (www.cylink.com) has a great demo for a PKI system. You can find the demo at https://pki.cylink.com/welcome.

When you first enter the demo for Cylink, you will receive a prompt to accept a new certificate (Figure 9.11). This certificate will allow you to communicate securely with Cylink.

In Figure 9.12, Cylink has created a new site certificate for you based on an RC4-40 key.

In Figure 9.13, you can determine how long you want to keep the certificate. The default is "Accept this certificate for this session."

Figure 9.14 shows a disclaimer for fraud. This is a true statement: You can have fraud, and then you can have encrypted fraud. Always be careful in your Internet transactions.

The screen in Figure 9.15 is really saying, "Are you done, and have you read every screen?"

Once the browser accepts the certificate, you can review it if you like. In Netscape select the "Show Security Information" icon . This will bring

FIGURE 9.11 *Cylink Certificate*

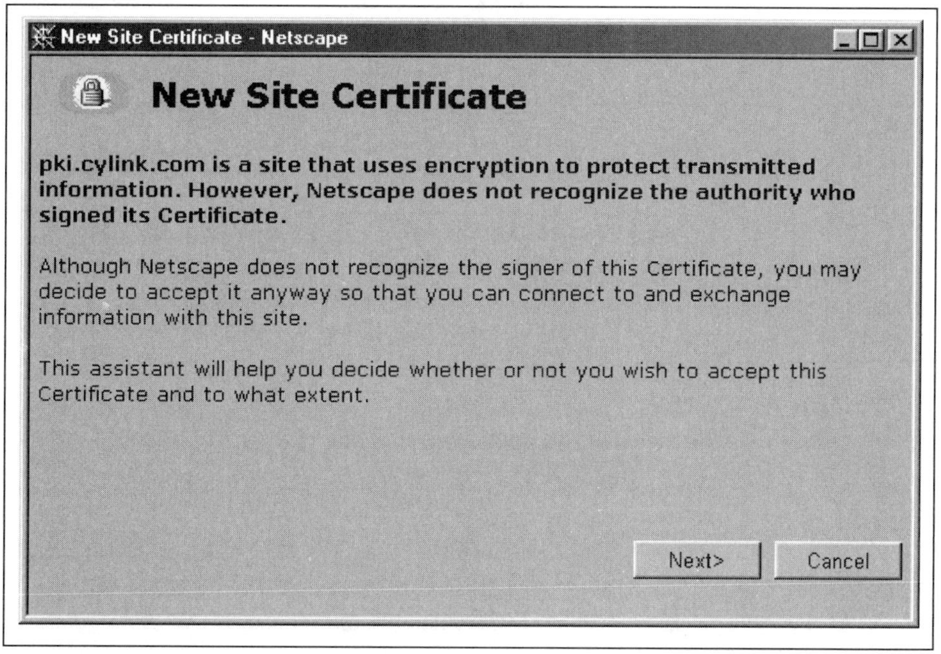

FIGURE 9.12 *New Cylink Certificate*

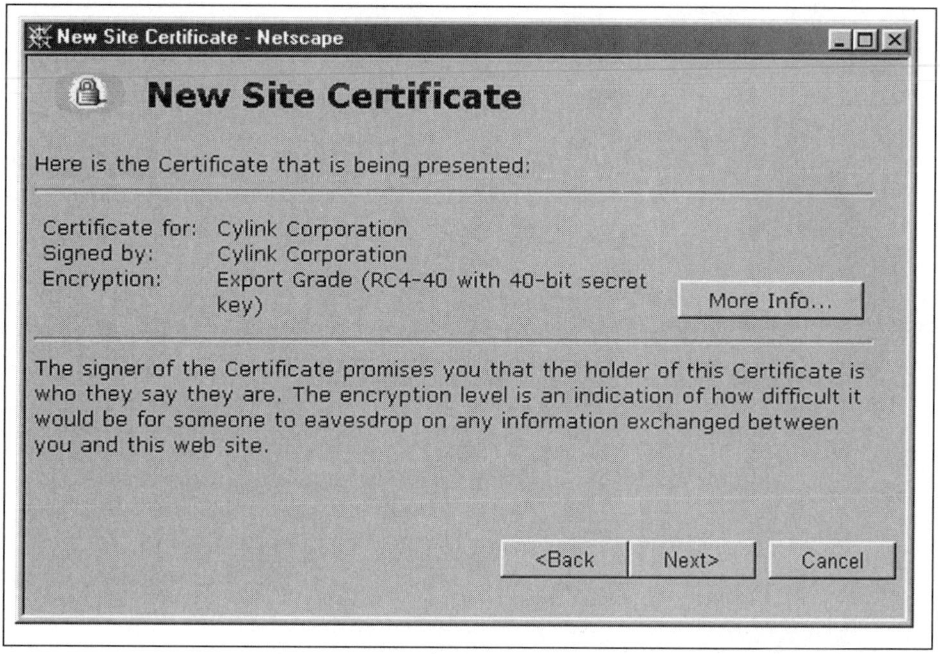

FIGURE 9.13 *Certificate Duration*

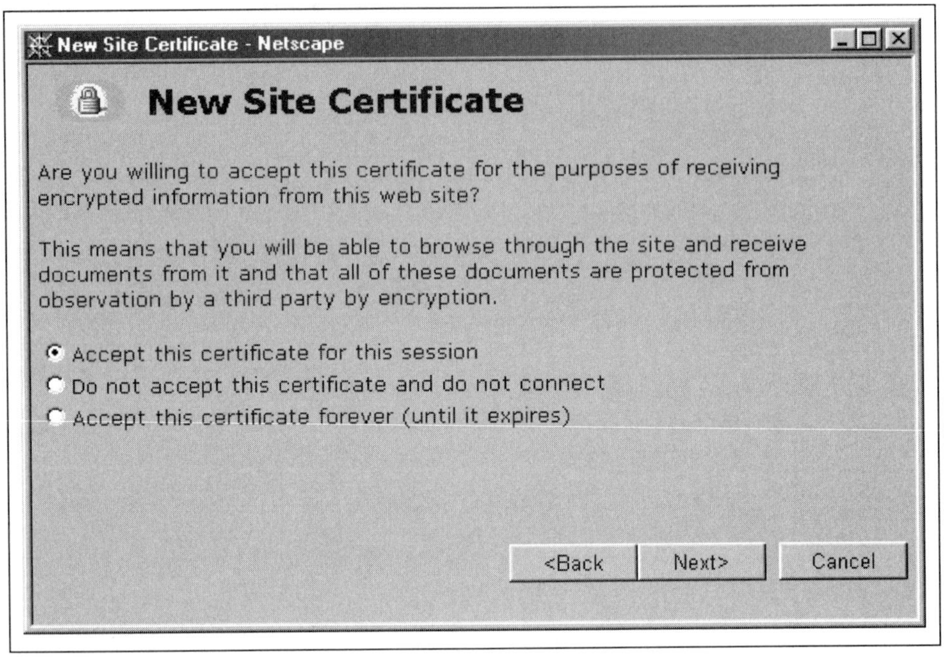

FIGURE 9.14 *Fraud Disclaimer*

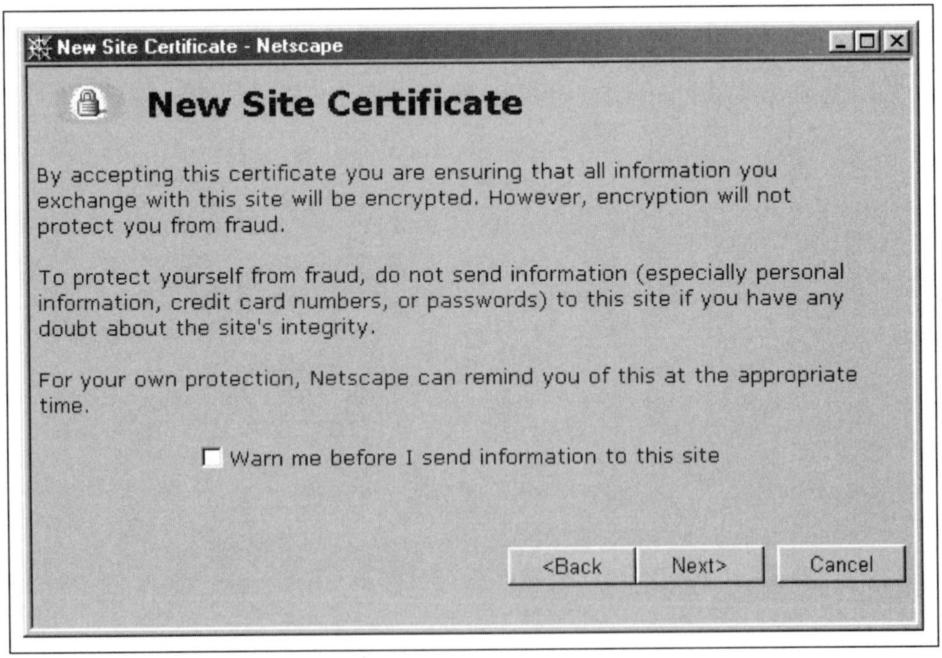

FIGURE 9.15 *Confirming Certificate*

up a dialog box showing several choices. Select "Web Sites," and then select the site you want to view. In our example we are looking at pki.cylink.com (Figure 9.16). Press Edit once you have selected the site.

The dialog box in Figure 9.17 will display. It will provide information about the certificate and who issued the certificate.

Follow the steps in the demo. You will do the following.

1. Generate a private key for your browser. (Make sure you enter a correct e-mail address.)
2. Pick up the certified key for your browser. Two messages will be sent to you. The first message will confirm that the request was sent to the correct e-mail address. You will select and launch a URL, and that will start a process that will send a second e-mail. The second e-mail will send your pickup information. This URL will send you to a server where you can pick up your certified certificate. The screen in Figure 9.18 shows an example of the pickup URL.

On the pickup screen press the Accept button. This starts the process for you to pick up your certificate.

Once you have completed all the steps, view the security settings for your browser. Figure 9.19 shows an example. This screen shot shows that

FIGURE 9.16 *Choosing a Web Site*

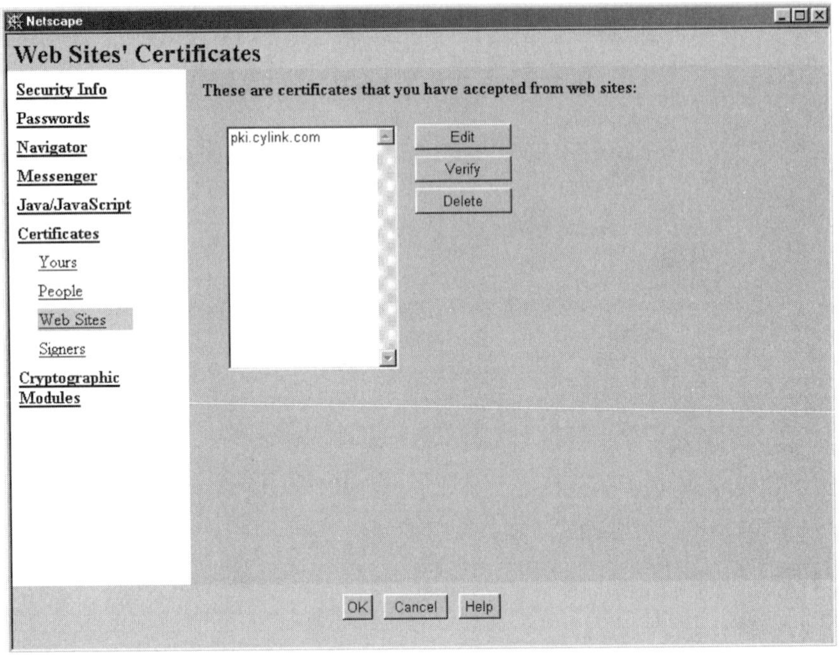

FIGURE 9.17 *Dialog Box*

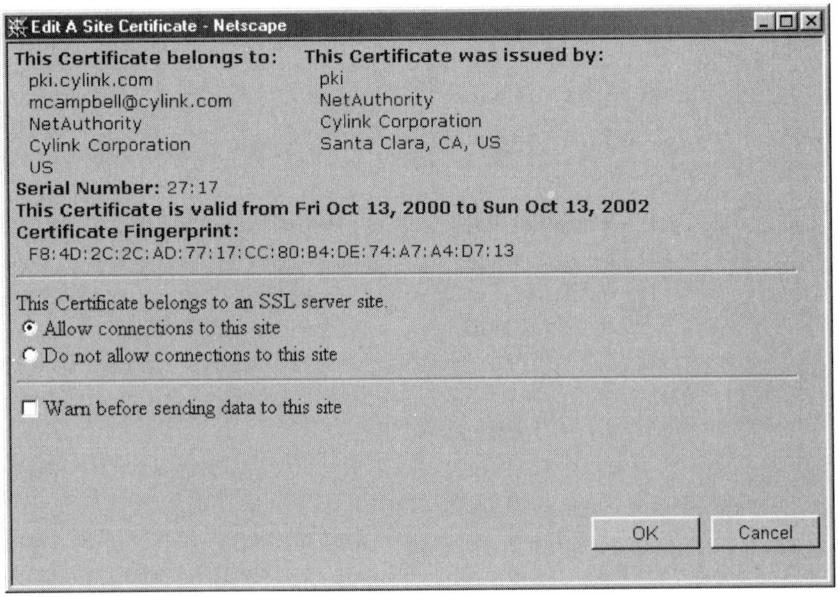

FIGURE 9.18 *Pickup URL*

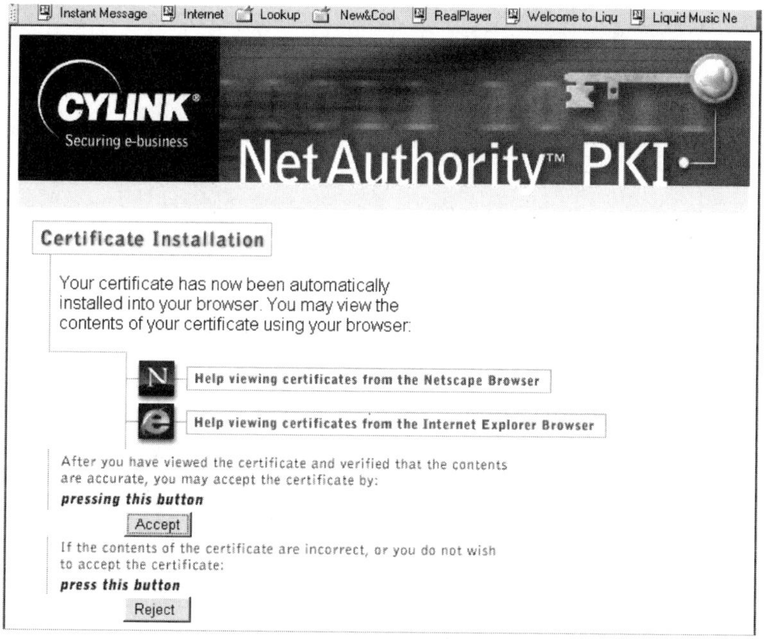

FIGURE 9.19 *Your Certificate*

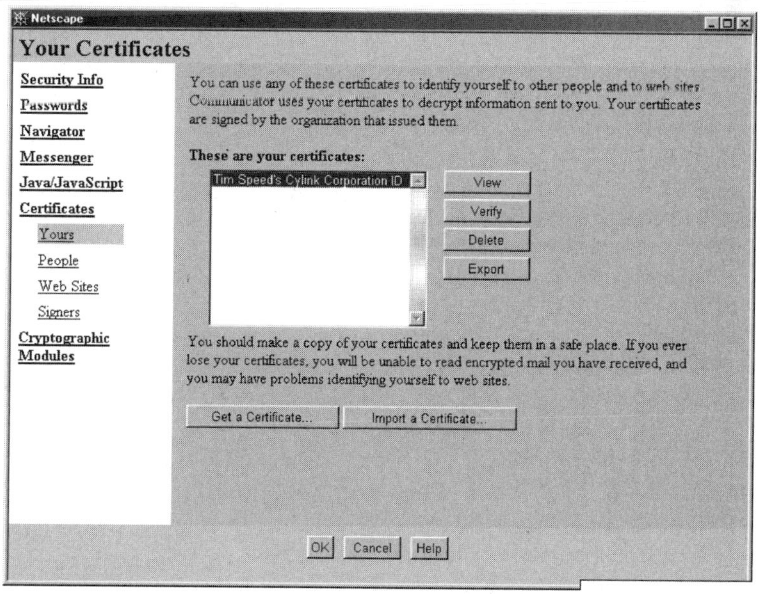

FIGURE 9.20 *Certificate Ownership*

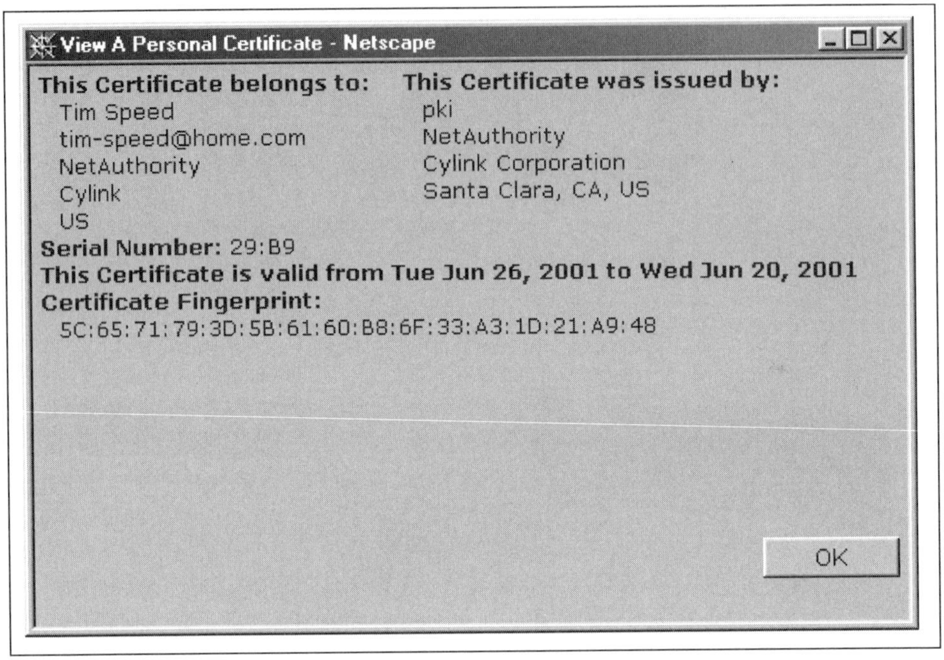

you have a certificate. You can press the View button to view the specifics about the certificate.

The screen shot in Figure 9.20 shows who owns the certificate and who issued the certificate. Also shown is the expiration date.

9.6 Certification Practice Statement

Note: This is a fictitious document.

1. Introduction

A Certification Practice Statement ("CPS") is defined by the Electronic Commerce and Information Technology Division of the American Bar Association as "A statement of the practices that a certification authority employs in issuing certificates." The CPS and supporting documentation explain the practices, procedures, and philosophies behind the issuance of certificates within The Company Cylink Certificate environment.

1.1 Scope

The scope will be limited to the Cylink Certificate environment. Certificates created within this environment are based on the Cylink Certificate systems.

1.1.1 Trademarks

Cylink—© 2000 Cylink Corp. All Rights Reserved. For questions or comments about this trademark, please contact Cylink Corp. P.O. Box 54952, 3131 Jay Street, Santa Clara, CA 95056-0952.

COPYRIGHT NOTICE. Copyright © 2000 Microsoft Corporation, One Microsoft Way, Redmond, Washington 98052-6399 USA. All rights reserved. See www.microsoft.com for more information

TRADEMARKS
Microsoft, Windows, Windows NT, Exchange, MSN, Outlook, The Microsoft Network, Windows98, Windows95, and/or other Microsoft products referenced herein are either trademarks or registered trademarks of Microsoft. See www.microsoft.com for more information

This list is not exhaustive. All other companies not explicitly mentioned or the names of actual companies and products mentioned herein may be the trademarks of their respective owners.

1.2 Overview

The Company Certificate Certification Practice Statement describes the practices and procedures of (i) the Certification Authorities, and (ii) User Registration Authorities operating under the Certification Authorities. This Certification Practice Statement also describes the terms and conditions under which The Company makes Certification Authority and Registration Authority services available in respect to Certificates. This Certification Practice Statement is applicable to all persons, entities, and organizations that fall under the influence of The Company Certificate environment including, without limitation, all applicants, administrators, users, new users, and any other persons, entities, or organizations that have a relationship with (i) The Company in respect to Certificates and/or any services provided by The Company in respect to Certificates, or (ii) any Registration Authorities operating under a Certification Authority.

1.3 Identification

This document is called the Certificate Certification Practice Statement.

1.4 Definitions

Applicant: means a person, entity, or organization applying for a Certificate, but which has not yet been issued a Certificate, or a person, entity, or organization that currently has a Certificate and that is applying for renewal of a Certificate. This can be a new user or a user with an expired certificate.

CA: Certification Authority
Canonical Name: This is a hierarchical name in canonical format. Example: CN = Joe Smith/OU = Dallas/O = The Company. Also can be known as a String Name.

Certificate: means a digital document that at a minimum: (a) identifies the Certification Authority issuing it, (b) names or otherwise identifies a Subject, (c) contains a Public Key of a Key Pair, (d) identifies its operational period, and (e) contains a serial number and is digitally signed by a Certification Authority.

Certificate Revocation List: this is a list of the user names of revoked Certificates that has been revoked by a CA Administrator. This is list that has been signed by the CA for authenticity.

Certification Authority: means an entity or organization that (i) creates and digitally signs Certificates that contain among other things a Subject's Public Key and other information that is intended to identify the Subject, (ii) makes Certificates available to facilitate communication with the Subject identified in the Certificate.

Certification Practice Statement: means a statement of the practices that a Certification Authority uses in issuing, managing, revoking, renewing, and providing access to Certificates, and the terms and conditions under which the Certification Authority makes such services available.

Compromise: means a suspected or actual loss, disclosure, or loss of control over sensitive information or data.

CPS: see Certification Practice Statement.

CRL: see Certificate Revocation List.

DN: Distinguished Name

DNS: Domain Name Server

DSA: Digital Signature Algorithm

The Company Operational Authority: is defined as the personnel who work for or on behalf of The Company and who are responsible for the operation of the Certification Authorities.

The Company Policy Authority: means that personnel who work for or on behalf of The Company and who are responsible for determining the policies and procedures that govern the operation of the Certification Authorities.

The Company Repository: means a collection of databases that contain information about Certificates provided by The Company in respect to Certificates, including among other things, the types of Certificates issued by the Certification Authorities

HTTP: Hypertext Transfer Protocol

IETF: means the Internet Engineering Task Force. The Internet Engineering Task Force is an international community of network designers, operators, vendors, and researchers concerned with the evolution of the Internet architecture and the efficient operation of the Internet.

ITU-T: International Telecommunication Union—Telecommunication Standardization Sector

Key Pair: means two mathematically related cryptographic keys, having the properties that (i) one key can be used to encrypt a message that can only be decrypted using the other key, and (ii) even knowing one key, it is believed to be computationally infeasible to discover the other key.

Certificate Certification Authority: means a Certification Authority operated by or on behalf of The Company for the purpose of issuing, managing, renewing, and providing access to Certificates.

Certificate Certifier: Certifier IDs and certificates form the basis of X.509 security. Using the certifier ID an administrator can issue certificates, based on the organization's naming tree, to servers and users when an administrator registers them. Authentication is a process that ensures server or user certificates are members of the same naming tree. For servers and users in different naming trees, will create cross-certificates to enable communication. To keep the certifier certificate file safe, an administrator defines where to store it as part of its registration process.

Certificate: A certificate is a unique electronic stamp that identifies a user or server.

A certificate contains:

- The name of the certifier that issued the certificate.
- The name of the user or server to whom the certificate was issued.

- A public key that is stored in both the Directory and the certificate file. Certificate uses the public key to encrypt messages that are sent to the owner of the public key and to validate the certificate owner's signature.
- An electronic signature.[1]
- The expiration date of the certificate.

Certificate Certification Practice Statement: means this document.

Certificate CPS: See Certification Practice Statement.

Operational Period: means, with respect to a Certificate, the period of its validity. The Operational Period would typically begin on the date the Certificate is issued (or such later date as specified in the Certificate), and ends on the date and time it expires as noted in the Certificate.

OU—Certifier—This is the certifier that is used to create users and servers. The OU certifier is created from the O root level certifier.

PA: Policy Authority

Password: A password is required in order to access a User ID or a Certifier ID.

PKI: Public-Key Infrastructure

PKIX: means an IETF Working Group developing technical specifications for PKI components based on X.509 Version 3 Certificates.

Private Key: means the key of a Key Pair used to decrypt an encrypted message. This key must be kept secret.

Public Key: means the key of a Key Pair used to encrypt a message. The Public Key can be made freely available to anyone who may want to send encrypted messages to the holder of the Private Key of the Key Pair. The Public Key is usually made publicly available in a Certificate issued by a Certification Authority and is often obtained by accessing a repository or database. A Public Key is used to encrypt a message that can only be decrypted by the holder of the corresponding Private Key.

RA: see Registration Authority.

Registration Authority: is a person that has the authority to initiate a new user registration process.

1. Note: In many cases the Signature private key and the Encryption Key are separate Keys. This can be accommodated via different vendors as well as Lotus Notes Id files (for X.509v3 user certificates).

Registration Server: This is the server that houses the registration engine and the certifier database.

Revoke or Revocation: means, with respect to a Certificate, to prematurely end the Operational Period of that Certificate from a specified time forward. Removing the person document from the Directory or adding the user to the CRL can control this.

RFC: Request for Comment

Secret Key: Certificate users can use the Secret Encryption Keys to encrypt documents without having to use their own encryption keys. The Secret Encryption Keys field can contain either the name of a key, which is automatically used to encrypt documents, or the field can be blank, allowing users to assign the encryption key.

Subject: means a person, entity, or organization whose Public Key is contained in a Certificate.

Subscriber: means a person, entity, or organization that has applied for and has been issued a Certificate. Also known as an end-user.

Subscription Agreement: means the agreement between a Subscriber and The Company a Registration Authority.

URL: Uniform Resource Locator (RFC1738)

1.5 Communities and Application

Use of the CA certificate is restricted to Administrators,

1.6 Certification Authorities

Only Certification Authorities authorized by The Company are permitted to issue Certificates.

1.7 Registration Authorities

In The Company Certificate public-key infrastructure, Registration Authorities under the Certification Authorities may accept Certificate Applications from Applicants and perform a verification of the information contained in such Certificate. If the information provided is verified according to the procedures established by The Company. Certification Authority may request a Certification Authority to issue a Certificate to the Applicant.

Only Registration Authorities authorized by The Company are permitted to submit requests to the Certification Authority for the issuance of Certificate. In the event that more than one Registration Authority is authorized to perform this function for Certificates issuance then The Company will post a list of such authorized Registration Authorities.

1.8 End Entities

End entities for the Certificate public-key infrastructure consist of:

- **Applicants**—An Applicant is a person, entity, or organization that has applied for, but has not yet been issued, a Certificate.
- **Subscribers**—A Subscriber is a person, entity, or organization that has been issued a Certificate. This can be a user or a server. An administrator acts as the subscriber for the server key ring file.
- **Registration Authority**—A person who has the authority to initiate a new user registration process. This can be for a new user or a migrated user.

1.9 Applicability

This, The Company Certification Practice Statement, is applicable to The Company Certificates issued by The Company Certification Authorities. Certificates are issued by Certification Authorities for use by The Company Users, Servers, and contractors.

1.10 Specification Administration Organization

The Certification Practice Statement is administered by The Company Operational Authority and is based on the policies established by The Company Policy Authority.

1.10.1 Contact Person

The contact information for questions about Certificates is:
The Company Inquiries
Tel:
Fax:
E-mail:

2. General Provisions

2.1 Obligations

2.1.1 Certification Authority Obligations

The Company Certification Authority shall:

- Provide Certification Authority services in accordance with the terms and conditions of the Certification Practice Statement.

- Upon receipt of a request from a Registration Authority operating under such Certification Authority, issues a Certificate in accordance with the terms and conditions of the Certification Practice Statement.

2.1.2 Registration Authority Obligations

A Registration Authority operating under a Certification Authority shall:

- Receive Certificate Applications in accordance with the terms and conditions of the Certification Practice Statement. This can be via a formal request or via a request into a registration tool.
- Perform verification of information submitted by Applicants when applying for Certificates, and if such verification is successful, submit a request to a Certification Authority for the issuance of a Certificate, all in accordance with the terms and conditions of the Certification Practice Statement

Note: In many CPS documents there is an obligation of the Registration Authority to implement the following:

- Submit requests to the CA that would issue a revocation of the certificate.
- Issue warning notices of certificate expiration.

These necessary tasks are implemented via a different set of administration considerations and are outside the scope of this document.

2.1.3 Subscriber Obligations

Subscribers and Applicants shall:

- Understand and, if necessary, receive proper education in the use of Public-Key cryptography and Certificates including Certificates.
- Provide, in any communications with The Company Certificate Administration or the Registration Authority, correct information with no errors, misrepresentations, or omissions;
- Read and agree to all terms and conditions of this section (2.1.3) of the Certification Practice Statement and Subscription Agreement.
- Refrain from modifying the contents of a Certificate.
- Use Certificates exclusively for legal and authorized purposes in accordance with the terms and conditions of The Company Certification Practice Statement and applicable laws.
- Only use a Certificate on behalf of The Company.
- Protect the Subscriber's (a.k.a. the Users) Private Keys.

- Notify The Company if Applicant submitted its Certificate to an independent third-party Registration Authority, such as an independent third-party Registration Authority.
- Immediately cease to use a Certificate if the certificate file has been compromised.
- Notify The Company immediately of any suspected or actual Compromise of the Subscriber's Private Keys and request the revocation of such Certificate file.
- Immediately cease to use the Subscriber's Certificate upon (a) expiration or revocation of such Certificate, or (b) any suspected or actual Compromise of the Private Key corresponding to the Public Key in such Certificate, and remove such Certificate from the devices and/or software in which it has been installed.
- Subscribers will not share certificate files with other users. Certificates and related information may be subject to export, import, and/or use restrictions. Subscribers shall comply with all laws and regulations applicable to a Subscriber's right to export, import, and/or use Certificates (files) or related information.

2.1.4 Frequency of Publication

The Certification Practice Statement may be reissued and published yearly.

2.1.5 Access Controls

The Company publishes the Certification Practice Statement.

2.2 Compliance Audit

Certification Authorities, The Company—operated Registration Authorities, and independent third-party Registration Authorities operating under the Certification Authorities shall be audited for compliance against the practices and procedures set forth in the Certification Practice Statement.

2.2.1 Frequency of Entity Compliance Audit

Certification Authorities, The Company-operated Registration Authorities, and independent third-party Registration Authorities operating under the Certificate Certification Authorities shall be audited once per calendar year for compliance with the practices and procedures set forth in the Certification Practice Statement. If the results of an audit report recommend remedial action, The Company or the applicable independent third-party

Registration Authority shall initiate corrective action within thirty (30) days of receipt of such audit report.

2.2.2 Identity/Qualifications of Auditor

The compliance audit shall be performed by a third-party audit team.

2.2.3 Auditor's Relationship to Audited Party

(An organization would add information about the auditor and the auditor's company, may include past history. The purpose of the section is to determine the conflicts of interest)

2.2.4 Topics Covered by Audit

The compliance audit shall test compliance of Certification Authorities, The Company-operated Registration Authorities, or independent third-party operated Registration Authorities under The Company Certification Authorities against the policies and procedures set forth in this Certification Practice Statement.

2.2.5 Actions Taken as a Result of Deficiency

Upon receipt of a compliance audit that identifies any deficiencies, the audited The Company Certification Authority, The Company-operated Registration Authority, or independent third-party operated Registration Authority under a Certification Authority shall use reasonable efforts to correct any such deficiencies in an expeditious manner.

2.2.6 Communication of Results

The results of all compliance audits shall be communicated, in the case of Certification Authorities, to The Company Operational Authority, and, in the case of any The Company-operated Registration Authorities under a Certification Authorities, to The Company Operation Authority, and in the case of third-party Registration Authorities operating under a Certification Authority, to the operational authority for such Registration Authority.

2.3 Confidentiality

Neither The Company nor any independent third-party Registration Authorities operating under The Company Certification Authorities, nor any Resellers, vendors, contractors, Co-Marketers shall disclose or sell Applicant or Subscriber names (or other information submitted by an Applicant or Subscriber when applying for a Certificate).

2.3.1 Disclosure of Certificate Revocation/Suspension Information

If a Certification Authority revokes a Certificate; the certificate will be placed into the defined CRL.

2.4 Intellectual Property Rights

The Company retains all right, title, and interest (including all intellectual property rights), in, to, and under all The Company generated Certificates, except for any information that is supplied by an Applicant or a Subscriber and that is included in a Certificate, which information shall remain the property of the Applicant or Subscriber.

3. Identification and Authentication

3.1 Initial Registration

To obtain a Certificate, an authorized representative of the Applicant must submit a request to the Registration Authority. Upon completion of the Certificate Application and acceptance of the terms and conditions of this Certification Practice Statement and the Subscription Agreement, a Registration Authority or a third-party authorized by a Registration Authority shall perform a verification of some of the information contained in the Certificate Application. If the verification performed by a Registration Authority is successful, the Registration Authority may, on its sole discretion, request the issuance to the Applicant of a Certificate from The Company Certification Authority. In the event of successful verification of a Certificate Application, the Registration Authority shall submit a request to a Certification Authority for the issuance of a Certificate.

3.1.1 Types of Names

The Subject names in a Certificate follow the X.500 Distinguished Name (DN) form. Certification Authorities shall use a single naming convention as set forth below. Each Certificate shall contain the following information:

(i) the "Country Name" (C) is not used.
(ii) the "Organization Name" (O) this has been defined as *The Company.*
(iii) the "Organizational Unit Name" (OU). The OU field will be used to distinguish between different organizational groups within an organization
(iv) the "Common Name" (CN), which is the fully qualified username.

3.1.2 Need for Names to Be Meaningful

Usernames should follow the Doc Standard for The Company—Doc #12345-a

3.1.3 Uniqueness of Names

Usernames should follow the Doc Standard for The Company—Doc #12345-a

3.1.4 Name Claim Dispute Resolution Procedure

Usernames should follow the Doc Standard for The Company—Doc #12345-a

3.1.5 Authentication of Individual Identity

Registration Authorities operating under The Company Certification Authorities shall perform a verification of any organizational identities that are submitted by an Applicant or a person requesting the Certificate for the application. The Registration Authority shall determine whether the organizational identity, e-mail address, or other user attributes have been provided into the Registration process. The information and sources used for the verification will be under the control of the person submitting the Certificate request. Examples:

- A new user—The authorized person that submits a request for a Certificate will have the responsibility to verify that the person that received the certificate is actually the intended recipient of the certificate.

The Company Policy Authority may, at its discretion, update verification practices to improve the organizational identity verification process. Any changes to verification practices shall be published pursuant to the standard procedures for updating the Certification Practice Statement.

3.2 Routine Recertification

Each Certificate shall contain a Certificate expiration date. The reason for having an expiration date for a Certificate is to minimize the exposure of the Key Pair associated with the Certificate. For this reason, when issuing a Certificate, The Company requires that certificates be recertified in order to be used beyond the expiration date. Details on the process are not included in this document. See Recertification requests Doc Standard for The Company—Doc #123456-b.

3.3 Certificate Request After Revocation

Certification Authorities and Registration Authorities operating under Certification Authorities do not renew Certificates that have been revoked. If a Subscriber wishes to use a Certificate after revocation, the Subscriber must apply for a new Certificate and replace the Certificate that has been revoked. In order to obtain another Certificate, the Subscriber will be required to complete the initial application process, including generation of a new Key Pair and submission of all information required for an initial application for a Certificate. Upon revocation of a Certificate, the Subscriber shall immediately cease using such Certificate and shall remove such Certificate from any devices and/or software in which it has been installed.

3.4 Revocation Request

Revocation Requests should follow the Doc Standard for The Company—Doc #22345-a

4. Operational Requirements

4.1 Certificate Application

To obtain a Certificate, an Applicant must follow the procedures described in the Certification Practice Statement and each tool that is being used to request the certificate.

4.2 Certificate Issuance

After performing a verification of the information provided by an Applicant with a Certificate Application, a Registration Authority operating under a Certification Authority may request that a Certification Authority issue a Certificate. Upon receipt of a request from a Registration Authority operating under a Certification Authority, that Certification Authority may generate and digitally sign a Certificate in accordance with the Certificate processes.

4.2.1 User Verification

It will be the responsibility of the requester to verify the necessary user attributes before submitting the request. The Certificate will be sent to an identity as specified in the form of each request.

4.3 Certificate Acceptance

Once a Certificate has been generated and given to the end user it will be the end user's responsibility to change their initial password and safeguard their certificate. The end user should receive the certificate via one delivery mechanism and the password via another delivery mechanism.

4.4 Certificate Suspensions and Revocation

4.4.1 Circumstances for Revocation

The Company shall be entitled to revoke and may revoke a Certificate at anytime for any reason. Some of these reasons may include:

- Compromise of such Certification Certifiers.
- Breach by the Subscriber of any of the terms of the Certification Practice Statement or the Subscriber's Subscription Agreement.
- A determination that a Certificate was not issued in accordance with the requirements of the Certificate Certification Practice Statement or the Subscriber's Subscription Agreement.
- Any other reason that may be reasonably expected to affect the integrity, security, or trustworthiness of a Certificate or a Certification Authority.

A Subscriber shall request revocation of their Certificate if the Subscriber has a suspicion or knowledge of a Compromise of the Subscriber's Private Key or a suspicion or knowledge of a change in the information contained in the Subscriber's Certificate or a change in circumstances that causes the information contained in Subscriber's Certificate to become inaccurate, incomplete, or misleading.

4.4.2 Who Can Request Revocation

Certificate suspension and revocation should follow the Doc Standard for The Company—Doc #52345-a

4.4.3 Procedure for Revocation Request

4.5 Security Audit Procedures

Significant security events in the Certification Authorities are automatically time-stamped and recorded into a log and time-stamped.

4.6 Records Archival

Records Archival should follow the Doc Standard for The Company—Doc #42345-a.

4.7 Compromises and Disaster Recovery

See Disaster recovery Doc Standard for The Company—Doc #72345-a.

5. Physical, Procedural, and Personnel Security Controls

5.1 Physical Controls

Access to the CA root Certifiers should be limited via access control. Access to the CA root certifiers should be logged. This log should indicate the following:

- Who used the root Certifier?
- What was the Certifier used for?

5.2 Procedural Controls

See Process and Procedural control document for The Company—Doc #892345-a.

5.3 Personnel Controls

Operational personnel for a Certification Authority will not be assigned other responsibilities that conflict with their operational responsibilities for the Certification Authority. The privileges assigned to operational personnel for a Certification Authority will be limited to the minimum required to carry out their assigned duties.

6. Technical Security Controls

6.1 Public Key Delivery

The Public Key to be included in a Certificate is delivered to directory automatically via the Registration Process.

6.2 User ID Delivery to Users

User ID delivery should follow the Doc Standard for The Company—Doc #942345-a

6.3 Computer Security Controls

The workstations and servers on which the Certificate Registration Authorities operate should be physically secured as required by The Company. In all cases Registration Authorities should never share passwords. The workstations and servers on which the Certification Authorities operate should be physically secured as required by The Company. The operating systems on the workstations on which the Certification Authorities operate enforce identification and authentication of users. Access to registration software databases and tools and audit trails is restricted as described in the Certification Practice Statement. All registration Servers should have tight Operating Systems (O/S) Level access and should have all required patches installed. Also the O/S should be audited for O/S level access. The Registration Server should have only required level services installed, example: FTP should never be installed on the Registration Server.

6.4 Life Cycle Technical Controls

The efficacy and appropriateness of the security settings described in this Certification Practice Statement should be reviewed at least once a year. A risk and threat assessment will be performed to determine if key lengths need to be increased or operational procedures modified from time to time to maintain system security.

7. Vendor Tools Controls

Vendor tool controls should follow the Doc Standard for The Company—Doc #7732345-a

8. Specification Administration

8.1 Contact Information

(An organization will place any specific contact information into this section—this should include the Company Name, and primary contact for the CPS.)

8.2 Specification Change Procedures

The Company may, at its discretion, modify the Certificate Certification Practice Statement and the terms and conditions contained therein from time to time. Modifications to the Certification Practice Statement that, in the judgment of The Company, should have little or no impact on Applicants, Subscribers, and, may be made with no change to the Certification Practice Statement version number and no notification to Applicants, Subscribers, and. Such changes shall become effective immediately upon publication.

8.3 Publication and Notification Policies

Prior to major changes to this Certification Practice Statement, notification of the upcoming changes will be published.

8.4 CPS Approval Procedures

This Certification Practice Statement and any subsequent changes shall be approved by The Company Policy Authority.

CHAPTER 10

Enterprise Security Scenarios

It is amazing that as soon as the world discovers a new technology, the hackers "discover" a mechanism to expose it. Directories in themselves are not new, but newer technologies are being hacked as soon as the standards are off the press. Let's take a look at CERT® Advisory CA-2001-18 (see http://www.cert.org/advisories/CA=2001=18.html). This advisory was published on July 16, 2001 and revised on August 13, 2001. It discusses issues with implementations of the Lightweight Directory Access Protocol (LDAP). It describes vulnerabilities with LDAP and many different vendor implementations. Here is a sampling of the list.

- iPlanet Directory Server
- IBM SecureWay
- Lotus Domino R5 Servers
- Critical Path LiveContent Directory
- Microsoft Exchange
- Network Associates PGP Keyserver

As you can see, this particular advisory impacts a wide audience.

Many products, including Active Directory, support LDAP. But like most software, if it is not properly implemented, LDAP-based directories can provide malicious hackers with a boatload of potentially sensitive information.

The most difficult phase of a directory-services implementation is the design stage. Critical choices made during this stage can remain with the organization for a long time. Poor out-of-the-box implementation can also lead to "default-based settings" and security exposures. Let's consider a scenario where we need to expose part of our directory within the DMZ for our corporate enterprise.

10.1 Filtered Directory

In Figure 10.1, the authoritative server is in the trusted network. Via an API and/or replication, a subset of the data is placed into the DMZ. In this example, this could be public data, such as the sales staff. This information could use the following schema.

- Name:
- Phone number:
- E-mail address:
- Public key:

This filtered data is replicated into the DMZ. Let's say we are using LDAP, and then we could use TCP ports 389 or 636. So from the trusted side of the DMZ, we would use the following firewalls rules.

- Trusted to inbound DMZ ports open—389 and/or 636.
- All other ports closed.
- Outbound DMZ to Trusted Network—all ports closed.

Now let's look at how you can serve the data. A user would access the Web server via the DMZ. This data could be public data and does not require authentication, but we may need to display dynamic data via the Web server. Again, if we were using LDAP, the Web server would access the directory server via TCP ports 389 or 636. The pages would be built dynamically using the data from the directory server. The end-user would never need to access the DMZ directory server. The only access to the directory server would be via the Web server. So from the untrusted Internet into the DMZ, we would use the following firewall rules.

- TCP port 80 and/or 443 would be open.
- All other ports are blocked.

FIGURE 10.1 *Filtered Directory*

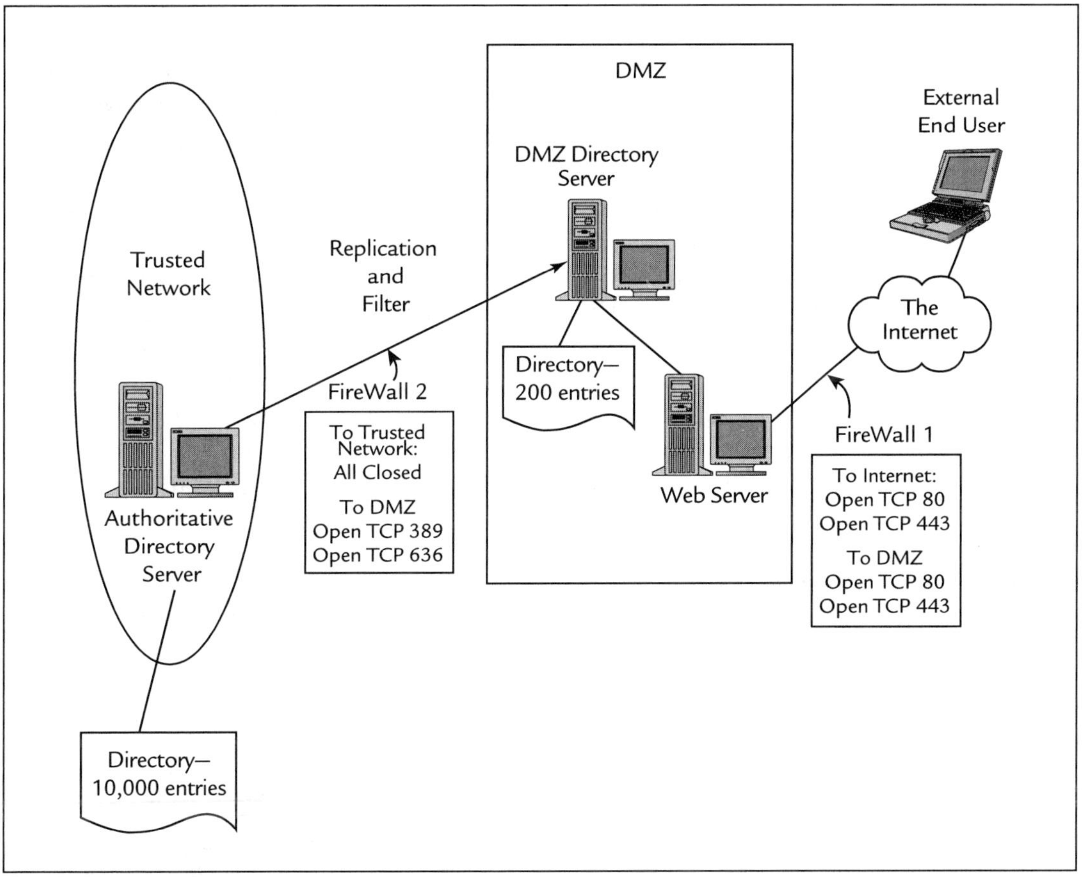

Again, you can see we don't need to expose port 389 or 636 because the Web server is the server providing the lookup to the DMZ directory server.

10.2 The 100 Percent LDAP Solution

Another situation would be where you have several different authentication mechanisms such as the following.

- Web services (Web pages)
- Instant messaging servers

- Specialized accounting or ERP system
- GroupWare and messaging services

Each system would manage the authentication and binding process by using its owns internal processes. A good example of this would be where the Laptop, shown in Figure 10.2, would access the Web servers. The browser, in this case, would attempt to access a protected page. The Web server would return an http status code of 401. This status code would, via the browser, display a Username and Password dialog box. The user at the laptop would fill in the correct credentials and then submit the information back to the Web server. The Web server in turn would start the binding process to communication with the LDAP server. If the authentication were successful, then a DN (distinguished name) would be returned from the LDAP server. We have discussed all this already, but here is the rub—let's say you were maintaining a different independent directory for each system. Most systems will have some type of directory system for maintaining user

FIGURE 10.2 *Ubiquitous LDAP*

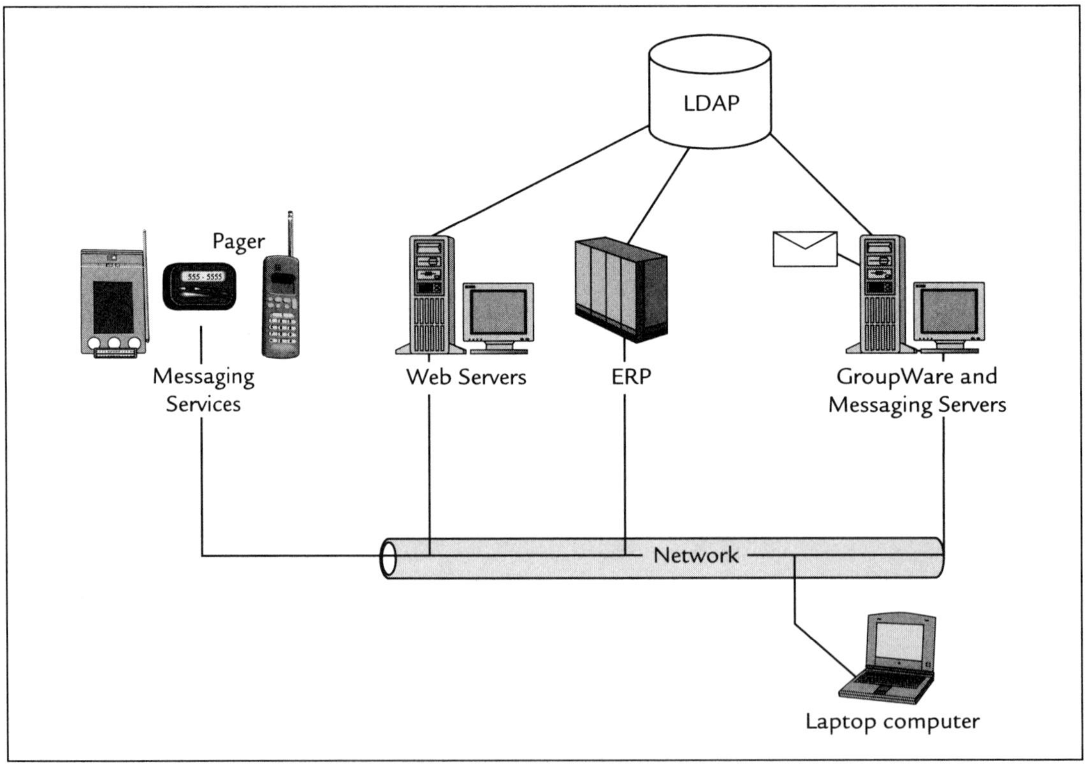

accounts. The challenge is to match up the DN with the expected naming conventions in each subsystem. This is one of those theories that looks *great* on paper but is difficult to implement. Here are some examples.

1. The Web server may expect a name, such as Bubba Smith.
2. The messaging server may want a name, such as Bubba Smith/Dallas/ The Company.
3. The ERP system may want a name, such as Bsmith.
4. The LDAP server returns (from a bind) CN = Bubba Smith/OU = Dallas/ O/The Company.

Now, with all these different names, you need to find a way to match these to each subsystem ACL structure—of course, groups would help.

So your first thought now to solve this problem would be to control the query and return strings from the services devices (the servers) into the LDAP server. Not all vendors support this type of flexibility. When you start to design your directory authentication system, be sure and analyze the LDAP interfaces and see how much control you have over the DNs.

10.2.1 Microsoft Windows NT 4.0 Solution

Microsoft Windows NT 4.0 (referred to as NT4 here) offers some solutions to managing logins into various subsystems. The Windows NT Challenge/ Response is one of those. A Windows NT authentication process, Challenge/ Response can occur when a user or service (such as IIS) tries to access any resource stored on another Windows NT machine across a network (such as viewing a shared resource on a server). Challenge/Response can also be used by IIS to authenticate a user browsing a Web site. The NT4 control directory is known as SAM, which is a database of user and group account information. In the case of a pure Microsoft Client solution, you would set up a process where users would access several computing services with a single logon. In Figure 10.3, the user at the laptop logs into the NT4 Domain via his or her NT4 workstation. With that single login, the user can access any resource in the Domain. (MS Domain trust relationships are not covered in this book.) Here is an example.

- The user would be able to access any of the NT4 servers and their shared resources.
- The user would be able to access the messaging server (MS-Exchange).
- The user would be able to access the Web server via http by using an IE5 browser that implements NT4 Challenge/Response.

FIGURE 10.3 *Microsoft Windows NT 4.0 Solution*

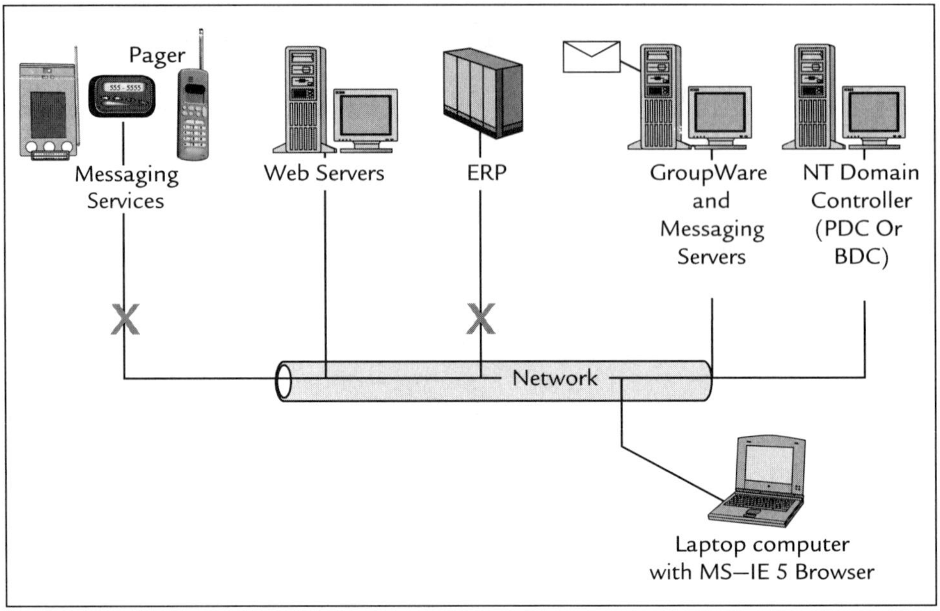

- If the ERP system and the online messaging services did not support NT4 authentication and/or NT4 Challenge/Response, then authentication would not work with these systems.

10.2.2 A Single Sign-on Solution

Today's heterogeneous computing environments often require users to obtain separate sign-on credentials. As we mentioned before, each product can have a different system for user authentication. Also, with a credential name, you can also have management of the password associated with each user. Here are some examples.

- Password length (number of characters)
- Password quality (use of words from a dictionary)
- Password expiration (passwords must be changed every X days)
- Strike-out mechanism (if a username is attempted three times without success, then the account is locked)

The mechanism used with NT4 is very different from that of Lotus Notes (R4 and R5). So as a result, users can have a variety of systems for offering credentials and a password with each one. Now, add on to this problem the issue of credential and password management.

- Lost usernames or IDs
- Lost passwords
- User renames

The more disparate systems you have, the more time and resources are required to support those systems.

Figure 10.4 shows an example of a single sign-on solution. Let's look at each step.

1. The user will offer credentials into the operating system and/or a plug-in on the laptop. Via software that is installed on the laptop, the credentials are passed to a secure server that will manage the passwords for each system.
2. If all credentials and passwords match, then the user is issued a token and/or marked as authenticated.
3. When the user attempts to access a resource on the network, like the Web server, the plug-in will log on to the requested resource with the proper credentials for that resources.
4. Finally, when the user connects to the targeted resources, authorization will be implemented. This process is normally managed by the resource being accessed and not the third party authentication service.

10.2.3 Kerberos

Kerberos, named after the dog in mythology who guarded the gates of Hades, is software that is used in a network to establish a user's identity. MIT (Massachusetts Institute of Technology) developed it in the mid-1980s. Kerberos uses a combination of encryption and distributed databases so a user can log in and start a session from any computer on the network. This can be a real advantage on a network with a lot of roaming users. The Kerberos protocol uses strong cryptography so a client can prove its identity to a server across a network connection. After a client and server have used Kerberos to prove their identity, they can also encrypt all of their communications for privacy and data integrity. Kerberos is freely available from MIT under a copyright permission notice very similar to the one used for the BSD operating and X11 Windowing system. MIT provides Kerberos in source form.

Kerberos is a network authentication system targeted for use on physically insecure networks. Kerberos is implemented by communicating over networks to prove their identity to each other while preventing eavesdropping or replay attacks. Data stream integrity is provided. Users or systems are given tickets that can be used to identify themselves to other systems, and secret cryptographic keys are provisioned for secure communication

FIGURE 10.4 *Single Sign-on Solution*

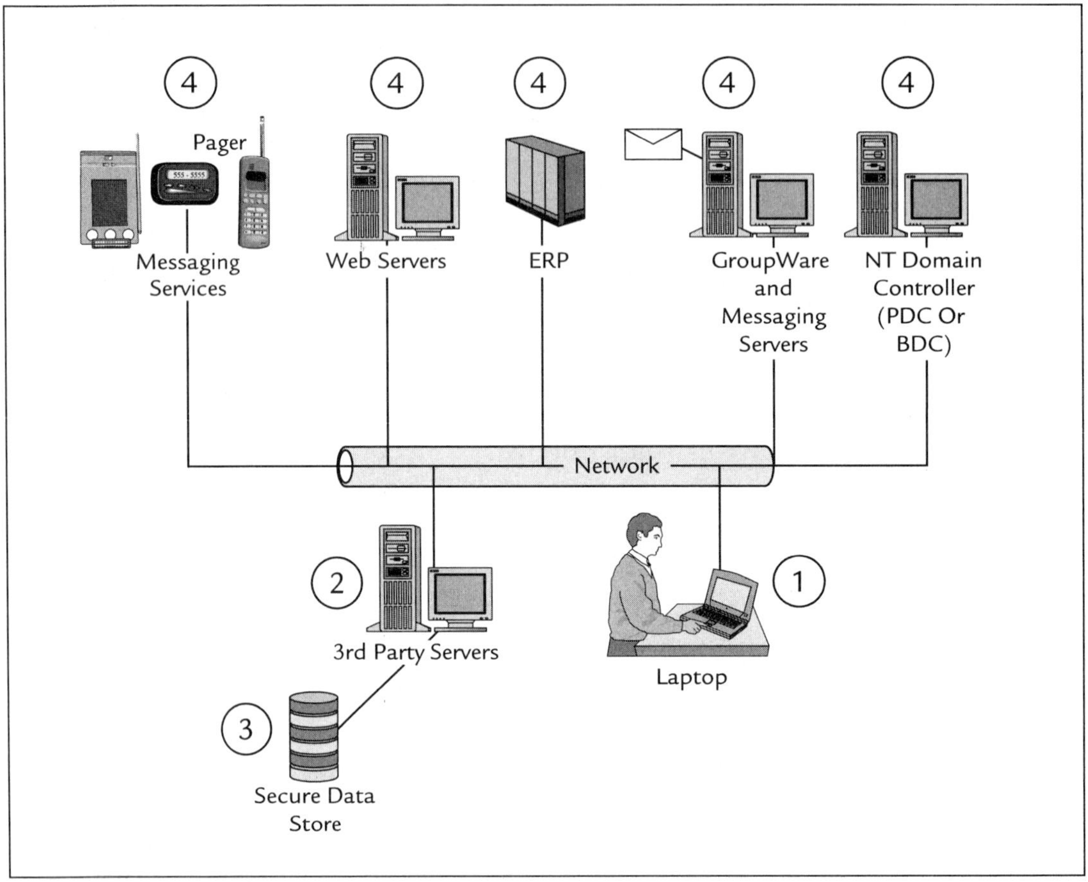

with other systems. A ticket is a small sequence of a few hundred bytes. Using this ticket system, an ubiquitous access system can be designed, allowing a single ticket to authenticate with many different security mechanisms. Overall Kerberos is used in application-level protocols. Remember the OSI reference model; Kerberos lives on Level 7.

The Kerberos protocol is composed of three subprotocols.

- Authentication Service (AS) Exchange
- Ticket-Granting Service (TGS) Exchange
- Client/Server (CS) Exchange

Figure 10.5 shows an overview of the Kerberos authentication service.

FIGURE 10.5 *Kerberos Authentication Service Overview*

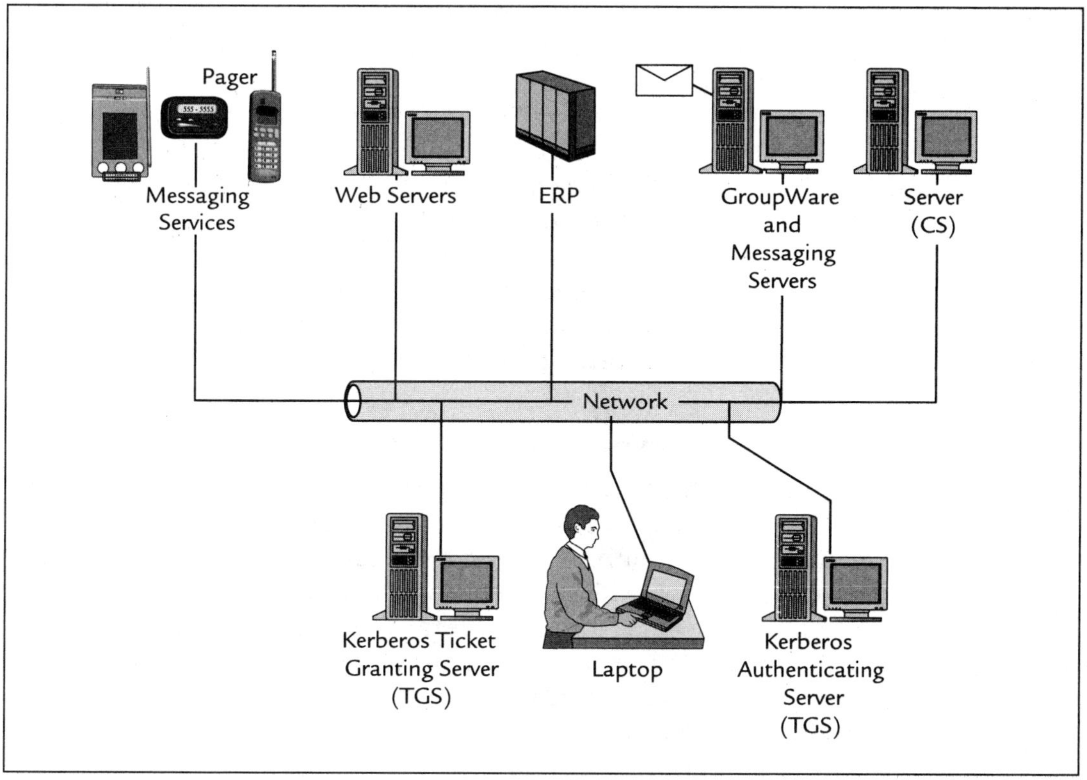

10.2.4 Authentication Service (AS) Exchange

The user accesses the network by typing a logon name and password. The Kerberos-enabled client converts the password to an encryption key and saves the result in a variable. The client then requests credentials from the Kerberos Key Distribution Center (KDC). When the KDC receives the request, it looks up the user in its database, gets the user's master key, decrypts the preauthentication data, and evaluates the timestamp inside. Once the user's identity has been validated, then the KDC creates credentials that the client can present to the ticket-granting service.

10.2.5 Ticket-Granting Service (TGS) Exchange

The Kerberos client on the user's workstation requests credentials for the service by sending a message to the KDC. This message consists of the identity of the service for which the client is requesting credentials and an authenticator message encrypted with the user's new logon session key. The KDC uses the logon session key to decrypt the user's authenticator message and evaluates for validity. If the authenticator passes the test, the KDC extracts the user's authorization data and creates a session key for the user to share with the targeted server. The KDC encrypts one copy of the service session key with the user's logon session key. The KDC embeds another copy of the service session key in a ticket, along with the user's authorization data, and encrypts the ticket with the server's master key. The KDC sends these credentials back to the client. When the client receives the reply, it decrypts the service session key with the user's logon session key and stores the service session key in its ticket cache. The client extracts the ticket to the server and stores that in its ticket cache.

10.2.6 Client/Server (CS) Exchange

Once a user has a ticket to a server, the workstation client can establish a secure communications session with that server. The client sends the server a message containing an authenticator message encrypted with the key sent by the KDC for the session with the server. Also sent is a ticket for sessions with the server and a flag indicating whether the client requests mutual authentication. The server receives the request and decrypts the ticket and then extracts the user's authorization data and the session key. The server uses the session key from the ticket to decrypt the user's authenticator message and evaluates the timestamp inside. If the authenticator message is valid, the server checks the mutual authentication flag in the client's request. If the mutual authentication flag is set, the server uses the session key to encrypt the time from the user's authenticator message and returns the result in a message of type Kerberos Application Reply. When the client receives the reply, it decrypts the server's authenticator message with the session key it shares with the server and compares the time sent back by the service with the time in its original message. If all this matches, then the client is assured that the service is genuine and the connection is validated.

There are several different versions and distributions of Kerberos. Most of them are based on an MIT distribution.

Versions of Kerberos V4

- MIT Kerberos V4
- Bones
- Transarc
- Digital UNIX

Versions of Kerberos V5

- MIT Kerberos V5
- OSF DCE Security
- Microsoft Windows 2000

In the United States and Canada, Kerberos is available via anonymous FTP from athena-dist.mit.edu (18.71.0.38).

10.2.7 A DNS Directory

Next up in our list of examples is the Domain Name System or DNS. The DNS system is how the Web and the Internet work. Without it, you would have a very difficult time determining what site you need to access and open. Now, how do you access a Web site? Let's say you want to go to a site. To do so, you will need an address. Let's use IP address 207.69.200.100. One number like this may be easy to use and remember, but what about remembering IP numbers for 20 or 30 sites? DNS solves this problem of having to remember hundreds or even thousands of IP addresses. Today we access Web sites via domain names. Domain names are a method of looking up addresses without having to remember some long number. Remembering a 32-bit number—the IP Address—(that really maps to a 48* bit number) can be difficult. Thankfully, the Domain Name System was created.

The following document (from Request for Comments: 1591) explains how domains work. (http://info.internet.isi.edu:80/in-notes/rfc/files/rfc1591.txt)

1.1 Domains

Getting where you want to go can often be one of the more difficult aspects of using networks. The variety of ways that places are named will probably leave a blank stare on your face at first. Don't fret; there is a method to this apparent madness.

If someone were to ask for a home address, he or she would probably expect a street, apartment, city, state, and zip code. That's all the information the post office needs to deliver mail in a reasonably speedy fashion. Likewise, computer addresses have a specific structure. These are the general forms.

A person's e-mail address on a computer: user@somewhere.domain

(continued)

A computer's name: somewhere.domain

The user portion is usually the person's account name on the system, although it doesn't have to be. Somewhere. The domain tells you the name of a system or location and what kind of organization it is. The trailing domain is often one of the following.

com	Usually a company or other commercial institution or organization, such as Convex Computers (convex.com).
edu	An educational institution, such as New York University, named nyu.edu.
gov	A government site—for example, NASA is nasa.gov.
mil	A military site, such as the Air Force (af.mil).
net	Gateways and other administrative hosts for a network (it does not mean all of the hosts in a network). One such gateway is near.net.
org	This is a domain reserved for private organizations that don't comfortably fit in the other classes of domains. One example is the Electronic Frontier Foundation, named eff.org.

Each country also has its own top-level domain. For example, the United States domain includes each of the 50 states. Other countries represented with domains include the following.

au	Australia
ca	Canada
fr	France
uk	The United Kingdom. These also have subdomains of categories like ac.uk for academic sites and co.uk for commercial ones.

The proper terminology for a site's domain name (somewhere. domain) is its Fully Qualified Domain Name (FQDN). It is usually selected to give a clear indication of the site's organization or sponsoring agent. For example, the Massachusetts Institute of Technology's FQDN is mit.edu. Similarly, Apple Computer's domain name is apple. com. While such obvious names are usually the norm, there are the occasional exceptions that are ambiguous enough to mislead, such as vt.edu, which on first impulse one might surmise is an educational institution of some sort in Vermont. Not so. It's actually the domain name for Virginia Tech. In most cases it's relatively easy to glean the meaning of a domain name. Such confusion is far from the norm.

The DNS is a distributed database of name-to-IP address mappings. Give the DNS the name of a computer, and it returns the address—for example, www.lotus.com is 198.114.68.10. To look up a name, the computer sends a request to a remote domain server. This sever will answer the query and return an actual 32-bit IP address. This address is then used by the application to access the resource and return the data that was requested. At one time these host names were maintained by the Network Information Center (NIC) in a single file (HOSTS.TXT), which was FTPed to all of the other hosts in the network. This is no fun, plus it would be easy to get the files out of sync. The design goals for the DNS system are as follows.

- The primary goal is a consistent name space.
- The lookup must be quick (taking 30 to 40 seconds to return an address would be too long).
- Due to the potential size of the DNS directory and the amount of updates, the database should be offered as a distributed service.
- Local caching of frequently (or localized names) should be offered to improve performance.

Each of these design criteria is accomplished by the current implementation of today's DNS architecture. Figure 10.6 shows the basic structure of

FIGURE 10.6 *DNS Zones*

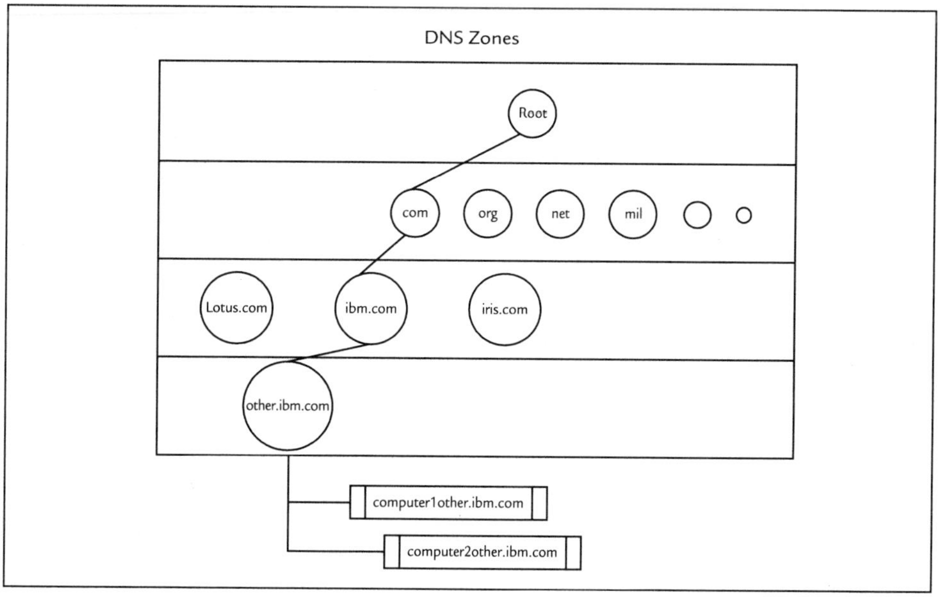

the DNZ lookup structure. Starting with the root level, you drop down to the "com" level. From there you get individual sites. With each site you get ownership of the zone. IBM is the owner of the Start of Authority (SOA) for IBM.com. Any changes are made by IBM and distributed from there.

For the most part, a DNS server is just a computer that's running DNS software. One of the most popular programs is BIND (Berkeley Internet Name Domain). You can also get DNS services via NT and Windows2000.

In Figure 10.7, the user, #1 will attempt to access the GroupWare messaging server, #2. The user will enter the name of the server, and the TCP stack will send a DNS query to the DNZ server. If successful, the DNS server, #3, will return an IP address. If not successful, the DNS will query the next server up the tree to see if it has the address for this name. This process happens very quickly. One process that can help speed up the lookup time is a caching server. In some cases, you can install a server that will cache the entries from the master server. So as a result of this architecture, a part of the DNS directory is keep local for quick lookups.

FIGURE 10.7 *DNS Lookup*

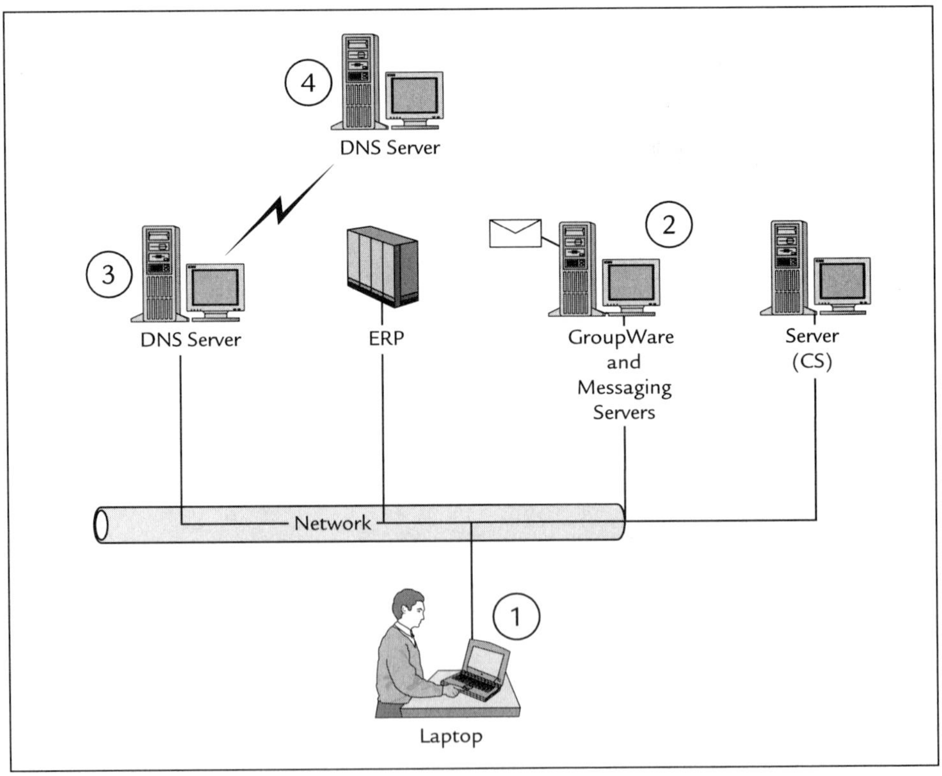

CHAPTER 11

Enterprise Security and Security Deployment Planning

11.1 Security Planning

This chapter is here because "Technology is useless without people." That may be an obvious statement to some, but to CIOs, IT management, and consultants it is the ultimate truth. Let's take a look at a simple problem. Suppose you want to offer a directory service to one person. For the most part, that is an easy task. Here are the basic steps.

- Define what the directory service will do (let's say, messaging and authentication services).
- Order a server.
- Contract with an ISP.
- Order the software.
- Install all of the hardware and software.
- Hand out the passwords.
- Turn on the service.

It's done! That was easy—for the most part. We should be able to accomplish this in about a week. It is amazing how many people will look at this simple exercise and say, "Well, that is easy. If it takes a week to do this, then we should be able to roll out the whole company in about two to three weeks." If your company has about 10 to 15 employees, then that may be true.

But what if you need to implement a new process/technology for 100,000 users? Now we have a challenge. This chapter leads you though many of the decisions processes required to implement a new technology. There are books, methods, and classes on this topic. If you get anything out of this chapter, it should be this: "Plan, Plan, and then plan a bit more." Guess what? We will start with *planning*.

Figure 11.1 shows the basic seven steps of an IT project. You will notice that the figure is a circle-spoke diagram. Normally, when you use a diagram like this, it is to denote that each part is equal in value. Most projects start out as a hierarchical exercise. They start with scope analysis and end with the rollout. The most successful projects are based on this model. Yes, you need to start with a strategic direction. It helps to have a map if you are driving across the country, but the planning and the execution must be balanced. Also, each element needs to be treated not only as an individual unit but as being tied to one another. The message here is "See the project as a sum of the parts, not just individual elements."

Table 11.1 lists the steps required to plan out your security infrastructure.

FIGURE 11.1 *IT Project Steps*

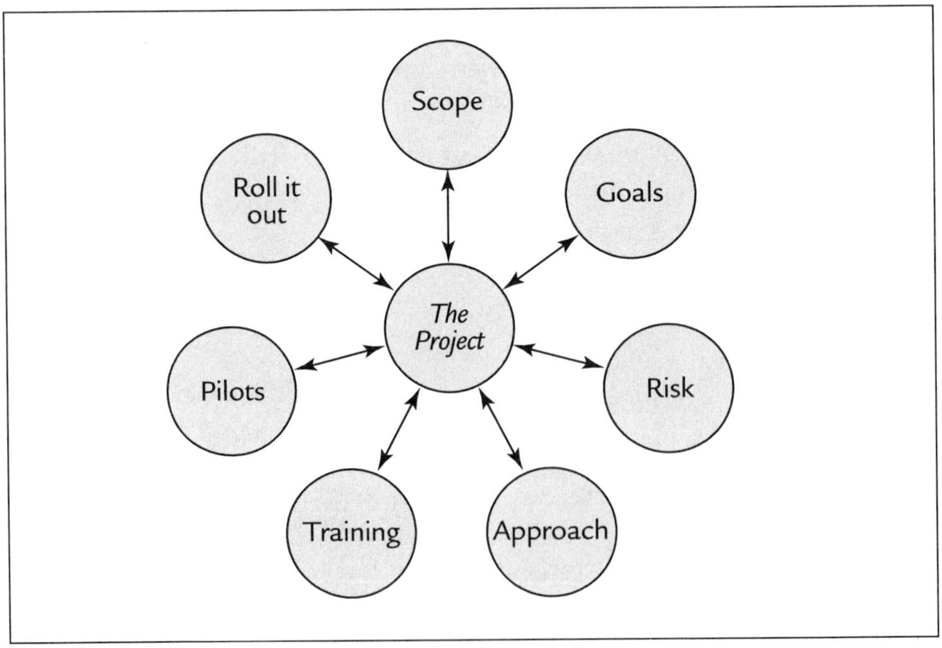

TABLE 11.1 *Security Plan*

Project Steps	Details
The Project Scope	This is where you identify the design and configuration of your IT infrastructure. Review—why are we doing this?
Goals and Objectives	List the goals and objectives for the implementation. List the service levels that you will want to maintain.
Risk Analysis	Risk analysis identifies risks associated with a project and how to mitigate those risks. One of the biggest risks is "vague requirements."
Project Approach	Detail the approach that you want to take. This should include both the business analysis and risk analysis. Determine the feedback mechanism so the project can have checkpoint and review cycles. Also, keep track of the cost and timing of the project.
Training	Determine what type of training is needed for users, vendors, employees, and so on.
Pilots	Pilot the process.
Roll out schedule	What, when, where, and how.

"It must be considered that there is nothing more difficult to carry out, nor more doubtful of success, nor more dangerous to handle, than to initiate a new order of things." (*The Prince* by Niccolo Machiavelli)

Change—it does not matter if you are installing a new system, an upgrade, or a fix. If your end-users see a change, then you need to plan for it. Here's an example: I was part of a project that moved users from an old green screen technology to a new graphical technology. To a technologist this is a great leap forward, with new features and cool graphics. But end-users only see "change," something frightening. In the process of this technological change, we did several surveys. Here are some of the responses we received.

"Wow, this is cool!"
"I don't understand how this is better."
"Will there be layoffs now?"
"Why do we need to make this change? It was working fine the way it was."
"Is this a virus?"
"I was not trained. How do you expect me to do my job without training?"

For the most part I have seen very few "failed" projects. There have been a few where the new technology is dumped and the customers goes back to what they had. I have seen many projects go over budget, run very behind schedule, and get very expensive. Why? The sad truth is that someone, inside or outside of the company, sold the "new software" as the best thing since sliced bread. Hence the problem. There are many reasons why companies choose to change their technology.

- New and improved release of software
- Features in a competitive version
- Faster, better, lower cost
- New software along with new processes will (remember process re-engineering?)
  - Increase sales
  - Lower costs
  - Increase profit
- And the best of the best
  - ROI—we will return our money in X months.
  - TCO—this cost less than this other product.

In the end, it really does not matter why the company decided to make a change of process and/or technology. It *does* matter if you can make the change a success.

As I said, it is very rare for a company to stop an IT project. Typically, once the company realizes that there is a problem, it is too late. Here is an example.

A company has decided to move from product X to Y. The estimated cost of moving from X to Y was $100,000, and the project would take about 6 months. The company starts the project, and 12 months down the road they realize that only 60 percent of the users have been moved. The total cost at this point is about $200,000. Here are the choices.

Dump the new product and go back to where you were. The problem with this answer is that you have expended a lot of money to get *this* far. The users are starting to learn the new processes and the new products. Also, there was some problem that drove the company to making this decision. If this process/product is not solving "the problem" or providing a competitive advantage, then you are in real trouble. This project should be killed and reverted back to where you were.

Continue and finish what was started. This is normally what companies do. They finish the job. The problem with this answer is that the company has now spent money that was not budgeted. This is when the following happens.

- The "I told you so" people come out of the woodwork.
- If the project really goes bad, the people (that started the project) will be moved into jobs they don't like or, in a worse case, lose their jobs.
- Money will be moved from another "critical" project to pay for this one.

Stop the project and run two systems in a coexistence mode. This case happens more often than companies deciding to return to the old technology. Companies will run two or more systems together at the same time. But the following problems can arise:

- It can be very expensive—the more subsystems you have, the higher the expense.
- With each type of software you have, the greater the potential for security patches and updates.
- Users with different subsystems can cost more to support.
  - — Confused users—different systems for different users
  - — Help desk procedures
  - — Migration costs
  - — Ongoing license cost of gateways (you will have this cost during the migration)

11.1.1 The Project Scope

You may be looking at the business as a whole or just a single process. So specify the scope of the project and the expected results. The scope is the starting point for any project. Take the time to develop a "high-level" description of what the project is about. In other words, "Why are we here?" This is also a great time to test assumptions about the project. At least take a look at the numbers, the TCO and/or the ROI. See if there are any fantasy numbers or assumptions. Remember the lessons of the dot coms. Many of those failed businesses had ROIs in months where the reality was centuries.

The scope should include some of the following documents.

- Business vision and mission statement
- The pains that got us here—business goals and drivers

- Critical Success Factors
- The "end state" technological vision

11.1.2 Goals and Objectives (High Level)

List out the goals and objectives of this particular project.

- Who is the project sponsor? (You *must* have someone with clout and power.)
- Who are the stakeholders?
- Build a team to manage the managers. This is a team that will deal with high-level managers. Keep these people happy, and you will have a successful project.
- What budget monies are available?
- What are the initial target dates?
- Define the high-level demographics (who, what, when, where).
- Define the project milestones.

The biggest problem that we see with new any technology implementation is the "ready, fire, aim" syndrome. List your goals before you start.

Risk Analysis

Risk analysis is needed to address "What can go wrong?" If you have an idea of what can get messed up on a project, then you can plan for it. Now here is the reality: Life happens. Things go wrong. But with some good planning, you can at least be ready for some of the bigger issues and problems. Here are some of the basics for your risk analysis.

- Make sure the project is realistic. If you are trying to migrate 100,000 users in 100 countries from one system to another in three months, then you need to be in a hospital.
- Make sure you have the budget in place to finish what you started.
- Make sure that you have the proper communication channels in place.
- Do you have the right resources allocated?
- Do you have good representation from the various divisions and departments in your company?
- Are there any other projects going on? Impact:
  - Overlaps
  - Resource issues
  - Funding issues

11.1.3 Project Approach and Project Plan

Most consulting companies will have project management approaches. Check with your favorite consulting firm for their approach. For the most part, it does not matter what approach you will use to manage your project. With that said, here are a few items that are critical to any project.

- Detail the deliverables.
- Detail the timing requirements—start date, end date.
- Define the checkpoints—these are sanity checks to see if you are on-track and on budget.
- Define how many pilots you will need.
- What are the cultural impacts of different countries?
- Define when you want to have the pilots.
- Define what you will pilot.
  - — The process
  - — The hardware
  - — The support system—help desk
  - — The training
  - — Ethical hackers
- Identify the owners of the project and the sponsor of the project. This sponsor may not necessarily be the project manger. I have seen many projects fail due to lack of sponsorship and budget.
- If possible, assign a full-time project manager to the project. The project manager should be a permanent employee. This is very important to have accountability. Again, I have seen many projects fail when a consultant runs a project without having accountability to an internal employee.
- Determine early on how you will communicate. E-mail may be part of your communication strategy. It would be better to have a formalized tracking system or a groupware system to track the activities. A Web page is good. Also, have regular meetings with your team and require weekly status reports.
- Have some type of system that will manage the scope. This is where formal project management systems and tools will help. (This is a book on security, not project management)
- Identify training needs as you create your plan. This will be used in the next step.

- Have a change control system. Manage and track changes to the project. Yes, this is different from scope—scope could be a change in "since we are doing process A then we can add on process B." That is a scope change. Change control is "We started using software rev 1.0. Now we will be using software rev 1.1." See the difference? If not, go and get a soft drink, then take a nap.
- Via some tracking system, be sure and set the priorities. You may be under a timeline and will need to complete some tasks before you can start others.
- Take the time to closely manage your vendors and your consultants. This is where you can find the "experts," but these experts can be very costly. Yes, we recommend using these experts, but we also know that you can blow your budget before you see any deliverables. I have seen many times where a vendor will be sitting in the break room at $200 per hour eating cookies. Why? Due to poor planning, the vendor was there to set up the server, but the server room was not ready. It was being painted.
- Create a test environment that is different from the pilot.
  - Testing is where you check out your process or tools in a "test" environment. This is the place where you use ethical hackers to "do their best" at hacking or destroying the process.
  - A pilot, in many cases, is actually working in a limited production setting. Use ethical hackers in the pilot to "test assumptions."
- Regarding vendors and consultants—make sure you have solid deliverables defined in your contracts.
- Finally—be ready for the politics. This is the worst issue that you will need to deal with, and as with any enterprise company, you will encounter it. For example, you will be in the middle of your pilot, and some high-level manager will question your whole approach. She will ask, "Why are we using vendor A when vendor B is better?" You are unaware that vendor B just took that manager out to the golf course and convinced the manager that a lot of money could be saved if you dumped vendor A. This is an old story. Just be ready to deal with these types of interruptions.

11.1.4 Training

There are companies that focus on training and training requirements. Again, check with your local vendor for help as needed. Training is critical to the success of any new process/project/product implementation. As with the "Project Approach" section, there are some basic steps you will need to take/implement.

- If you have created a good project plan/approach, then you should have identified "training opportunities." List these opportunities and then look at each opportunity to determine the steps needed to meet these opportunities. This step entails listing each opportunity and its basic requirements.
- The next step is to decide the initial content. This is a high-level scope to make sure that it meets the requirements as specified in the project plan. As part of the process is the identification of the medium that will be used for training.
  - Classroom
  - CBT
  - Web pages
  - Books
  - Online training
- Once the initial content has been confirmed as well as the media, teams should be created that will create the content for training.
- Determine the locations and timing of the training.
- Finalize the development of the training materials.
- Pilot the training

11.1.5 Pilots

Use the pilots to test assumptions, systems, process, and user training. Have several pilots. If you have an enterprise business, then have individual pilots at different levels of implementation. If you are rolling out a product to 100,000 desktops, then you should pilot with 10 users and learn from the results. Then pilot with 100 users, and learn from those results. With each pilot, you will be checking for the following.

- Is the rollout process designed correctly?
- What is the potential impact to the business?
- What needs to be done differently?
- What are the cultural impacts of different countries?
- Is the scaling of the process working, and will it work for more users?

- What automation is needed to roll out the process?
- Use the pilot to determine if the training is obtaining the desired results.
- Use the pilot to determine if the documentation is as required.

11.1.6 Rollout Schedule

Now you need to create the rollout schedule and implement it. It is time to make it happen. Use of tools, like Microsoft Project and/or Lotus Notes, can help track and manage the process. As you make your rollout schedule, consider the following factors.

- Resource requirements
- When will the software be ready?
- When will the hardware be ready?
- When will the physical support structure be ready: networks, server rooms?
- Resources include the people doing the work. Identify vacation schedules, training.

List dependencies.

- The server room must be ready before you can install the server.
- If SSL is required, a vendor must be selected and contacted for certificates.
- IP address must be acquired and/or assigned before the routers can be configured.

Be mentally ready to make adjustments to the schedule. The more complex the project, the greater the possibility that issues will force a change to the schedule. Publish the schedule and set milestones. Use markers that will tell you, the implementation team, and management where you are in the project.

11.2 Security Hardware and Software Reference Guide

This section lists hardware and software tools that may be used in securing your work or home PC and laptop.

11.2.1 Encryption

Company name: Armadillo Limited
Address: P.O. Box 667694; Charlotte, NC 28266
Phone number: (704) 987-5003
E-mail address: (704) 896-7818
URLs: http://www.armadillousa.com/gatekeeper.htm
Category: Encryption
Product name: GateKeeper™
Product Description: Smart-card based 1024-bit RSA, RC4, 3DES file and email encryption system. GateKeeper is a personalized encryption system designed for data security of individual users in a corporate and/or personal environment. By using 1024-bit RSA, RC4, Triple-DES (3DES) encryption methods and the proven security of the smart card, the GateKeeper™ protects the integrity and confidentiality of the user's files (documents, texts, spreadsheets, graphics, etc.), program files (stored in data disk, hard drive, etc.), and/or messages transmitted through the Internet. GateKeeper utilizes encryption methods that have been tried, tested, and developed in the US; 1024-bit RSA, RC4, and 3DES are widely used by telecommunication corporations, financial institutions, and government agencies in the US. GateKeeper is a hardware/software-combined system that supports Windows™ 95, 98, and 2000 operating systems. GateKeeper is ideal for individuals or small- to medium-sized businesses seeking to protect the vital contents on a computer and private information transferred through the Internet. GateKeeper is convenient, easy-to-use, virtually tamperproof and is available for immediate purchase directly from the publisher's Web site at www.armadillo.com.hk/gatekeeper.htm. The product comes complete with a smart card, smart card reader, power adapter, and software on CD-ROM.

Company name: CyPost Corporation
Address: 900–1281 West Georgia; Vancouver, BC V6E 3J7
Phone number: (604) 904-4422
E-mail address: info@cypost.com
URL: http://www.cypost.com
Category: Encryption
Product name: Navaho Lock with Voice
Product description: Encrypted voice e-mail. Navaho Lock with Voice allows users to record, compress and encrypt private voice email for transmission across any digital network without sacrificing the tone, feeling, or integrity of the message. Navaho Lock with Voice also reduces the time spent typing traditional text-based email messages. A summary of new major features follows.

- Electronic Shredder. Navaho Shredder offers a high level of disk sanitization allowing users to securely delete files and documents from any computer. Navaho Shredder has been designed to meet and exceed the US Department of Defense standard (DOD 5220.22-M) for data removal. The program is currently capable of overwriting data stored on disk a total of nine times, exceeding the DOD standard for data removal.
- Built-in Compression. Navaho Lock with Voice automatically compresses all documents and files by as much as 70%, thereby maximizing disk space and dramatically reducing transmission times.
- Choice of Encryption Strength. Navaho Lock with Voice offers the widest selection of encryption standards including 40-, 56-, 112-, 128-, and 168-bit key-lengths and algorithms to meet the individual security needs of your business. Users are able to customize security settings and select unique pass phrases by contact or group.
- New Drag-and-Drop User Interface. Further improving ease of use and increasing user productivity, the new drag-and-drop user interface allows users to encrypt, compress, or shred files by simply dragging and dropping them into the Drop area.

Company name: DSEnet
Address: 5201 South Westshore Blvd.; Tampa, FL 33611
Phone number: (813) 902-9597
E-mail address: questions@dsenet.com
URL: www.dsenet.com
Category: Encryption
Product name: DSEnet Encryption
Product description: DSEnet Encryption provides users with the ability to securely encrypt and store their information. There is no better way to keep intruding hackers, nosy coworkers, pesky younger siblings, and cunning competitors from your critical information. Encrypt documents, spreadsheets, presentations, e-mail attachments, graphs, charts, images, music, and most files residing on your computer with DSEnet Encryption. DSEnet Encryption is an easy-to-install, quick-to-learn and simple-to-use software utility that secures data stored on a computer's hard drive.

Keys:

- encryption prevents unwanted access
- easy to learn and operate, little training required
- easy to use explorer style interface
- encrypts individual files, groups of files and folders
- DSEnet Encryption occupies only 4 MB of disk space.

- user key and password combination protects data
- strong 256-bit encryption algorithm

Operating requirements: Microsoft Windows 95, 98, Me, NT 4.0, 2000 Professional / Advanced Server, 32MB-RAM.

11.2.2 Filters

Company name: Armadillo Limited
Address: P.O. Box 667694; Charlotte, NC 28266
Phone number: (704) 987-5003
E-mail address: (704) 896-7818
URL: http:/ /www.armadillousa.comlmaincatalog.html
Category: Filters
Product name: R.A.T. Control™
Product description: Smart-card based Internet filtering/blocking system—the only parental control software that is 100% effective against accessing nonapproved Internet sites. **R.A.T.™ Control is the first 100% effective Internet blocking/filtering product to combine hardware and software security.**

Using R.A.T.™ Control, parents select appropriate Web sites according to their own values, taste and their children's maturity level. When supervision is not available, the system shelters children in a library of parent-approved sites and prevents their intentional or accidental access to objectionable sites.

R.A.T.™ Control combines the use of a high-security smart card key with personalized password security to create a seamless lockout system to provide the most effective protection against access to unapproved sites. Parents actively choose which Web sites are good for their children instead of relying on filtering software to block out known objectionable sites and sites that use objectionable keywords.

This product is convenient, easy-to-use, and virtually tamperproof. User friendly, R.A.T.™ Control employs clear graphics and icons that users of all ages can navigate with ease. Parents can also give each site a name and description for the convenience of their children.

R.A.T.™ Control is available for immediate purchase direct from the publisher's Web site, http://www.armadillo.com.hk/maincatalog.html. The product comes complete with a smart card, reader, and software (CD-ROM).

Company name: Charles River Media
Address: 20 Downer Avenue, Suite 3; Hingham, MA 02043
Phone number: (800) 382-3505

E-mail address: info@charlesriver.com
URL: www.charlesriver.com
Category: Filters
Product name: Internet Watchdog
Product description: Allows the user to record and monitor computer activity.

Company name: surfControl a Division of JSB
Address: 100 Enterprise Way, Mod A-1; Scotts Valley, CA 95066
Phone number: (831) 431-1400
E-mail address: surfsales@CONTROL.com
URL: www.surfcontrol.com
Category: Filters
Product name: surfCONTROL Family of Products
Product description: Controls the use of your Internet.

Company name: Blue Ocean Software, Inc.
Address: 15310 Amberly Drive, Suite 370; Tampa, Florida 33647
Phone number: (813) 977-4553
E-mail address: info@bluocean.com
URL: www.blueocean.com
Category: Filters
Product name: Track-It
Product description: Record keeping system.

Company name: SonicWall, Inc.
Address: 1160 Bordeaux Drive; Sunnyvale, CA 94089-1209
Phone number: (408) 745-9600
E-mail address: sales@sonicwall.com
URL: www.sonicwall.com
Category: Filters
Product name: SonicWALL DMZ
Product description: Provides protection from hackers and content filters.

11.2.3 General Protection

Company name: CyPost Corporation
Address: 900–1281 West Georgia; Vancouver, BC V6E 3J7
Phone number: (604) 904-4422
E-mail address: info@cypost.com
URL: http://www.cypost.com

Category: General protection
Product name: Navaho ZipSafe
Product description: Navaho ZipSafe is the easiest and fastest way to ensure that no one reads confidential data on hard disks, network drives, or floppies. Navaho ZipSafe compresses (by up to 70%) and protects data in one step, enabling you to organize documents files and folders instantly for secure storage or transport.

- Built-in compression. Reduces file size on hard drives and floppy disks by as much as 70%.
- Drag-and-drop feature. Application works behind the scenes to allow users to encrypt and compress files by simply dragging and dropping them into the Drop area.
- Shredder. This feature makes files unrecoverable to programs that rebuild files after deletion.
- Choice of encryption. Navaho ZipSafe supports a variety of algorithms including 40-, 56-, 112-, 128-, and 168-bit.
- Works with all file formats. Navaho ZipSafe quickly and easily encrypts and compresses digital images, spreadsheets, Word documents, files, folders, and even entire directories.

Company name: Delta Design UK.com
Address: 10 Wratting Road; Haverhill, Suffolk, CB9 0DD, United Kingdom
Phone number: n/a
E-mail address: marketing mail@deltadesignuk.com / for publication: mail@deltadesignuk.com
URL: http://www.deltadesignuk.com/
Category: General protection
Product name: Net-Commando 2000
Product description: Hacker protection/prevention/detection, Trojan horse virus protection/prevention/detection/removal, system analysis and Internet tracing. This package uses various methods of detection, prevention and monitoring to deny remote access to your computer. It does this by monitoring areas of your computer where Internet viruses aim their auto-start procedures. It warns of hackers attempting to access your computer, and provides an address for you to backtrack them—as well as tools to assist you in reporting the hacker to the ISP. The program also includes many system analysis tools, including NetStat (protocol statistics), which lists all open ports and allows one to terminate an established TCP port.

Company name: Finjan Software
Address: 2860 Zanker Road, Suite 201; San Jose, CA 95134

Phone number: (408) 324-0228
E-mail address: info@finjan.com
URL: www.finjan.com
Category: General protection
Product name: SurfinShield Corporate
Product description: SurfinShield Corporate is a centrally managed PC security solution that proactively monitors the actual behavior of downloaded active content including executables, scripts, ActiveX, and Java. By monitoring code behavior in its protected "SafeZone," SurfinShield enforces its security policy and automatically blocks malicious activity before damage can be inflicted. Unlike traditional anti-virus technology, SurfinShield represents a new way to combat Trojans, Internet worms, and hostile Web pages based on code behavior, not by static signature recognition. Because SurfinShield does not rely on database updates, it defends against new variants, unknown, and "yet-to-be-created" attacks on the "first strike."

Features and Benefits:

- Behavior Monitoring. Checks active content in realtime in SurfinShield's sandbox including Executables, ActiveX controls, Java applets, Scrap files (.shs), and all Windows scripting host files (e.g., .VBS, .JS, .WSH, etc.). Companies can have protection from all "ILOVEYOU" type worm attacks without having to wait for anti-virus updates.
- Palm-to-PC Sync Protection. Palm Pilots can be used to deliver malicious programs or Trojans to PCs using the synchronization process. SurfinShield monitors all Palm OS-based PDA sync processes for executable programs and protects PCs from sync attacks.
- Multimedia Surveillance Protection. SurfinShield now protects against audio/video recording from Trojans by preventing the PC microphone or camera from automatically being turned on and by monitoring network connections.
- White Listing. Applications from trusted partners enables secure e-business. Companies can allow trusted applications to enter the network with full permissions while unknown code is still subject to monitoring.
- Application Auto-Launch Blocking. Prevents Microsoft Office Suite applications from being automatically launched by Web browsers, Microsoft Outlook and Qualcomm's Eudora e-mail client.
- SurfinConsole™. Centralized management console enables security managers to easily implement and enforce group and individual security policies for all computer users throughout an organization.
- Smart Kill. SurfinShield can identify and surgically kill specific malicious codes. Applications and Web browsers are left undisturbed and user productivity is not hindered.

- Mobile PC Protection. SurfinShield Corporate's monitoring "engine" resides on the PC and will continue to operate when taken on the road. This results in ongoing protection for PC users who are connecting to the Internet from outside the corporate network.

SurfinShield Corporate consists of a console, a server, and a client module. The central console is designed for ease of use, allowing administrators to set both granular and corporate-wide security policies. The central server holds security policies and logs the security events of each desktop. Should one client face an attack, it will update all other SurfinShield Corporate clients, automatically blocking the hostile element upon contact. The client module of SurfinShield Corporate houses the behavior monitoring "engine." The client is not dependent on the server for protection and will continue to defend against attacks when removed from the corporate network.

A "first strike" is the first time a new malicious code attack is launched. First-strike security uses content inspection and behavior-monitoring technology to detect and prevent malicious attacks before damage is caused. Because Finjan products do not rely on database updates, they defend against new variants, unknown, and even "yet-to-be-created" attacks on the "first strike."

SurfinShield Client System Requirements:

- Pentium 133 processor and above
- Windows 9x/ME/NT 4.0/2000
- 16-MB RAM (32-MB RAM recommended)
- 15-MB of free disk space

SurfinShield Server System Requirements:

- Pentium 266 processor and above
- Windows NT 4.0/2000/Solaris 2.6
- 64-MB RAM (128 MB recommended)
- 24 MB of free disk space

SurfinConsole System Requirements:

- Pentium 200 processor and above
- Windows 9x /NT 4.0/2000
- 64-MB RAM (128 MB recommended)
- 15 MB of free disk space

Company name: Intego, Inc.
Address: 6301 Collins Avenue Suite #1806; Miami, Florida 33141
Phone number: (305) 868-7920
Contact name: Olivier Depoorter
E-mail address: odepoorter@intego.com
URL: www.intego.com

Category: General protection
Product name: ContentBarrier
Product description: Blocks all offensive material from the Internet. Intego, a leading provider of Macintosh Internet security utilities announced ContentBarrier thorough and efficient Internet filtering software for Macintosh. ContentBarrier 1.0 helps parents protect their children by monitoring Internet usage to avoid contact with dangerous Web sites, chat rooms, email, newsgroups, and downloads.

ContentBarrier allows parents to select or customize specific categories of potential danger, log Internet usage, control access days and times, and receive email alerts when certain activity occurs. ContentBarrier works with multiple users, so if there are several children in a household, different criteria can be set according to their age. ContentBarrier has a high-content filter engine for sophisticated filtering. Its pre- defined categories let you choose what you don't want your children to see. Inappropriate Web sites are blocked, thus shielding your children from things they are too young to see. ContentBarrier also supports the new version of Intego's NetUpdate, the automatic software update engine. Users can program updates for specific days and times, and NetUpdate will check the Intego server to find out if updates are available for all of Intego's Barrier products installed on your computer.

Laurent Marteau, CEO, Intego, reported that "When children surf the Internet, they can see whatever they want, unless a parent is there to watch over their shoulders." He went on to say that "ContentBarrier sets up a protective wall around your computer making the Internet a safer place for children."

ContentBarrier features:

- Blocks and filters all offensive material from the Internet
- Multiple users—if you have several children, you can adjust the settings for their age and maturity
- Multiple levels of protection
- Predetermined categories for safe and easy content filtering (sexually explicit sites, violence, hate/racism, online chat, etc.)
- Limits Internet access by day and time
- Allows you to inspect your child's computer and make a full inventory of all pictures, movies, music files or Web pages
- Anti-predator function to block predatory language in chat sessions
- Trusted site selection—you can set the program to block all sites except those you select
- Keeps a detailed log of each user's Internet sessions. Records traffic data for an overview of Internet use

- Automatic updates with Intego's NetUpdate function
- Password protection to prevent unauthorized users from changing program settings
- Automatic e-mail notification of certain events

ContentBarrier is also used by companies to restrict inappropriate employee Web site usage. Many employees do their shopping on the Internet, play network games, send and receive personal e-mail or download MP3 files while at work, thereby reducing productivity and using valuable network bandwidth. ContentBarrier can solve this problem by blocking access to many different types of sites, and contains specific categories of Web sites designed for business use.

If your employees spend their working time surfing sexually explicit sites, this not only reduces productivity, but it may even expose you to liability for sexual harassment. Sending private e- mail over your mail server can also expose you to liability , and even prosecution, as your business is responsible for what circulates on its network.

ContentBarrier business features:

- Helps increase productivity and optimizes bandwidth; and
- protects your company from liability.

System requirements are a Mac OS compatible computer with a Power PC processor, OpenTransport, Mac OS 8.1 or higher, and 32-MB RAM. It is also compatible with Mac OS 9.1. A Mac OS X version will be available Q1 2001. Also available in French and Japanese versions.

ContentBarrier is available immediately from retailers including buy.com, CompUSA, MacZone, Outpost.com, Computertown, Club Mac, MacWarehouse, MacMall, ComputerWare, Computer Store Northwest, J&R, Microcenter, CDW, Developer Depot, and from 200 Apple Specialists (see list on the Intego Web site), and online at httQ://www.intego.com.

Company name: Intego, Inc.
Address: 6301 Collins Avenue Suite #1806; Miami , Florida 33141
Phone number: (305) 868-7920
Contact Name: Olivier Depoorter
E-mail address: odepoorter@intego.com
URL: www.intego.com
Category: General protection
Product name: Internet Security Barrier
Product description: The Internet Security Suite for the Mac. Intego, a leading provider of Macintosh Internet security utilities announced Internet Security Barrier, a total Internet security suite for the Macintosh. Internet Security Barrier includes NetBarrier and its three powerful modules: Firewall,

Antivandal, and Internet Filter; VirusBarrier, the acclaimed antivirus program for Macintosh; and ContentBarrier, the thorough and efficient Internet filtering program for a full security suite to protect Macs from all Internet dangers. This suite is the perfect solution to Internet security problems.

Intego's programs have received many awards in the US, Europe, and Asia, for example, awards from *Macworld, MacHome, MacNN,* and *MacAddict*. In France, *UniversMacWorld* recently gave NetBarrier their 2000 trophy for the best Internet program.

Internet Security Barrier 1.0 also supports the new version of Intego's NetUpdate, the automatic software update engine. Users can program updates for specific days and times, and NetUpdate will check the Intego server to find out if updates are available for all of Intego's Barrier products installed on your computer.

As noted by Laurent Marteau, CEO, Intego, "Security issues are the biggest computer problem in recent years." And, continuing, he noted, "Hackers, viruses, and inappropriate content are a plague. Our goal was to develop a full suite of security software for the Macintosh, so Mac users can be protected from every security risk. We're proud to be able to offer such a comprehensive package."

Internet Security Barrier Features include:

- NetBarrier's fully customizable Firewall
  - Anti-vandal to protect your computer from hacker attacks
  - Internet Filter
  - Spam Filtering
  - Ad banner blocking
- VirusBarrier's protection against all known viruses
  - Protection against Word and Excel macroviruses
  - Scans compressed files—checks all types of archives recognized by Stuffit Expander (Zip, CompactPro, DiskDoubler, tar, BZip, arc, etc.)
  - Turbo Mode makes scanning from 5 to 40 times faster
  - Contextual Menu module for quick virus scanning
- ContentBarrier's predetermined categories for safe and easy content filtering (sexually explicit sites, violence, hate/racism, online chat, etc.)
  - Blocks and filters all offensive material from the Internet
  - Multiple users—if you have several children, you can adjust the settings for their age and maturity
  - Multiple levels of protection

System requirements are a Mac OS compatible computer with a Power PC processor, OpenTransport, Mac OS 8.1 or higher, and 32-MB RAM. It is also compatible with Mac OS 9.1. A Mac OS X version will be available Q1 2001. Also available in French and Japanese versions.

Internet Security Barrier is available immediately from retailers including buy.com, CompUSA, MacZone, Outpost.com, Computertown, Club Mac, MacWarehouse, MacMall, ComputerWare, Computer Store Northwest, J&R, Microcenter, CDW, Developer Depot, and from 200 Apple Specialists (see list on the Intego Web site) and online at htm://www.intego.com.

Intego, the i-security software company, publishes security software for the Macintosh, and its products are currently sold in 65 countries. With three essential products, Intego focuses on all aspects of the computer security market—antivirus protection, intrusion prevention, and content control.

In less than two years, NetBarrier has become the world leader in personal firewalls for the Macintosh. VirusBarrier, Intego's acclaimed antivirus solution, has been a resounding success since its launch in July 2000. And ContentBarrier, Intego's new parental control program, was to be available to reinforce its product line in January 2001.

Intego was founded in May 1999 by a group of highly motivated engineers and high-profile marketing, finance, and sales managers to leverage their extensive knowledge of network security and the Mac environment to corporate, individual, and educational users worldwide. Intego has grown 500% in the year 2000, and 2001 will help maintain this exceptional growth through the release of other new and innovative computer security products. The privately held company has headquarters in Miami, Florida, and Paris, France.

Company name: MFX Research
Address: 19–23 Bridge Street; Pymble New South Wales 2073 Australia
Phone number: +61 2 9440 0200
E-mail address: info@mfxr.com
URL: www.mfxr.com
Category: General protection
Product name: MFX Verify
Product description: MFX Verify is a toolset designed to monitor and protect the condition of your applications and operating systems files from ANY form of corruption, decay, or degradation.

MFX Verify continuously checks critical system and application files. As soon as any corruption is detected, regardless of the cause, the files are immediately restored to their original state.

Examples of some of the day-to-day problems solved by MFX Verify:

- Your PC "hangs."
- Your system has not closed properly.
- Your .exe or .dll files have become corrupted.
- You inadvertently delete a monitored file.
- A virus attaches to an .exe file.

In all of the forementioned examples, MFX Verify immediately detects what has happened, and undoes any damage done to the file. MFX Verify is unique—and because it is complementary to other utility software, it "plugs the holes" in the control of systems and applications. Unlike other "so-called" restoration systems, MFX Verify operates by making a byte-by-byte comparison, not simply a checksum, file size, or date stamp comparison. It offers users the ability to define which files they wish to protect. The major cause of errors in PCs is the corruption of application and system executable and library files. By keeping these files in their original condition, "up time" is dramatically improved. Rather than permitting a problem to occur, and then trying to fix it, MFX Verify prevents the problem from happening in the first place. MFX Verify also permits the frequency of scan to be run continuously or set at intervals. MFX Verify operates in a fully automated or user-selected format, on compiled file types, such as .exe, .com, .dll, and .sys. MFX Verify is very fast—the throughput is up to 20Mb/s. With full log and reporting facilities, MFX Verify maintains the integrity of the files from the time of installation. MFX Verify SDK provides the same protection on Windows NT and 2000 systems.

Company name: MFX Research
Address: 19–23 Bridge Street; Pymble New South Wales 2073 Australia
Phone number: +61 294400200
E-mail address: info@mfxr.com
URL: www.mfxr.com
Category: General protection
Product name: MFX ValidSite
Product description: This product allows the user to control the information that is published on their Web site. ValidSite from MFX Research ensures that ONLY the information YOU want to display is publicized on your Web site. ValidSite's unique "file trap procedure" provides for:

- Total and automatic revalidation of a Web site's contents.
- Regular updates to the sites contents, ensuring that only the correct information is being seen by visitors to the site.
- Permits approved updates of information on the site; and
- Eliminates any site rebuild costs should an attack take place.

Should a hacker enter the site, ValidSite will automatically remove all traces of the attack. ValidSite dramatically reduces Web site maintenance and updates costs. ValidSite is simple to use, does not require any extra hardware, requires little or no systems knowledge, and can be installed in seconds. ValidSite ensures that only the "authorized version" of your site can be viewed by your customers, staff, investors, or any visitor to the site.

As more companies are relying upon their Web sites to act as both a shopfront for their products and services, and as a window to their company, the need to protect the contents of their Web site is critical. The protection of this investment is paramount to companies and organizations. Full details of ValidSite can be obtained from the MFXR Web site.

Company name: MFX Research
Address: 19–23 Bridge Street; Pymble New South Wales 2073 Australia
Phone number: +61 294400200
E-mail address: info@mfxr.com
URL: www.mfxr.com
Category: General protection
Product name: MFX WebSiteLock
Product description: Protect your Web site from attack and alteration. WebSiteLock is the world's first software toolset to "lock" and protect the contents of an organization's Web site.

- Automatically monitors and secures your Web site.
- Can constantly monitor all files on a Web site.
- Monitors each byte, and at the first change, reverts to the original and correct byte.
- Permits an immediate and automatic rebuild of any "tampered" files with the original files.
- Immediate reporting of any attack to the System Administrator.
- Not just an Intrusion Detection System, WebSiteLock actually maintains the integrity of your Web site.
- Prevents the Web site files from being corrupted, which is essential for the protection of full e- Commerce sites.
- Can protect both dynamic and static files.
- Allows authorized users to make changes to the Web site, but blocks everyone else.
- Protects your critical firewall files.

As more and more companies rely upon their Web sites to act as both a shopfront for their products and services, and as a window to their company, the need to protect the contents of their Web site has become critical. The protection of this investment is paramount to companies and organizations.

Significant amounts of interest, time, and money are invested in firewalls and other software and hardware solutions to prevent intrusion. In spite of this, we all know that even the most secretive and security-conscious organizations have been "hacked"—from our own Prime Minister's site to the CIA site in Washington. Commercial sites such as Nike and MGM have been entered and details altered, deleted, or added. Many smaller companies and organizations have been targeted and the costs suffered by the disruption have been experienced by all sectors of business, the utilities, and the government. Hackers often attack a site out of curiosity, mischief, and "fun" to prove how clever they are—not necessarily to prove how negligent you are. Regardless of the motive, the impact is the same—You pay *for* the consequences! ! ! Because your firewall alone, is never enough.

Further, the damage being caused by someone from within, or someone with inside knowledge who has recently left the company, can be of greater impact. This person can be far more "focused" and specific in the damage he or she may cause. WebSiteLock is aimed at organizations that have their own server(s) to manage their site.

Company name: Palisade Systems Inc.
Address: 2625 North Loop Drive, Suite 2120; Ames, IA 50010
Phone number: (515) 296-6500 or (888) 824-0720
E-mail address: info@palisadesys.com
URL: http:llwww.palisadesys.com
Category: General protection
Product name: PacketPup
Product description: PacketPup is free-to-download software available from www.packetpup.com that quickly and easily shows you whether you should be concerned about bandwidth allocation on your network. PacketPup tracks the use of file-sharing and streaming applications such as Napster, Gnutella, iMesh, RealAudio/RealVideo, Scour Exchange, Shoutcast, and Windows Media, displaying its data in graphical form. It then provides a Return on Investment (ROI) interface that helps you determine both usage and how much that usage costs your organization. If PacketPup shows you that you have a bandwidth problem, PacketHound, a hardware-based blocking appliance, is a great solution.

PacketPup protects PC networks by alerting administrators to possible bandwidth and security issues associated with the use of file-sharing and streaming applications. Used unchecked, these applications (including Napster, Gnutella, RealAudio/RealVideo, etc.) can make PCs vulnerable to problems, clogging network bandwidth and exposing the network to security holes by opening backdoors and creating virus vulnerabilities.

Company name: Palisade Systems Inc.
Address: 2625 North Loop Drive, Suite 2120; Ames, IA 50010
Phone number: (515) 296-6500 or (888) 824-0720
E-mail address: info@palisadesys.com

URL: http://www.palisadesys.com
Category: General protection
Product name: PacketHound
Product description: PacketHound is a network appliance that allows system administrators to manage or block access to bandwidth- and productivity-eating Internet technologies such as Napster, Gnutella, iMesh, RealAudio/RealVideo, Scour Exchange, and Windows Media. PacketHound protects your organization by allowing you to impose a flexible, organization-specific rule set. You can, for example, block an entire network, or block all access except in one computer lab, or block on a machine-by-machine basis. You can also use time-based rules to shut down access during critical hours but allow it at other times.

PacketHound protects PCs from the bandwidth and security issues associated with the use of file-sharing and streaming applications. Networked PCs are vulnerable to the actions of others on the network; if others are running Napster or Gnutella, all computers have less bandwidth and are potentially vulnerable to security issues—network use of peer-to-peer clients can open security holes and expose an organization to viruses and Trojan horses.

Company name: Pedestal Software
Address: 11 Medway Branch Road; Norfolk, MA 02056
Phone number: (888) 664-7174
E-mail address: info@pedestalsoftware.com
URL: http:/ /www.pedestalsoftware.com
Category: General protection
Product name: SecurityExpressions
Product Description: Enterprise security management, administration, reporting, and lockdown. SecurityExpressions automates the process of deploying, assessing, and maintaining consistent security policies on networks of Windows NT and 2000 systems. It helps organizations with security management and large-scale systems lockdown. SecurityExpressions helps protect Internet PCs by locking them down according to industry-standard guidelines. Security "expressions," similar to mathematical ones, are at the core of this host and application policy management system. SecurityExpressions first assesses the vulnerability state by seeing how well the PC complies with the lockdown policy. Changes are recommended for non-compliant settings and SecurityExpressions automatically fixes them either interactively or in unattended mode. History logging provides an audit trail of changes and modifications may be rolled back to their previous state if problems arise.

Company name: Secure Computing Corporation
Address: One Almaden Boulevard, Suite 400; San Jose, CA 95113
Phone number: (800) 379-4944
E-mail address: NA
URL: www.securecomputing.com
Category: General protection
Product name: SafeWord Plus
Product description: Supports smart cards, Secure Computing's Server for Virtual Smart Card, and general smart cards.

Company name: Secure Computing Corporation
Address: One Almaden Boulevard, Suite 400; San Jose, CA 95113
Phone number: (800) 379-4944
URL: www.securecomputing.com
Category: General protection
Product name: Sidewinder 5
Product description: Provides internal and perimeter security.

Company name: Texar Software Corp.
Address: 1101 Prince of Wales Drive; Ottawa K2H 9N6, Canada
Phone number: (613) 274-2200
E-mail address: info@texar.com
URL: www.texar.com
Category: General protection
Product name: Secure Realms
Product description: An access control solution that controls access to both legacy-based applications and to the Web.

Company name: WatchGuard Technologies
Address: 316 Occidental Ave. S., Suite 2000; Seattle, WA 98104
Phone number: (206) 521-8340
E-mail address: information@watchguard.com
URL: www.watchguard.com
Category: General protection
Product name: WatchGuard LiveSecurity System w/FBII Plus and w/FBI-Fast VPN
Product description: Provides VPN and security for the Internet.

Company name: Webroot Software, Inc.
Address: P.O. Box 3531; Boulder, CO 80307
phone number: (800) 772-9383

Category: General protection
E-mail address: Infocom@webroot:com
URL: www.webroot.com
Product name: Window Washer™
Product description: Window Washer is a utility, not unlike ScanDisk, Disk Defragmenter, etc., that every computer should have, whether it is used in the home or office. Window Washer automates the cleaning of all unnecessary system and Internet files. In the case of system files, Window Washer cleans the following:

- Recycle Bin. This area continues to hold deleted information long after it is useful. Deleting its contents is important for home users as many do not know the Recycle Bin does not empty itself. In the case of businesses, this serves the important function of completely removing sensitive material.
- Registry Streams. This area tracks programs that are used most often. Clearing the Registry Streams is important for home users since it contains useless data that continually takes up space. In the case of businesses, eliminating this information prevents others from finding information regarding the computer's recent activity.
- Windows Run & Find History. These memory blocks were created for convenience, but only take up space in the average consumer's computer. On business computers, they can also act as an open window into the user's activity.
- CHK Scan Disk Files. These files can be used to reconstruct old, deleted files. Eliminating these files removes useless fragments and, in the case of businesses, prevents other users from reconstructing old files.
- Recently Viewed Pictures. Deleting these items can protect children from inappropriate material parents do not wish them to view. For businesses this can prevent the theft of online schematics and PowerPoint presentations.
- Recently Opened Documents. Removing the information stored in this area keeps others from discovering which documents have been opened recently.
- MS Office 97 and 2000 Tracks. These files are similar to Recently Opened Documents. By deleting the MS Office tracks, a user keeps secret the documents that have recently been modified, whether it is changes to a home checking account or changes to the company's new formula for household cleaners.
- Windows Temporary Files Folder. By eliminating these files users prevent anyone from determining which programs have recently been installed and what items have been downloaded.

This list is considerably expandable through the use of Window Washer's free plugins (now over 130) and the custom cleaning feature. The plugins enable the user to clean programs sucn as Adobe Acrobat Reader, MSN Instant Messenger, Real Player, etc. For browsers such as Internet Explorer, Netscape, Opera, Neoplanet, etc., Window Washer cleans:

- Cache. This area stores accessed Internet pages. By deleting this, users do not have to worry about anyone seeing which sites have recently been viewed.
- Cookies. By deleting the cookies from a user's browser, it prevents third-party services from tracking the sites to which the user has gone.
- History. By deleting this, the user prevents others with access to the computer from being able to find out which sites have been visited. This can help keep research and financial information secret.
- Mail Trash. This function of Window Washer completely eliminates emails once they have been removed from the deleted folder in mail managers. Many users believe that when the deleted items folder is emptied the emails are gone forever. Window Washer completely secures old correspondence by deleting them from the system entirely.
- Drop Down Address Bar. As this area tracks all URLs that have been input into the browser, deleting this information helps secure a user's browsing history.
- Auto Complete Data Forms. By removing this information, home users can protect their credit card information and business users can keep login and password information secure.
- Downloaded Program Files. Deleting this information gives both home and business users the comfort of knowing that no one can discover which Internet programs have been downloaded onto the computer.

The functionality of Window Washer offers the user two major benefits— privacy and performance. Whether it is the home user who doesn't want friends, spouses or children to view his or her latest letter to the IRS or whether it is a business person writing a letter to the human resources department, Window Washer protects their privacy according to DOD standards.

In the process of protecting the user's privacy Window Washer also recovers valuable hard drive space, restoring overall performance to the machine's original speed. As I'm sure you know, unless these areas are routinely cleaned, they accumulate rapidly, using more and more hard drive space. Most computer users are not aware of how to clean these areas and those who do know tend to avoid doing so because of the tedious and boring nature of the task.

The Windows™ operating system was designed for convenience and ease of use, not security. Hackers can enter computer systems through a variety of surreptitious means. This enables them to access private information, thereby compromising an individual's safety and right to privacy. Window Washer, when used routinely, plugs many of the security holes left open by the operating system's original design.

Window Washer is currently available on the Webroot Web site, http://www.webroot.com, and through a variety of Internet resellers. In the retail channel, Window Washer is carried by AOL, CompUSA, Fry's Electronics, Hastings, and others.

Company name: Webroot Software, Inc.
Address: P.O. Box 3531; Boulder, CO 80307
Phone number: (800) 772-9383
Category: General protection
E-mail address: Infocom@webroot:com
URL: www.webroot.com
Product name: WinGuardian
Product description: As children begin to use computers at younger and younger ages, they often become sophisticated enough to disable filtering and blocking software. WinGuardian is a Windows TM monitoring utility that is an alternative to filtering and blocking for parents, schools, and other organizations. This helpful tool runs completely hidden and is able to monitor everything a user does on a system. WinGuardian can keep track of which programs a user runs, log any text that is typed into a program, log all Web sites that are visited, and even capture screenshots at specified intervals. The logs can be reviewed to determine if a user is running inappropriate programs such as games or visiting Web sites that the system owner considers offensive. Alternatively, WinGuardian can display an acceptable use policy (AUP) on the computer screen. A user must read the AUP and then click on the AGREE button before he or she is allowed to access the system. Knowing that the system is being monitored is a strong deterrent from using inappropriate programs or viewing inappropriate Web pages. WinGuardian also gives you the option to "lock down" the Windows 95/98/Me environment so that users can only run authorized programs.

Company name: World Wide Digital Security, Inc. (WVVDSI)
Address: 4720 Montgomery Lane, Suite 800; Bethesda, MD 20814
Phone number: (301) 656-0521, ext. 0085

E-mail address: isolav@wwdsi.com
URL: http:llwww.wwdsi.com
Category: General protection
Product name: SAINT™ (System Administrator's Integrated Network Tool)
Product description: The most current version is bundled with SAINTwriter and/or SAINTexpress™. Older versions can be downloaded separately. SAINT is a vulnerability assessment tool used to scan networks for vulnerabilities that hackers might exploit to gain access. SAINT also supports extensive documentation on how to use the product, about the vulnerability, and how to fix the vulnerability. SAINT provides links to more information on the vulnerabilities found, and when possible, links to sites where patches can be downloaded to fix vulnerabilities. SAINT provides a variety of scanning intensity options ranging from *light* to *heavy plus*. Additional options include the SANS Top 10 and user-customized scans.

Company name: World Wide Digital Security, Inc. (WVVDSI)
Address: 4720 Montgomery Lane, Suite 800; Bethesda, MD 20814
Phone number: (301) 656-0521, ext. 0085
E-mail address: isolav@wwdsi.com
URL: http:llwww.wwdsi.com
Category: General protection
Product name: SAINTwriter™
Product description: SAINTwriter is a report writing module that attaches seamlessly to SAINT. SAINTwriter allows the user to generate easily various types of reports, ranging from executive summaries to technical detail reports. Users can quickly and easily create customized reports and save the report formats for future use.

Company name: World Wide Digital Security, Inc. (WVVDSI)
Address: 4720 Montgomery Lane, Suite 800; Bethesda, MD 20814
Phone number: (301) 656-0521, ext. 0085
E-mail address: isolav@wwdsi.com
URL: http:llwww.wwdsi.com
Category: General protection
Product name: SAINTexpress™
Product description: SAINTexpress is an automatic service that updates SAINT every time it is used. When a SAINT scan is initiated, SAINTexpress checks the WWDSI Web site to see if a newer version of SAINT is available. If available, SAINTexpress downloads the newer version of SAINT and runs the scan using this newer version. This guarantees that the scan is testing for the most recently discovered vulnerabilities and using the most ad-

vanced version of SAINT. This service is important because SAINT is updated at least once every two weeks or whenever a new critical vulnerability is discovered.

Company name: World Wide Digital Security, Inc. (WVVDSI)
Address: 4720 Montgomery Lane, Suite 800; Bethesda, MD 20814
Phone number: (301) 656-0521, ext. 0085
E-mail address: isolav@wwdsi.com
URL: http:llwww.wwdsi.com
Category: General protection
Product name: WebSAINT™
Product description: WebSAINT is WWDSI's Web-based vulnerability assessment scanner. The network scan is run from the WWDSI Web site and the report of the findings is sent to the user via secure http. WebSAINT is designed for people who are responsible for the security of their networks but do not have the time or expertise to download and configure the software, perform the scan, and create the reports.

11.2.4 Personal Firewall

Company name: Computer Peripheral Systems, Inc. (CPS)
Address: 5096 Bristol Industrial Way, Suite B; Buford, GA 30518
Phone number: (770) 945-0643
E-mail address: cpsinc@randomc.com
URL: http://www.cpscom.com
Category: Personal firewall
Product name: Mini Firewall
Product description: Hardware security product for LANs with modem connections. Used to prevent modem connections to the Internet from gaining backdoor access to the corporate LAN. It connects between the modem and the LAN and physically breaks the LAN connection when the modem is in use. The LAN connection is re-established when the modem goes back on-hook or after user-specified software is executed.

Company name: DSEnet
Address: 5201 South Westshore Boulevard; Tampa, FL 33611
Phone number: (813) 902-9597
E-mail address: questions@dsenet.com
URL: www.dsenet.com
Category: Personal firewall
Product name: DSEnet Firewall

Product description: DSEnet Firewall is a personal firewall that protects networked PCs from remote attacks. Install DSEnet Firewall on a PC using the friendly interface, and apply the necessary access rights for the Internet. DSEnet Firewall is an ideal low-cost solution for small- to medium-sized businesses, home offices and home users. Now, connecting to the Internet does not require the resources or support of a large corporate security infrastructure. Put DSEnet Firewall on a PC and browse the Internet safely and securely.

Use DSEnet Firewall to restrict access to specific services for example, web browsing, or email. Even advanced rules can be created on a per user basis. Allow and block various users from Web addresses, ports, and protocols. Parents can blacklist Web sites that are off limits to children, or whitelist only the acceptable Web sites children are allowed to browse. Businesses can limit employees to work-related Web sites, prevent downloads and restrict Internet e-mail.

DSEnet Firewall can be accessed with the icon located in the lower right corner of the taskbar. Logging in provides users with their profiles. The Configuration Panel is accessible only with an administrator password. All user profiles, settings and rights can be configured in this panel.

DSEnet Firewall:

- Prevents unauthorized access from the internet
- Stealth mode hides your PC from the Internet world
- Runs seamlessly while surfing the Internet
- Great help files and instructions
- Basic users can use the firewall with minimal effort
- Computer wizards can, in detail, control every TCP and UDP port
- Runs on Windows 95, 98, and NT 4.0
- Control access to unacceptable Web sites
- Low-cost solution with no additional hardware required
- Supports multiple user profiles
- Simultaneously notifies the user and blocks intrusion attempts
- Flexible control of Web browsing
- Restricts access by IP address, URL, port and protocol
- Easy to install and easy to use explorer style interface

System Requirements: Win 95,98, NT, Me, 2000; 32-MB RAM & TCP/IP

Company name: Intego, Inc.
Address: 6301 Collins Avenue, Suite # 1806; Miami, Florida 33141
Phone number: (305) 868-7920
Contact name: Olivier Depoorter
E-mail address: odepoorter@intego.com

URL: www.intego.com
Category: Personal Firewall
Product name: NetBarrier
Product description: First personal firewall for the Mac. Intego, a leading provider of Macintosh Internet security utilities, announced that it has won the prestigious International award, the UniversMacworld Award for the Best Internet Software of 2000 for NetBarrier. NetBarrier is the first personal Firewall for Macintosh with Firewall, Antivandal, and Internet Filter components that make NetBarrier the all-in-one solution for complete personal Internet security .

Intego has won over 20 awards in the US, Europe, and Asia, among which are awards from *Macworld; MacHome, MacNN, and MacAddict.* In just two years, NetBarrier has become the worldwide leader in personal firewall software for the Mac. In the words of Laurent Marteau, CEO, Intego, "We are extremely excited about winning this international award for our Internet security software. To be chosen the Best Internet Software among this fast-paced Internet community is truly an honor."

NetBarrier provides three powerful modules: Firewall, Antivandal, and Internet Filter to make NetBarrier the all-in-one solution for complete personal Internet security. Designed with maximum ease of setup and use, NetBarrier is the "must have" in Internet security software. New security features in NetBarrier 2.0 include control of unwanted Internet cookies, banner ads, and spam, the ability to filter personal information sent when connected to a Web site, updates to the program's Firewall settings, gauges to monitor data traffic by protocol or application, and log exporting. NetBarrier 2.0 also supports the new version of Intego's NetUpdate, the automatic software update engine. Users can program updates for specific days and times, and NetUpdate will check the Intego server to find out if updates are available for all of Intego's Barrier products installed on your computer.

Again, quoting Laurent Marteau, CEO of Intego: "All Macs connected to the Internet are susceptible to security problems without exception. Some Internet users falsely believe that using a modem or ISDN dial-up connection does not expose them to hackers. Hackers can get in through flaws in the OS. For example, a flaw discovered in port 49152 of Mac OS 9 allows hackers to send data that instantly freezes up a Mac, a problem that NetBarrier solves easily."

New NetBarrier Features include:

- Quick access to many settings via a new Control Strip module
- New Aqua interface
- Spam filtering
- Filtered spam is deleted directly on POP3 servers

- Filtering of message subject, author, and sender
- Filtering of URLs
- Updates to the program's Firewall settings
- Definition of port intervals
- Predefined rule sets
- Ability to monitor data traffic by protocol or application
- Blocks cookies and counts the number of cookies received
- Allows the user to erase cookies received by Internet Explorer, Netscape Communicator, and iCab
- Blocks banner ads
- Allows the user to filter information sent when connected to a Web site
- Choose to not send your type of computer and browser
- Choose to not identify the last Web page visited
- Support for the new version of NetUpdate
- Information on Macintosh network configuration

System requirements are a MacOS compatible computer with a Power PC processor, OpenTransport, Mac OS 8.1 or higher, and 32-MB RAM. It is also compatible with Mac OS 9.1. A Mac OS X version will be available Q1 2001. Also available in French and Japanese versions.

NetBarrier is available immediately. It can be purchased from www.intego.com, from retailers including buy.com, CompUSA, MacZone, Outpost.com, Computertown, Club Mac, MacWarehouse, MacMall, ComputerWare, Computer Store Northwest, J&R, Microcenter, CDW, Developer Depot, and from 200 Apple Specialists (see list on the Intego Web site) and online at htm://www.intego.com.

Company name: Network ICE
Address: 2121 S. El Camino Real, Suite 1100; San Mateo, California 94403
Phone number: (650) 532-4100
E-mail address: info@networkice.com
URL: www.networkice.com
Category: Personal Firewall
Product name: BlackICE Defender
Product description: An easily installed personal firewall combined with a hacker detection system. Everyone on the Internet is at risk of attack by hackers. "Always-on" DSL or cable modem, and dial-up Internet connections provide hackers with the ability to violate the security of your computer.

BlackICE Defender is an industrial-strength anti-hacker system that automatically blocks unauthorized intrusions into your computer. It scans your DSL, cable modem, or dial-up Internet connection looking for hacker activity. When it detects an attempted intrusion, it automatically blocks traffic from that source, keeping intruders from accessing your computer. BlackICE Defender works silently in the background, keeping hackers at bay so you can safely stay connected to the Internet.

BlackICE Defender installs automatically and is up and running in a matter of seconds. It has a simple easy-to-use interface, provides audible or visual alerts, and a display that identifies who's trying to break into your computer.

BlackICE technology has been recognized with over 12 industry awards for superior technology and usability by leading publications such as *Business Week, PC World, Network World, PC Computing, PC Magazine, Info World,* and *Internet Week*.

Company name: Open Door Networks, Inc.
Address: 110 S. Laurel Street; Ashland, OR 97520
Phone number: (541) 488-4127
E-mail address: sales@opendoor.com/doorstop/
URL: http://www.opendoor.com/doorstop/
Category: Personal Firewall
Product name: DoorStop Server Edition
Product description: A software-based "firewall" product for Macintosh servers. Unlike conventional firewalls, which are usually expensive dedicated hardware devices, DoorStop is software that you install directly on the servers you wish to protect. DoorStop is significantly easier to set up and use than a hardware firewall and provides the same capabilities at lower cost. With DoorStop, you can specify precisely which machines should have access to which services, and you can keep track of both allowed and denied access attempts to those services. DoorStop works well with a wide range of Macintosh-based Internet servers, including AppleShare IP, WebSTAR, and Open Door's ShareWay IP product line. This product or service will protect a PC on the Internet by acting as a machine-specific firewall to deny TCP access attempts as desired. Also logs access attempts.

Company name: Open Door Networks, Inc.
Address: 110 S. Laurel Street; Ashland, OR 97520
Phone number: (541) 488-4127
E-mail address: sales@opendoor.com
URL: http://www.opendoor.com/whosthere/
Category: Personal Firewall
Product name: Who's There? Firewall Advisor
Product description: Who's There? Firewall Advisor helps users analyze and react to access attempts detected by their firewall. Who's There? is

essential for understanding the ever-increasing access attempts from the Net. It provides advice and helps users take action to combat access attempts. It works with Open Door's DoorStop and Symantec's Norton Personal Firewall for Macintosh. This product or service will protect a PC on the Internet by allowing users to understand and react to access attempts detected by their machine-specific firewall.

Company name: Presinet Sytems
Address: 645 Fort Street, Suite L109; Victoria, BC V8W 1G2
Phone number: (250) 405-5380
E-mail address: Solutions@PresiNET.com
URL: http://www.PresiNET.com
Category: Personal Firewall
Product name: Deadbolt Managed Internet Firewall and Virtual Private Networking Services
Product description: PresiNET provides a range of managed Internet Firewall security services, Network Activity Reporting, and Virtual Private Networking services for small to enterprise-sized organizations for their computer networks of 1 to 250 units. As part of the service, PresiNET provides its robust firewall server, firewall management and reporting services, event and activity monitoring services, expert consulting, and support wherever your business is located.

Company name: SOLSOFT
Address: 130 rue Victor Hugo; 92300 Levallois Perret, France
Phone number: 00 33 1 47 15 55 00
E-mail address: info@solsoft.com
URL: www.solsoft.com/np-lite/
Category: Personal Firewall
Product name: Solsoft NP™-Lite 4.1
Product description: Solsoft NP-Lite 4.1 is a free version of Solsoft NP™ specially created for Linux users. Combining a powerful visual interface and compiler engine, Solsoft NP-Lite automatically translates visual representations of a security policy into consistent, error-free IP Filters. Solsoft NP-Lite configures up to three interfaces on Linux IP Firewall 2.0.x, Linux IP Chains 2.2.x and Linux NetFilter version 1.2. Solsoft NP-Lite 4.1 is a free security solution and can be downloaded from Solsoft's Web site (www.solsoft.com/np-lite/).

Solsoft NP-Lite is the ideal solution for any user or small companies directly connected to the internet (ADSL, Cable, high-speed connection) that want to protect themselves without wasting time.

Company name: SonicWALL, Inc.
Address: 1160 Bordeaux Drive; Sunnyvale, CA 94089
Phone number: (408) 745-9600
E-mail address: info@sonicwall.com
URL: www.sonicwall.com
Category: Personal Firewall
Product name: SonicWALL SOHO2 Internet Security Appliance
Product description: Integrated Internet Security. The SonicWALL SOHO2 Internet Security Appliance is a high-performance, integrated security platform. It includes a stateful packet inspection firewall, IP address management, and support for an expanding array of SonicWALL security services, including VPN (virtual private networking), network anti-virus, and content filtering. The SonicWALL SOHO2 is an ideal solution for broadband connected small offices to provide Internet security for all the computers on a LAN. By offloading security from each PC on the LAN to a high-performance appliance, security is dramatically enhanced.

11.2.5 Physical Security

Company name: Codex Data Systems, Inc.
Address: 143 Main Street; Nanuet, New York 10954
Phone number: (845) 627-0011
E-mail address: sales@codexdatasystems.com
URL: www.codexdatasystems.com
Category: Physical Security
Product name: PC PhoneHome
Product description: Tracks and locates a stolen computer throughout the world.

Company name: Digital Asset Protection
Address: 617 Myrtle Street; Arroyo Grande, CA 93420
Phone number: (877) 752-7364
E-mail address: Info@DAProtect.com
URL: www.DAProtect.com
Category: Physical Security
Product name: Lock & Go™
Product description: Lock & Go offers premier mechanical protection for notebook computers. Nearly 700 pounds of resistance offers a level of asset protection unmatched by traditional cables. For quick and effective notebook protection the Lock & Go simply snaps into place, no awkward

cabling is required. Upon your return, one twist of the key allows you to access your computer.

Company name: Digital Asset Protection
Address: 617 Myrtle Street; Arroyo Grande, CA 93420
Phone number: (877) 752-7364
E-mail address: Info@DAProtect.com
URL: www.DAProtect.com
Category: Physical Security
Product name: DAP Watchman™
Product description: The DAP Watchman is a standalone electronic alarm that may be used to protect a single piece of computer hardware or other electronic equipment. Ideally suited for the SOHO, or isolated equipment distributed throughout a large facility. If the sensor is removed, or the wire severed, an 85-dB tone notifies personnel in the vicinity of an attempted theft.

Company name: Digital Asset Protection
Address: 617 Myrtle Street; Arroyo Grande, CA 93420
Phone number: (877) 752-7364
E-mail address: Info@DAProtect.com
URL: www.DAProtect.com
Product name: DAP Marshall™
Category: Physical Security
Product description: Ideally suited for environments that contain notebooks that are frequently taken on the road, the DAP Marshall is a standalone electronic alarm system for computer hardware that combines state-of-the-art asset protection with hassle-free mobility. The DAP Marshall's infrared remote access allows the end-user to engage the system from a distance of up to 20 feet and protects your computer hardware without compromising the mobility of portable equipment.

Company name: Digital Asset Protection
Address: 617 Myrtle Street; Arroyo Grande, CA 93420
Phone number: (877) 752-7364
E-mail address: Info@DAProtect.com
URL: www.DAProtect.com
Category: Physical Security
Product name: DAP Sentry™
Product description: Ideally suited for environments with distributed computer hardware, the DAP Sentry is a standalone electronic alarm system that allows for complicated configurations with minimal impact. Touch

pad or optional remote infrared access allows authorized users to quickly and effectively engage the system.

Company name: Digital Asset Protection
Address: 617 Myrtle Street; Arroyo Grande, CA 93420
Phone number: (877) 752-7364
E-mail address: Info@DAProtect.com
URL: www.DAProtect.com
Category: Physical Security
Product name: DAP Guardian™
Product description: The DAP Guardian is a standalone electronic alarm system for computer hardware that pinpoints the exact location of a security breach. In the event of an attempted theft of your high-tech equipment, the information provided by the alarm panel allows your personnel to execute an effective stealth response.

Company name: Digital Asset Protection
Address: 617 Myrtle Street; Arroyo Grande, CA 93420
Phone number: (877) 752-7364
E-mail address: Info@DAProtect.com
URL: www.DAProtect.com
Category: Physical Security
Product name: DAP Monitor™
Product description: The DAP Monitor is an integrated system ideally suited for unsupervised environments where round-the-clock protection of computer hardware is critical. The DAP Monitor provides an interface with a central alarm system point panel. The DAP Monitor uses a zone within a normally open or normally closed alarm loop circuit to protect computer equipment and allows organizations to take advantage of their existing access control infrastructure.

Company name: Fastening Solutions, Inc.
Address: 15230 Burbank Boulevard, Suite 106; Van Nuys, CA 91411
Phone number: (818) 994-3698; (800) 232-7836
Category: Physical Security
Product name: LockGuard
Product description: Provides fastening protection in combination with a key and lock security system. Can be used with PCs, and peripherals.

Company name: Kensington Technology Group ACCO Brands
Address: 2855 Campus Drive; San Mateo, CA 94403
Phone number: (650) 572-2700

Category: Physical Security
Product name: Notebook MicroSaver Security Cable
Product description: A lock and cable device that can be attached to the security slot of a desktop sytem or notebook.

Company name: PC Guardian
Address: 1133 E. Francisco Boulevard; San Rafael, CA 94901-5427
Phone number: (415) 459-0190; (800) 288-8126
E-mail address: pcg@pcguardian.com
URL: www.pcguardian.com
Category: Physical Protection
Product name: Perma Dome Cable Anchor
Product description: Security cable anchor.

Company name: PC Guardian
Address: 1133 E. Francisco Boulevard; San Rafael, CA 94901-5427
Phone number: (415) 459-0190; (800) 288-8126
E-mail address: pcg@pcguardian.com
URL: www.pcguardian.com
Category: Physical Protection
Product name: Partition Furniture Cable Anchor
Product description: Security cable anchor that can be inserted into cublic walls.

Company name: Philadelphia Security Products, Inc.
Address: 405-R Baily Road; Yeadon, PA 19050
Phone number: (800) 456-1789
E-mail address: info@flexguard.com
URL: www.flexguard.com
Category: Physical Security
Product name: FLEXGUARD security system
Product description: Anti-theft security hardware for laptop computers, desktop computers, and other electronic equipment.

Company name: Se-Kure Controls, Inc.
Address: 3714 Runge Street; Franklin Park, IL 60131-1112
Phone number: (847) 288-1111; (800) 322-2435
E-mail address: secure@se-kure.com
URL: www.se-kure.com
Category: Physical Security
Product name: Laptop Holder #PTR-200

Product description: Provides protection for the glass screen with a metal enclosure.

11.2.6 User Authentication

Company name: American Biometric Company
Address: DFW Engineering & Development Ltd.; 3429 Hawthorne Road; Ottawa, Ontario, K1G 4G2 Canada
Phone number: (613) 736-5100; (888) 246-6687
Category: User Authentication
Product name: BioMouse Fingerprint Scanner
Product description: Plug and play peripheral that uses a desktop fingerprint scanner to replace password protection.

Company name: Ankari
Address: 3429 Hawthorne Road; Ottawa, Ontario K1G 4G2 Canada
Phone number: (613) 736-5100, or 1-(888) 246-6687
E-mail address: info@ankari.com
URL: www.ankari.com
Category: User Authentication
Product name: BioMouse
Product description: Combined fingerprint scanner and smart card reader. The BioMouse Plus integrated fingerprint scanner and smart card reader lets you store credentials on a secure portable token whose use depends on a method of positive identification that cannot be lost, stolen, shared or forgotten—your fingerprint. When applied to Internet security, a user can store a Verisign digital certificate on a smart card and use a fingerprint instead of a password to enter secure Web sites.

Company name: Ankari
Address: 3429 Hawthorne Road; Ottawa, Ontario K1G 4G2 Canada
Phone number: (613) 736-5100, or 1-(888) 246-6687
E-mail address: info@ankari.com
URL: www.ankari.com
Category: User Authentication
Product name: Trinity
Product description: Trinity is a software authentication infrastructure that enables secure and convenient verification of user identities to protect access to a wide range of platforms and applications. Trinity allows a user to consolidate all their Web-based passwords into a single digital identity and protect that identity through the use of a biometric or smart card.

Company name: Litronic Inc.
Address: 17861 Cartwright Road; Irvine, CA 92614
Phone number: (949) 851-1085
E-mail: info@litronic.com
URL: www.litronic.com
Category: User Authentication
Product name: NetSign
Product description: Stores identity on a Smart Card which is compatible with Newscape2 and Microsoft@suites. This allows the user to conduct secure transactions over the Internet.

NetSign secures the Internet for communications by adding smart card functionality to Microsoft and Netscape email/browser packages. A user's digital identity is stored on the smart card to increase security. Mission-critical security functions such as private key storage and digital signature are performed on the smart card for significantly greater security that is completely portable for use with a desktop or laptop at the office, from home, or while traveling.

NetSign includes SecureDial , SecureStart@, and CardStart features that enhance network and desktop security and control desktop applications.

NetSign CardStart Features:

- Automatic registration of new certificates
- Windows log-off capabilities when the smart card is removed from the reader
- Automated launching of applications upon insertion of the smart card into the reader

NetSign SecureDial Features:

- Secure remote network access using the RAS, RADIUS, TACACS or PPTP protocols to enable smart card secured dial-up sessions and ISP access
- Storage of account information on the smart card to protect dial-up passwords

NetSign SecureStart Features:

- Log-on protection for Windows 95/98 and Windows NT PCs requiring the insertion of the user's smart card and PIN for PC access (Windows 2000 support provided through native Windows 2000 Logon)
- Locking capabilities for Windows PC NT stations upon the removal of the user's smart card
- System lock override with the use of an administrator card

Browser and E-mail Security Features:

- Authenticated Web page access with SSL
- Digitally signed and encrypted e-mail using S/MIME (VeriSignTM Digital ID included)

- Form and object signing using Microsoft Internet Explorer 4.0 or higher, Outlook 98/2000 or Outlook Express 4 or higher, or Netscape Communicator 4.05 or higher
- Support for custom smart-card enabled Java applets

Company name: Litronic Inc
Address: 17861 Cartwright Road; Irvine, CA 92614
Phone number: (949) 851-1085
E-mail: info@litronic.com
URL: www.litronic.com
Category: User Authentication
Product name: Profile Manager
Product description: Allows the user to create and maintain smart cards and to expert PKCS#12 files using a variety of Certificate Authorities.

Profile Manager provides organizations with a flexible solution by offering token interoperability. Because Profile Manager can initialize and maintain both smart cards and the exporting of PKCS#12 files, organizations can implement an adaptable PKI scheme that supports a multilevel security approach. Profile Manager is integrated with a variety of Certificate Authorities (CAs) offering trusted certificate issuance and integrated directory service. The CAs currently supported are Microsoft@ Certificate Management Sytstem, and CyberTrust@. In addition, Profile Manager supports international standards such as SSL, S/MIME, PKCS#11, and PC/SC while enabling the generation of X509v3 certificates, RSA keypairs, and other custom data objects.

Efficiency and security are critical to the success of a large-scale PKI deployment. Profile Manager enables organizations to quickly generate security tokens for any user in the system. To increase efficiency and to decrease the risk of third party interception, token generation is removed from the user's desktop and performed by the security administrator for fail-safe installation of the certificate on the token. Security administrators can control security by generating and backing-up keys and certificates in a restricted environment.

Profile Manager conveniently integrates with your existing employee or customer database so that the security administrator does not have to re-key user data for token personalization. User information can be imported from several sources including existing ASCII files, directories, and various databases. For large-scale deployments, Profile Manager integrates with DatacardTM printers to provide bulk smart card initialization and custom printing.

The ability to recover user information, including keys and certificates, is necessary to replace lost or damaged tokens. Profile Manager provides optional secure database integration for the recovery of token information. User data and profile information is encrypted with the security administrator's Triple DES key/PIN-protected smart card and stored in the database. The security administrator can access this information from the database to issue a user a duplicate smart card when a card is lost or damaged.

The routine maintenance of a PKI can be burdensome for security administrators without the proper tools for the management of security tokens. Profile Manager can be used to modify user privileges or alter user data by adding, deleting or modifying items on an existing user token. If necessary, a user's keys and certificates can be revoked using Profile Manager. Data on a card or other token can be changed and updated after that token has been issued using Profile Manager. Changing user data after token issuance also creates a new backup entry in the database.

Profile Manager Supports:

- Hardware key generation
- Integration with leading X.509v3 Certificate Authorities.
- Security policy profiling
- Integration with various databases and directories
- Bulk token issuance .Key recovery
- Certificate revocation

Profile Manager Includes: Profile Manager Software. Two NetSignia™ Smart Card Reader/Writers, Argus 2000 PC Card Reader/Writer, Chrysalis Luna 2 PCMCIA Token, thirteen smart cards.

Company name: Mytec Technologies, Inc.
Address: 1220 Sheppard Avenue E., Suite 200; Toronto, M2K 2S5 Canada
Phone number: (416) 467-6000
E-mail address: sales@mytec.com
URL: www.mytec.com
Category: User Authentication
Product name: Mytec® Gateway
Product description: Compares the user's fingerprints with those contained in an encrypted template.

Company name: Recognition Systems, Inc.
Address: 1520 Dell Avenue; Campbell, CA 95008
Phone number: (408) 364-6960
E-mail address: Sales@regosys.com
URL: www.handreader.com
Category: User Authentication
Product name: Id3D-R Handkey

Product description: A biometric access control system that responds to and recognizes people.

Company name: Secure Computing Corporation
Address: One Almaden Boulevard, Suite 400; San Jose, CA 95113
Phone number: 1-(800) 379-4944
URL: www.securecomputing.com
Category: User Authentication
Product name: SafeWord 5.1
Product description: Allows authentication methods to be mixed and matched as needed.

Company name: SHYM Technology Inc.
Address: 75 Second Ave.; Needham, MA 02494
Phone number: (781) 455-1100
E-mail address: info@shym.com
URL: www.shym.com
Category: User Authentication
Product name: snAPPSecure™
Product description: Allows the user to securely move offline processes onto the Web. The snAPPsecure targets organizations moving offline processes to the Web to achieve increased efficiencies. Most of these organizations do not have the vast resources required to implement a custom-built infrastructure for strong authentication and eSignatures. Initial target market segments include healthcare, manufacturing, financial services, pharmaceuticals, and government. Every organization is working rapidly and furiously to determine which core processes should be e-enabled. However, without the necessary security precautions, mission-critical Web, e-mail, and enterprise applications, such as SAP and PeopleSoft, are at serious risk. The latest version of Microsoft's server operating system, Windows 2000, has been developed with built-in security capabilities including a standards-based public key infrastructure (PKI) to deliver a complete Internet-enabled business operating system. SHYM's snAPPsecure utilizes no-cost certificates from Microsoft's Windows 2000 as a low-cost and easy to deploy solution for small and medium enterprises to secure critical applications.

SHYM's snAPPsecure is a turnkey application security solution powered by the Microsoft Windows 2000-based public key infrastructure (PKI) that dramatically accelerates the deployment of application security using digital certificates to protect today's e-business initiatives. The snAPPsecure allows organizations to look beyond individual security point solutions to a complete product solution that is centrally managed, covering all organizational domains. Also, snAPPsecure lets organizations easily leverage the integrated PKI of Windows 2000 with their choice of Web, e-mail and client/server applications without the time-consuming and costly custom integration traditionally needed for a complex and powerful PKI security. Further, snAPPsecure combines PKEnable', SHYM's flagship product, the Windows 2000 Certificate Server and professional services to enable organizations to rapidly secure critical e-business applications in just a few days, as opposed to the months of integration needed with today's digital certificate toolkits.

SHYM's application library includes support for popular Web, e-mail, and enterprise applications, providing snap-in application security, eliminating the pain of integrating and maintaining custom development. However, snAPPsecure does not require a homogeneous Windows 2000-based network. It provides clean integration with existing Windows NT, Novell, and UNIX environments.

Today, enterprises engaging in business over public networks are doing it at a great risk. The idea of conducting high-value transactions, such as contract negotiations and the exchange of product ideas with today's security technology gives most organizations reason for concern. The PKI is poised to meet these security needs with its combination of strong authentication, message integrity, and eSignature capabilities, but PKI is still too difficult to integrate, manage and deploy. Recent PKI projects that were expected to be in full-scale deployment are still mired in the pilot stages, while other projects have been completely cancelled. Those very few who have started to roll out a PKI now realize that just issuing certificates is not enough, and that there must be a way to validate that credentials are trusted to perform certain transactions. SHYM's snAPPsecure is the solution to this problem because it makes PKI less expensive, faster to deploy, and easier to manage.

SHYM's snAPPsecure enables organizations to leverage the underlying digital certificate capabilities of their Windows 2000 operating system, thereby leveraging digital certificates for greater efficiency and competitive advantage. snAPPsecure enables e-processes that result in greater efficiencies and competitive advantage. SHYM's snAPPsecure also removes application security integration barriers, making the product far easier to install and manage. With Microsoft's integrated PKI software, customers can deploy PKI-based security services quickly, easily and, most importantly, cost effectively. SHYM's solution lets organizations reap the promise of streamlined business processes, without breaking the bank or missing the market window. SHYM's solutions have the added advantage of being both snap-in simple, and customized to fit each organization's needs. A snAPPsecure pilot implementation can usually be installed in one day as opposed to weeks or months.

SHYM's snAPPsecure allows companies to build strong strategic online relationships with suppliers, distributors, customers, and other entities. They can share important business information knowing that interactions are private, that the identity of each party is authenticated, and that any agreements cannot be forged or repudiated. These assurances allow companies to replicate the best practices of the brick and mortar marketplace in the e-business realm.

Company name: Silanis Technology Inc.
Address: 398 Isabey, 2nd Floor; Saint Lauren, Quebec H4T 1V3
Phone number: 888-SILANIS (745-2647)
E-mail address: info@silanis.com
URL: www.silanis.com
Category: User Authentication
Product name: ApproveIt
Product description: Silanis ApproveIt is an award-winning, electronic signature software that enables organizations to securely capture multiple, legally binding signatures in electronic documents and Web forms without additional hardware, software or programming. Supported software includes Microsoft Word, Excel, Outlook, Adobe Acrobat, JetForm FormFlow, PureEdge and X.509 v3 digital certificates.

Company name: Secure Computing Corporation
Address: One Almaden Boulevard, Suite 400; San Jose, CA 95113
Phone number: 1-(800) 379-4944
URL: www.securecomputing.com
Category: User Authentication
Product name: SmartFiler
Product description: Allows control of Web access throughout the entire organization.

11.2.7 Virus Protection

Company name: Computer Associates International, Inc.
Address: 1 Computer Associates Plaza; Islandia, NY 1788-7000
Phone number: (516) 342-5224; (800) 225-5224
E-mail address: info@ca.com
URL: www.ca.com
Category: Virus Protection

Product name: eTrust AntiVirus
Product description: Provides antivirus protection. Has built-in identifiers of new virus.

Company name: F-Secure, Inc.
Address: 675 N. First Street, 5th Fl.; San Jose, CA 95112
Phone number: (408) 938-6700; (888) 432-8233
E-mail address: info@f-secure.com
URL: www.F-Secure.com
Category: Virus Protection
Product name: F-Secure Anti-Virus
Product description: Provides protection against virus and other attacking codes for both mobile and site-based workers.

Company name: InDefense
Address: 303 Potrero Street, #42–204; Santa Cruz, CA 95060
Phone number: (831) 471-1413; (877) 472-3372
E-mail address: info@indefense.com
URL: www.indefense.com
Category: Virus Protection
Product name: Achilles' Shield
Product description: Provides a patented protection from virus. It detects worm, viral, and Trojans.

Company name: Intego, Inc.
Address: 6301 Collins Avenue, Suite #1806; Miami, Florida 33141
Phone number: (305) 868 7920
Contact name: Olivier Depoorter
E-mail address: odepoorter@intego.com
URL: www.intego.com
Category: Virus Protection
Product name: VirusBarrier
Product description: Provides anti-virus protection for the Mac.
VirusBarrier features are as follows:

- Simple, fast and nonintrusive
- Scans compressed files and checks all types of archives recognized by Stuffit Expander (Zip, CompactPro, DiskDoubler, tar Bzip, arc, etc.)
- Turbo Mode makes scanning from 4 to 40 times faster
- Contextual Menu module for quick scanning
- Self-protection ensures that VirusBarrier doesn't get infected
- Scans RAM after detection of system viruses

- Faster manual scans
- Compatible with Mac OS 9.1

The upgrade from VirusBarrier version 1.x is free for registered users. Available from the Intego Web site, www .intego.com. System requirements are a Mac OS compatible computer with a Power PC processor, OpenTransport, Mac OS 8.1 or higher, and 32-MB RAM. It is also compatible with Mac OS 9.1 A Mac OS X version will be available Q1 2001. Also available in French and Japanese versions.

VirusBarrier is available immediately from retailers including buy.com, CompUSA, MacZone, Outpost.com, Computertown, Club Mac, MacWarehouse, MacMall, ComputerWare, Computer Store Northwest, J&R, Microcenter, CDW, Developer Depot, and from 200 Apple Specialists (see list on the Intego Web site), and online at httQ://www.intego.com.

In less than two years, NetBarrier has become the world leader in personal firewalls for the Macintosh. VirusBarrier, Intego's acclaimed antivirus solution, has been a resounding success since its launch in July 2000. And ContentBarrier, Intego's new parental control program, was available to reinforce its product line in January 2001.

Intego was founded in May 1999 by a collection of highly motivated engineers and high-profile marketing, finance and sales managers to leverage their extensive knowledge of network security and the Mac environment to corporate, individual and educational users worldwide. Intego grew 500% in the year 2000, and 2001 will help maintain this exceptional growth through the release of other new and innovative computer security products. The privately held company has its headquarters in both Miami, Florida and Paris, France.

Company name: McAfee
Address: 3965 Freedom Circle; Santa Clara, CA 95054
Phone number: 1-(888) VIRUS-NO
URL: www.mcafeeb2b.com
Category: Virus Protection
Product name: VirusScan TC
Product description: As the Internet becomes the hub of an increasing number of business transactions, and users—especially mobile users—depend on network availability to perform mission-critical functions, bandwidth becomes an essential resource for IT to manage. And in a circular scenario, this trend leads to a lack of available bandwidth. VirusScan TC (Thin Client) not only requires less bandwidth to deploy and manage than any other antivirus solution on the market today, but it intelligently uses the little bandwidth it does require. Working in concert with McAfee's ePolicy

Orchestrator, which sets the standard for enterprise anti-virus management, VirusScan TC allows you to centrally update, configure, manage, and gather information about your entire network, while minimizing the bandwidth impact to your network.

Because ePolicy Orchestrator uses standard protocols to communicate between the desktop and the server (secured HTTP), managing remote sites across the Internet is a breeze. Got an office in Australia, but no VPN connectivity between here and there? Using ePolicy Orchestrator and VirusScan TC you're still secure. Remote users who dial in for e-mail and became frustrated with their anti-virus protection because it took a long time to download updates will forget they ever had a problem once VirusScan TC is installed. Not only is the download speed of VirusScan TC's incremental update technology quicker, but you will have the peace of mind that secured agent-server communication gives you.

Company name: Midwest Systems, Inc.
Address: 1303 Corporate Center Drive; Eagan, MN 55121
Phone number: (651) 406-4100; (888) 800-8339
E-mail address: moreinfo@midwest-sys.com
URL: www.midwest-sys.com
Category: Virus Protection
Product name: Midwest Systems
Product description: A services company that specializes in storage, network, and messaging solutions that are secure.

Company name: SaferSite
Address: 2130 Walnut Bottom Road; Carlisle, PA 17013
Phone number: (717) 243-6588
E-mail address: brose@safersite.com
URL: www.safersite.com
Category: Virus Protection
Product name: PestPatrol
Product description: PestPatrol detects and can delete any malicious non-virus software found on PCs. Everyone knows what a virus scanner is and what it does. What people don't realize is that there is a wide variety of malicious software that can be more harmful than viruses, and they are not being detected by your antivirus software.

"Pests" represent a whole new category of things, which threaten the stability and integrity of your computer or network. You may not have been aware that these threats exist. Wouldn't you be surprised to find files containing information about hacking your PBX, password cracking, mail bombing, or a variety of hacker tools on your network or even on your own computer?

Where Do These Pests Come From? In some instances, these pests can be planted on your machine by "hackers." Such things as Trojans, worms, or hostile applets are among the most common items that arrive from the "outside." Other items can be brought into your network, knowingly or unknowingly, by your own employees. In any event, as a Webmaster or system administrator, you should be aware that they exist . . . and that they can be a source of disruption.

Some pests can cause a great deal of damage, and some can live on your machine without you even knowing about them. There are thousands of pests and new ones are found each day and added to SaferSite's PestPatrol database. You should be as rigorous about scanning for pests as you are about scanning for viruses.

There are dozens of categories of pests. Some include: worms, Trojans, spyware, hacker toolkits and password crackers. With such a large variety of pests out there, doesn't it make sense to protect your network from these types of things? PestPatrol only needs a few minutes to identify unwanted pests on your entire network. PestPatrol can also be updated in seconds to detect new pests as soon as they are discovered.

Company name: Trend Micro, Inc.
Address: 10101 N. De Anza Boulevard, 2nd Fl.; Cupertino, CA 95014
Phone number: (408) 257-1500; (800) 228-5651
E-mail address: sales@trendmicro.com
URL: www.antivirus.com
Category: Virus Protection
Product name: InterScan Virus Wall
Product description: A three-in-one product that scans SMTP mail, HTTP, and FTP traffic. All this is done in real time.

Company name: Trend Micro, Inc.
Address: 10101 N. De Anza Boulevard, 2nd Fl.; Cupertino, CA 95014
Phone number: (408) 257-1500; (800) 228-5651
E-mail address: sales@trendmicro.com
URL: www.antivirus.com
Category: Virus Protection
Product name: ScanMail for OpenMail
Product description: A virus protection system for Hewlett-Packard's e-mail.

GLOSSARY

ActiveX. ActiveX controls are software modules based on Microsoft's component object model (COM) architecture. They add functionality to software applications by incorporating modules with the basic software package.

Application. Part of the OSI reference model (see OSI-open systems interconnection). The application layer is also known as layer 7, the highest layer in the OSI model.

Arpanet. The network that became the basis for today's Internet. Funded by the US military, the Arpanet was composed of a number of individual computers connected by leased lines and that used a packet-switching scheme.

Attack. An attempt to subvert or bypass a system's security.

Authentication. Verification of a claimed identity.

Back Orifice. This is a program that can let unwanted people **access and control your computer** by way of its Internet link. It runs on Windows 95/98 systems. Once installed, Back orifice (BO) runs invisibly. It has to be **run** to be installed, but it is seldom recognizable to the victim. It can be packaged with legitimate software, attached to any program or file, or run all by itself. It installs itself quietly, usually erasing the original, and opens an "orifice" into your system. It is configurable in a variety of ways. Back orifice allows a very high degree of access and control by the remote operator, who uses a simple pushbutton client program to access the "server" on your machine. Once "in" your system, he can perform practically any of your computer's functions, most of them without any outward indication to the user at the console. The hacker can see passwords, run a DOS session, use your computer as a relay point for communications (so as to make himself untraceable), read your mail, track your keystrokes . . . , and lots more. Back orifice has been in use since August, 1998.

Biometric. Biometric is a unique, measurable characteristic or trait of a human being used for automatically recognizing or verifying identity.

Bubba. A dude who does not know much about computers and drives a truck.

Bubbette. A dudette who does not know much about computers and drives a truck.

Certificate Authority (CA). A CA is an authority that issues and manages security credentials for a PKI.

The CA Private Root Key. A cryptographic key known only to the CA. It is used to certify the user or server certificate requests.

Cat. A small furry animal.

Cable Modem. A device that enables you to hook your PC to the Internet via a cable connection from your TV cable provider.

CERT. The CERT Coordination Center is an organization that grew from the computer emergency response team formed by the Defense Advanced Research Projects Agency (DARPA) in November 1988 in response to the problems generated during the Internet worm incident. http://www.cert.org/

Certificate. digital identifier linking an entity and a trusted third party in order to confirm the entity's identification. Typically stored in a browser or a smart card.

Certificate Owner. A person or system is bound to the certificate. The owner is the person who has access to view and manipulate the certificate.

Certificate Policy. A set of rules that indicates the applicability of a certificate to a particular environment or application with common security requirements.

Certification Authority (CA). A trusted entity issuing certificates to end-users or systems.

Certification Practice Statement (CPS). This is a statement of the practices which a certification authority (CA) employs in issuing certificates.

Cipher. Alternative term for an encryption algorithm.

Ciphertext. Text (or data) that has previously been encrypted.

CRL. The certificate revocation list. A database of certificates no longer valid within a given PKI infrastructure.

Cryptography. This is a discipline that embodies principles, means, and methods for the transformation of data in order to hide its information content, prevent its undetected modification, and prevent its unauthorized use.

CSMA/CD. Carrier sense multiple access/collision detect or CSMA/CD is the protocol for carrier transmission access in Ethernet networks.

DAP. Directory access protocol.

DARPA. Defense Advanced Research Projects Agency (DARPA), is a research branch of the US Department of Defense (DOD), was one of the founder's projects that led ultimately to the development of the Internet.

Data Link. Part of the OSI reference model, this layer provides error control and synchronization for the physical level.

DDOS. This is a distributed denial of service attack. This DOS attack exploits several machines to make the attack.

Denial-of-Service Attacks (DOS Attack). This is any act intended to cause a service to become unavailable or unusable. In an Internet environment, a service might be an application such as a web or mail server, or a network service.

DES. Data encryption standard is a method of data encryption using a private (secret) key. The DES uses a 56-bit key to each 64-bit block of data.

Digital Certificate. A digital certificate is an electronic mechanism that binds a set of credentials to a particular person or system. A CA will issue the certificates.

Digital Signature. This is data appended to, or a cryptographic transformation of a data unit that allows a recipient of the data unit to prove the source and integrity of the data unit and protect against forgery.

DMZ. The demilitarized zone is a network inserted as a "buffer zone" between a company's private, or trusted network and the outside, untrusted, network.

DNS. A DNS system is a method by which Internet domain names are converted into IP addresses.

Dog. Another small furry animal. Or a computer that will not work properly or consistently.

DSL. Digital subscriber line.

Decryption. The process of transforming ciphertext back into plaintext.

Encryption. A process of disguising information so that it cannot be read or interpreted by an unauthorized person.

Ethel. Based on our extensive research (about 5 minutes), this person may have loved William Shakespeare at some point in time.

Ethernet. A network that is specified in a standard IEEE 802.3. Xerox, DEC, and Intel originally developed Ethernet.

Ethical Hackers. These are legal hackers and this means they will hack into your system only after obtaining legal and company permission. These hacking companies are paid to perform this operation and will provide a report on their findings after hacking into your systems.

Firewall. This is hardware and/or software that will protect the trusted resources of a private network user from attacks by untrusted networks.

Footprinting. Also known as profiling, this is the process of obtaining data about a particular individual or company. This information can be obtained from various resources, including public resources.

FTP. File transfer protocol uses TCP/IP ports 21 and 22.

Hacker. A bad person who wants to get into your computer systems without authority.

HTTP. Hypertext transfer protocol is the protocol used via the www. See http://www.w3.org/Protocols/ for more information.

HTTP 1.0. http://www.w3.org/Protocols/rfc1945/rfc1945

HTTP 1.1. ftp://ftp.isi.edu/in-notes/rfc2616.txt

HTTPS. (Secure hypertext transfer protocol) is a protocol developed by Netscape that will encrypt the data at the "network" layer. See SSL for more info.

IEFT. Internet Engineering Task Force http://www.ietf.org

IMAP. (Internet message access protocol) is a standard for accessing electronic mail from a server. Typically used on port 143 or IMAP for SSL is on 993.

IP. Internet Protocol is a method by which data is sent from one computer to another on any network (public or private).

IPSec. Internet protocol security is a standard (in development) for security at the network layer of network communication. This protocol can be used with **VPN**. Virtual private network.

ISDN. Integrated services digital network.

ISO. International Organization of Standards http://www.iso.ch/

ISP. Internet service provider is a company that provides individuals and/or companies access to the Internet and other related services.

Key. A series of numbers used by an encryption algorithm to transform plaintext data into encrypted data.

Key Generation. The process for creating keys in a browser. See <keygen>tag at http://users.knoware.n1/users/schluter/doc/tags/TAG/_KEYGEN.html

Key Management. Systemic processes associated with the secure generation, transport, storage, and destruction of encryption keys.

Key Recovery. This is a PKI key management process associated with the retrieval of a key lost by the keyholder.

Key Serial Number. This is a 128-bit number associated with a certificate.

KEYRING FILE. This is a file that can house the certificate.

L2F. Layer two forwarding protocol used in VPNs.

L2TP. Layer two tunneling protocol used in VPNs.

LDAP. This is the Internet standard for simple directories for use in messaging and similar applications.

LDIF. LDAP data interchange format is a file format used to import or export data from a lightweight directory access protocol directory. These files are ASCII text files. In many cases the files can be exported from one source and imported into another type of software, for example, export data from the LDAP directory and then import it into a private data source to register users.

Local Registration Authority (LRA). Evaluate and approve or reject certificate applications on behalf of a CA.

Macro. A macro is a series of instructions designed to simplify repetitive tasks within a program such as Microsoft Excel or Word. Macros execute when a user opens a file that has been associated with a program. Example, Bubba.doc is associated with Microsoft world.

Macro Virus. A macro virus is an evil (or it may not be evil but it is malicious) macro. These macro viruses are written with an embedded macro programming language and they attach to a document file.

Mapped Drives. Network drives assigned local drive letters and locally accessible. For example, the directory path \\MAINNT\Jsmith\ might be mapped as drive E: on a computer.

Marcel Marceau. French MIME who, as far as we know, has nothing to do with e-mail or encryption.

MD2—Message Digest. An algorithm that takes as input a message of arbitrary length and produces as output a 128-bit "fingerprint" or "message digest" of the input. http://info.internet.isi.edu:80/in-notes/rfc/files/rfc1319.txt

MD5—Message Digest. An algorithm that takes as input a message of arbitrary length and produces as output a 128-bit "fingerprint" or "message digest" of the input. http://info.internet.isi.edu:80/in-notes/rfc/files/rfc1321.txt

MIME. Multipurpose Internet mail extensions is a method to exchange different kinds of data files on a network: video, audio, images, and others. MIME will be transported via the SMTP protocol.

Modem. A modem is a device that modulates an outgoing digital signal from a computer into analog signals for a twisted pair telephone line and demodulates the incoming analog signal and converts it to a digital signal for the digital device.

NIC. Network interface card.

NNTP. Network news transfer protocol is a protocol used by computers for managing the notes posted on UseNet newsgroups.

Nonrepudiation. Cryptographic assurance that a message sender cannot later deny sending a message, or that the recipient cannot deny receipt.

Nontrusted Network. This is a network that is defined by a company as not being trusted. In many cases this would include the Internet.

Open Systems Interconnection. OSI open systems interconnection, also known as the OSI reference model. This describes a standard for how messages should be transmitted between any two points in a network. The reference model defines seven layers that take place at each end of a communication.

Password Attacks. A password attack is an attempt to obtain a user's password. Hackers can use cracking programs, password dictionaries, and password sniffers in password attacks.

PCI. Peripheral component interconnect is an interconnection system between a microprocessor and its attached devices in which expansion slots are spaced closely together for high-speed operation.

PGP. See www.pgp.com for information and product descriptions.

Physical. The first layer of the OSI reference model. This layer connects the bit stream through the network at the electrical and mechanical levels.

Physical Access. This can define access to a particular computer or site. Physical access should be controlled in a security environment.

PIN. Personal identification number.

Ping. This is a program that lets you verify that a particular IP address exists and can accept requests. Ping is typically used as a diagnostic.

Ping of Death. A technique that hackers use to overwhelm a computer with ping requests.

PKCS. Public-key cryptography system is a set standard protocol developed by RSA for secure information exchange. http://www.rsasecurity.com/

PKI. Public key infrastructure.

PKIX. A set of standards for PKI from the IETF. See http://www.ietf.org

POP. Point-of-presence is a location where a network can be accessed.

Pop3. Post office protocol 3 is a standard protocol for receiving e-mail. POP3 typically uses TCP/IP port 110.

Port. In our definition it is a mechanism for TCP to communicate with an application.

POT. This is an illegal substance. As far as we know there is no relationship to POTS.

POTS. "Plain old telephone service."

PPP. Point-to-point protocol is a protocol for communication between two computers.

PPTP. Point-to-point tunneling protocol is a protocol that allows corporations to extend their own corporate network through encrypted "tunnels" over a non-trusted network (a good example would be via the Internet).

Presentation. Another layer of the OSI reference model. This layer can be part of an operating system that converts incoming and outgoing data from one presentation format to another.

Private Key. A cryptographic key known only to the user, implemented in public key cryptography in decrypting or signing information.

Protocol. The special set of rules for communications that computers use when sending signals between and among other computers.

PSTN. Public switched telephone network.

Public Key. A cryptographic key implemented in public key cryptography to encrypt data to the key's owner, or to verify the key owner's signature. The public key can be published, for example in LDAP, without revealing the owner's corresponding private key.

Public Key Infrastructure (PKI). See PKI, PKIX, and PKCS.

Public/Private Key Pair. A form of asymmetric encryption where all parties possess a pair of keys, one private and one public, for use in encryption and/or digital signing of data.

RC2. A block cipher encryption method. Data is encrypted in blocks instead of by character (stream cipher/RC4). Block ciphers are slower than stream ciphers as data is encrypted only when a block is full. http://info.internet.isi.edu:80/in-notes/rfc/files/rfc2268.txt

RC4. A stream cipher encryption method. Each plaintext symbol/character is dynamically translated to ciphertext.

Registration Authority. As part of PKI, this is the mechanism or person involved in verifying and enrolling users.

RFC. Request for comments is an Internet document or standard that is the result of committee drafting and subsequent review by interested parties; see http://www.ietf.org

RSA. This is the encryption algorithm invented by Rivest, Shamir, and Adleman (RSA) in 1976.

S/MIME. Secure multipurpose mail extensions, a standard for secure e-mail.

Script Kiddies. These are entry-level hackers, newbies and cyberpunks. They have little skill, use other hackers' programs, and cause malicious damage such as the defacing of Web sites.

Service Provider. See ISP.

Session. Another layer of the OSI reference model; this layer sets up, coordinates, and terminates conversations, exchanges, and dialogs between the applications at each end.

Sex. If you don't know what this is then you need a lot of help.

Shared Drive. A disk drive made available to other computers on a local network. Most shared drives use the universal naming convention to differentiate themselves from other drives.

SLA. Service level agreement.

Smart Card. A small plastic card with a microprocessor that can store information (e.g., X.509v3 certificate).

SMTP. Simple mail transfer protocol is a TCP protocol that is used for sending and receiving e-mail, normally over TCP port 25.

Snail mail. Postal mail that is delivered by a person.

Sniffer. A software program that monitors network packets. Hackers use sniffers to capture IP data transmitted via a network.

SSL. Secure sockets layer was created by Netscape for managing the security of message transmissions in a network.

Stupid User. This is a computer user who is really stupid.

TCP. Transmission control protocol.

TCP/IP. Transmission control protocol and Internet protocol.

Transport. This OSI layer ensures complete data transfer and manages the end-to-end control and error checking.

Trinoo. A tool used by hackers as a DDOS.

Tripwires. A mechanism or tool that detects hack attacks and alerts someone (like an administrator) to the attack.

Trojan. A program (a.k.a. Trojan horse) in which malicious or harmful code is placed inside an apparently harmless program or utility. This Trojan is constructed in such a way that it can get control of various parts of the PC (or any computer) OS and inflict damage. We don't know if any links between a Trojan horse and the ©1999 Carter-Wallace Trojan® Brand Condoms. So don't get the two confused, one is a computer virus and the other can keep you from getting or giving a virus.

Trusted Network. This is a network that has been defined by a company as trusted.

UDP. User datagram protocol.

URL. Uniform resource locators (http://info.internet.isi.edu:80/in-notes/rfc/files/rfc1738.txt).

USB. Universal serial bus.

VBS. Visual basic script. Visual basic script is a programming language that can invoke a system function. Some of these functions can include starting, using, and shutting down other applications without the user's knowledge.

Vinton Cerf. The father of the Internet.

Virus. A virus is a piece of programming code that causes some unexpected and usually undesirable event on a computer.

Virus Hoaxes. Hoaxes are not viruses, but usually deliberate e-mail messages that warn people about a virus or other malicious software program. Some hoaxes cause as much trouble as viruses by causing massive amounts of unnecessary e-mail. Look out for these types of messages:

- Fake comments from government sources.
- Warnings about alleged new viruses.

VPN. Virtual private network.

WAP. Wireless access protocol.

Worms. Viruses that attack several computers.

www. World Wide Web.

X.500. A directory standard; see http://www.itu.int/

X.509. A certificate standard; see http://www.itu.int/ and http://www.ietf.org

Index

A
Acceptable use policy, 81–85, 107
Access
  control, 21, 104
  server room, 74–75
  zones, 74
Achilles' Shield, 220
ACT2™ (Access Control Facility Two), 16, 19
Aggregation, 61
American Biometric Co., 213
Ankari, 213
Approvelt, 219
Architecture. *See* Directory architecture
Armadillo Limited, 183, 185
ASN.1 (abstract syntax notation number one), 130, 132
Attributes, 5, 57
Auditors, responsibilities of, 103
Audits, 123
Authentication, 13–14, 21, 36–39, 113, 123
  hardware and software tools, 213–219
  Kerberos, 165–169
Authentication Service (AS) exchange, 167
Authoritative sources, use of, 57–60

B
Background checks, 99
Backups, 75–76
Basic constraints, 116
BigFoot, 9
BioMouse, 213
BioMouse Fingerprint Scanner, 213
BlackICE Defender, 206–207
Blue Ocean Software, Inc., 186
Bolt-on security, 64

C
CERT Advisory, 159
Certificate Authority (CA), 113
Certificate Revocation List (CRL), 124, 125–126
Certificates, 39–40
  closed system for, 117–118
  comparison of systems, 119–120
  example of, 120–121
  life cycle, 124
  open system for, 118–119
  root key, 123
Certification, 113
  path constraints, 116–117
Certification Practice Statement (CPS), 122–124
  authentication and identification, 152–154
  definitions, 144–147
  description of, 142–157
  general provisions, 148–152
  introduction, 142–148
  operational requirements, 154–155
  security controls, 155–157
  specification administration, 157
Change cases, 24
Change control, 107
Charles River Media, 185–186
Client/Server (CS) exchange, 168–169
Codex Data Systems, Inc., 209
Competitive asset, 68–74
Compliance, 107
Computer Associates International, Inc., 219–220
Computer Peripheral Systems (CPS), Inc., 203
Computers, security and, 77, 83, 100
Confidentiality, 21
Consultative Committee on International Telephone and Telegraphy (CCITT), 132
Container, 6
ContentBarrier, 190–191
Corporate report structure, 88–89
Corporate security policy document (CSPD)
  auditing, 99
  background checks, 99
  data classification requirements, 99
  facility requirements, 99
  messaging, 101–107
  mission statement, 92–93
  personal computers or handheld devices, use of, 100
  purpose of, 91
  roles and responsibilities described, 93–95
  security life cycle, 95–97
  training, 97–99
Costs, security and, 65–68
CPM, 46
Cylink™, 136–142
CyPost Corp., 183–184, 186–187

D
DAP Guardian™, 211
DAP Marshall™, 210
DAP Monitor™, 211
DAP Sentry™, 210–211
DAP Watchman™, 210
Data
  classification, 103–104
  handling conflicting, 57–60
Databases, differences between directories and, 26–27
Deadbolt Managed Internet Firewall, 208
Delta Design UK.com, 187
DES (Data Encryption Standard), 112
Developers, responsibilities of, 103
Diffie-Helman, 109
Digital Asset Protection, 209–211
Digital signatures, 112, 114
Directories
  See also Enterprise directory
  applications for, 4, 8–9
  historical view of, 41–43
  meta-, 2–3, 9, 29–33
  objects, 5
  privacy, 44–45
  role of, 1–2, 17–19
  schema, 5–6, 23
  security, 5, 19–22
  services , 6–9
  types of, 15–17
  virtual, 30
Directory Access Protocol (DAP), 10
  Lightweight Directory Access Protocol compared to, 28–33
Directory architecture
  critical elements, 26–27
  defined, 23, 24–26
  implementations, 27
Directory Information Base (DIB), 10
Directory Information Tree (DIT), 53
Disaster recovery, 96
Distinguished names (DNs), 11, 14, 127
  unique, 61
Distributed information system, 6
Domain Name System/Service (DNS), 9, 17, 43, 50, 169–172

Domains, 169–170
DoorStop Server Edition, 207
DSEnet, 184–185, 203–204
Dynamic Host Configuration Protocol (DHCP), 100

E
E-mail
  directory use by, 16
  encryption of, 114
  home or office, 4
  messaging, 46–50
  mobile, 4
  wireless mobile, 4
Encryption, 21
  of e-mail, 114
  hardware and software tools, 183–185
  techniques, 111–113
Enterprise directory, 16, 19
  aggregation, 61
  attributes, 56
  authoritative sources, use of, 57–60
  contents of, 51–53
  design, 53–56
  Directory Information Tree, 53
  security, 63–85, 173–223
  uniqueness criteria, 60–61
eTrust AntiVirus, 220
Executives, responsibilities of, 102
Extensible schema, 7

F
Fastening Solutions, Inc., 211
Fax, 4
File system directory, 46
Filtered directory, 160–161
Filters, hardware and software tools, 185–186
Finjan Software, 187–189
Firewalls, 80
  hardware and software tools, 203–209
Flat names, 6
FLEXGUARD security system, 212
Focused directories, 9
F-Secure, Inc., 220

G
GateKeeper™, 183Goals and objectives, project, 175, 178

H
Hackers, 71
Hierarchical names, 6
HTTP, 25

I
IBM, 112
Id3D-R Handkey, 216–217
IDs, 38–39
Incident handling, 96, 101, 106–107
Incident reporting, 98–99
InDefense, 220
Instant messaging, 4
Intego, Inc., 189–193, 204–206, 220–221
International Standards Organization (ISP), 10
International Telecommunications Union (ITU), 10, 132
Internet Engineering Task Force (IETF), 132–133
Internet fraud, 69–74
Internet Security Barrier, 191–193
Internet Security Guidebook, 68
Internet Watchdog, 186
InterScan Virus Wall, 223
Isolation, 22
IT projects
  planning, 173–177
  steps in, 174

K
Kensington Technology Group ACCO Brands, 211–212
Kerberos, 165–169
Key
  See also Public-private key
  escrow, 125, 126
  recovery systems, 125–126
  use of term, 11, 127

L
Laptop Holder #PTR-200, 212–213
Legal department, responsibilities of, 102–103
Lightweight Directory Access Protocol (LDAP), 5, 9
  authentication, 13–14, 36–39
  clients, 27, 127
  compared to Directory Access Protocol, 28–33
  development of, 10–11
  enabled applications, purchased, 27
  entries, 11–12, 127
  internal applications, 27
  referrals, 12–13, 36–38, 127
  security issues, 11, 159
  security scenarios, 159–172
  service model, 127–128
  transaction logs, 13, 127–128
  version 3 features, 11
Lightweight Directory Import Format (LDAP), 40
Litronic Inc., 214–216
Local area networks (LANs), 46, 47
Lock & Go™, 209–210
LockGuard, 211
Lotus Notes, 7, 9

M
Mainframe Security, 15–16, 19
McAfee, 221–222
MD2, MD4, and MD5 (Message Digest), 113
Media, security and, 76
Messaging policy document, 101–107
Messaging tools, 3, 46–50
Metadirectories, 2–3, 9, 29–33
MFX Research, 193–196
MFX ValidSite, 194–195
MFX Verify, 193–194
MFX WebSiteLock, 195–196
Microsoft
  Active Directory, 5
  Internet Explorer, 29
  NT, 8, 77, 163–164
Midwest Systems, Inc., 222
Mini Firewall, 203
MIT, 165
MS-DOS, 46
Mytec® Gateway, 216
Mytec Technologies, Inc., 216

N
Name constraints, 117
Namespace, 6
National Institute of Standards and Technology (NIST), 112
Navaho Lock with Voice, 183–184
Navaho ZipSafe, 187
Net-Commando 2000, 187
NetSign, 214–215
Network ICE, 206–207
Network Operating System (NOS), 15, 19, 45–46
Network security policy, 77–81, 100–101, 103
Nonrepudiation, 21–22, 114, 122
Notebook MicroSaver Security Cable, 212
Novel's NDS, 5

O
Objects, 5
Olivier Depoorter, 204–206
Open Door Networks, Inc., 207–208
Open Systems Interconnection (OSI), 10
Operating systems (OSs), 45–46

P
PacketHound, 197
PacketPup, 196
Packet sniffers, 80
Paging service, 4
Palisade Systems Inc., 196–197
Partition Furniture Cable Anchor, 212
Passwords, 38–39, 105–106, 164–165
PC Guardian, 212
PC PhoneHome, 209

Pedestal Software, 197
People Finder, 9
PeopleSoft™, 30
Perma Dome Cable Anchor, 212
PestPatrol, 222–223
Philadelphia Security Products, Inc., 212
Physical security
  hardware and software tools, 209–213
  policy, 74–77, 103
Pilots, 175, 181–182
Planning, 173–177
Policy constraint, 117
PresiNET Systems, 208
Privacy, 44–45
Process owner, responsibilities of, 102
Process security, 64–68
Profile Manager, 215–216
Protection, hardware and software tools, 186–203
Public-key cryptography standards (PKCS), 130–135
Public Key Infrastructure (PKI), 40
Public-private key
  components of, 113–124
  development of, 109
  encryption techniques, 111–113
  how it works, 110–111

Q

Quality attributes, 24

R

RACF™ (Remote Access Control Facility), 16, 19
R.A.T. Control™, 185
RC2, 112
RC4, 112
Recognition Systems, Inc., 216–217
Referrals, 12–13, 35–36, 127
Replication, 7
RFC1959, 13, 128, 129
Risk analysis, 175, 178
Risk management, 96
Rivest, Ron, 109, 113
Rivest, Shamir, and Adelman (RSA), 109, 130

S

SaferSite, 222–223
SafeWord 5.1, 217
SafeWord Plus, 198
SAINT™, 202
SAINTexpress™, 202–203
SAINTwriter™, 202
Scaling ability, 8
ScanMail for OpenMail, 223
Schema
  defined, 5–6, 23
  extensible, 7
Search feature, 6
Secure Computing Corp., 198, 217, 219
Secure Realms, 198
Secure Sockets Layer (SSL), 11
Security, 5
  See also Corporate security policy document
  committee, 88–91
  defined, 20–21
  importance of, 19–20
  life cycle, 95–97
  Lightweight Directory Access Protocol and, 11
  Mainframe, 15–16, 19
  report structure, 89
  responsibilities, 101–104
  scenarios, 159–172
  what makes a directory secure, 21–22
Security, enterprise, 63
  acceptable use policy, 81–85, 107
  access zones, 74
  appraisal costs, 66
  backups, 75–76
  bolt-on, 64
  commitment and, 68–69
  competitive asset, 68–74
  for computers, 77, 100
  external costs, 66
  firewalls, 80
  internal costs, 66
  Internet fraud, 69–74
  of media, 76
  monitoring tools, 81
  network security policy, 77–81, 100–101, 103
  packet sniffers, 80
  physical security policy, 74–77, 103
  policies and procedures, 69, 71–73, 74–85
  prevention costs, 65
  process, 64–68
  server room access, 74–75
  spoofing, 80
  tools, 69
  viruses, 64, 83–84, 100
SecurityExpressions, 197
Security officer, responsibilities of, 102
Security planning
  goals and objectives, 175, 178
  pilots, 175, 181–182
  project approach, 175, 179–180
  project scope, 175, 177–178
  risk analysis, 175, 178
  roll out schedule, 175, 182
  steps, 174, 175
  training, 175, 180–181
Security policies
  See also Corporate security policy document
  acceptable use, 81–85, 107
  guidelines, 69, 71–73
  network, 77–81, 100–101, 103
  physical, 74–77, 103
Se-Kure Controls, Inc., 212–213
Server room access, 74–75
SHA-1 (secure hashing algorithm), 113
SHYM Technology Inc., 217–219
Sidewinder 5, 198
Silanis Technology Inc., 219
SLAPD program, 17
SmartFiler, 219
S/MIME (Secure/Multipurpose Internet Mail Extensions), 111, 113
snAPPSecure™, 217–219
Sneakers, 71
SOLSOFT, 208
SonicWALL, Inc., 186, 209
Spoofing, 80
Stanford Linear Accelerator Center (SLAC), 71
surfControl, 186
SurfinShield Corporate, 188–189

T

Technology, reasons for changing, 176
Telephones, 4
Texas Software Corp., 198
Ticket-granting service (TGS) exchange, 167–168
Track-It, 186
Training, 97–99, 107, 175, 180–181
Trend Micro, Inc., 223
Trinity, 213
Triple DES, 112

U

Uniqueness criteria, 60–61
URL syntax, 13, 128
Use cases, 24
User authentication, hardware and software tools, 213–219
Users, responsibilities of, 103

V

Validation and expiration, 114
Virtual directory, 30
Virtual Private Networking Services, 208
VirusBarrier, 220–221
Viruses, 64, 83–84, 100
  hardware and software tools, 219–223
VirusScan TC, 221–222
Voice mail, 4

W
WatchGuard Technologies, 198
Webroot Software, Inc., 198–201
WebSAINT™, 203
White Pages, 16
Who's There? Firewall Advisor, 207–208
Window Washer™, 199–201
WinGuardian, 201
World Wide Digital Security, Inc., 201–203

X
X.500, 10, 39, 50
X.509, 13, 39–40, 114–115, 128, 132–133
X.509v2, 115
X.509v3, 115–116

Y
Yahoo, 9
Yellow Pages, 16

Z
Zoomit Corp., 3